A Practical Business Chinese Reader
（Revised Edition）

基础实用商务汉语

（修订版）

关道雄　编著

Daoxiong Guan

北 京 大 学 出 版 社

北　京

内 容 简 介

　　本书是为已有一定基础的汉语学习者编写的基础商务教程。全书以一个美国商务代表团访问中国为线索,依次介绍了商务活动的各项环节和相关的社交、礼仪活动。课文的语言简练,生动,富于幽默感。所附的材料大都是商务活动中的真实原件,力求把学生带入到真实的环境中去。练习形式多样,活泼,富于启发性。全书循序渐进,内容既前后衔接,又相对独立,便于教学。本书是一部高质量的教材。

图书在版编目(CIP)数据

基础实用商务汉语(修订版)/关道雄编著. –北京:北京大学出版社,2003.9
(对外汉语教材系列)
ISBN 7-301-04678-2

Ⅰ.基… Ⅱ.①关… Ⅲ.对外汉语教学-商务-教材 Ⅳ.H195.4

中国版本图书馆 CIP 数据核字(2000)第 68177 号

书　　　名:**基础实用商务汉语(修订版)**
著作责任者:关道雄
责 任 编 辑:徐 刚 郭 力
标 准 书 号:ISBN 7-301-04678-2/H·0560
出　版　者:北京大学出版社
地　　　址:北京市海淀区中关村北京大学校内　100871
网　　　址:http://cbs.pku.edu.cn/cbs.htm
电　　　话:邮购部 62752019　发行部 62754140　编辑部 62752028
电 子 信 箱:zpup@pup.pku.edu.cn
排　版　者:兴盛达激光照排中心　(010)82715400
印　刷　者:北京大学印刷厂
发　行　者:北京大学出版社
经　销　者:新华书店
　　　　　　787 毫米×1092 毫米　16 开本　20.5 印张　323 千字
　　　　　　2003 年 9 月第 2 版　2005 年 6 月第 3 次印刷
定　　　价:45.00 元

To our students whose love of Chinese

encouraged us to complete this book.

修订版前言

《基础实用商务汉语》一书自 2000 年出版以来,先后为国内外一些学校选用作教材。其韩文版亦于 2002 年由韩国多乐院有限公司在汉城出版。此次修订再版,除了订正原稿中的错误并更换、补充了若干课文中的部分内容以外,主要对每课的练习作了大幅度的扩充和调整。修订后的词汇总表共收入生词 1040 个,句型总表共收入句型 154 个。

需要说明的是,本书的原作者之一遇笑容教授因为出任加州大学海外学习项目驻华中心主任,此次未能参与修订工作。但是本书得以成稿问世却是与她的长期关心、支持与参与分不开的。北京大学出版社的徐刚先生和郭力女士从本书的撰写到修订出力甚多,在此一并表示感谢。

关道雄
2003 年 3 月于加州大学圣塔芭芭拉校区
东亚语言文化研究系

Preface for the Revised Edition

Since it was first published in 2000, *A Practical Business Chinese Reader* has been adopted as a textbook by schools in China and overseas. The Korean edition (*Ok! Business Chinese*) was published by Darakwon Inc. at Seoul in 2002. This revised edition has corrected some mistakes and partially replaced or replenished content in several lessons. However, the majority of the revision was made to the exercises in each lesson. Almost all the exercises have been rewritten or redesigned. As a result, the number of the exercises in this book has increased by as many as 3—4 times. There are only slight changes in vocabulary and sentence patterns. A total of 1040 new words and 154 sentence patterns has been introduced in the revised edition.

It was very unfortunate that Professor Hsiao-Jung Yu, the co-author of the original edition of this book, could not work on the new version of the book this time. She was appointed as director of the UC EAP (University of California Education Abroad Program) Study Center at Beijing last year and has committed herself completely into this immense responsibility. There is no doubt that it would have been impossible for me to complete this book from the very beginning without her support, concern, and contribution. Many thanks also go to Mr. Xu Gang and Ms. Guo Li at Peking University Press. Their continuous support and help have made the revision successful.

Daoxiong Guan
Department of East Asian Languages and
Cultural Studies at University of California,
Santa Barbara, March, 2003

初版前言

近年来,商务汉语在海外汉语教学中逐渐引起了相当的注意。在美国,目前已经有不少大学相继开设了商务汉语课程。一些大学甚至正在计划、酝酿开设层次不同、训练重点不同的系列商务汉语课。显然,商务汉语正开始成为对外汉语教学中的新热点。

商务汉语课的出现无疑与中国经济的迅速发展有着密切的关系。可以肯定地说,只要中国经济继续保持良好的发展趋势,商务汉语课的发展将是非常有潜力的。但是,作为一门新的学科,商务汉语面临着众多急需解决的问题。其中,编写、出版适合对外汉语教学所使用的商务汉语课教材的任务尤为迫切。这就是我们编写《基础实用商务汉语》的起因。

《基础实用商务汉语》一书的主要适用对象定位为至少已经学习了一年到一年半汉语、对主要的现代汉语语法结构已有所了解的学生。其已经掌握的词汇量应当在一千左右,即大致相当于《汉语水平词汇与汉字等级大纲》中甲级词的水准。在编写体例与架构上,《基础实用商务汉语》一书共分为十六课,以一个美国商务代表团访问中国为线索,依次介绍了商务谈判的各项主要环节和其他相关的商务、社交活动。内容上既前后衔接又相对独立,以便任课教师根据需要调整自己的课程教学安排。就难易程度而言,前八课稍易,后八课较难。每课包括:

1. 主题对话;
2. 阅读短文;
3. 词汇和句型;
4. 练习和活动;
5. 附录。

全书最后编有总附录,包括全部课文的英译、词汇总表、句型总表、重要网址、中国地图和主要参考书目。全书共计列出生词 1010 个,句型 152 个。通过这本课本的学习,学生可望达到中级或中级以上的汉语水平。

把本书设计在上述的汉语水平层次上是基于这样的考虑:

我们认为,商务汉语的学习应该在已经初步具有了一定的汉语语言能力的基础上进行。商务汉语课不需要也不应该在"商业"的名目之下再教授发音、识字或是最基本、最常用的汉语词汇和语法。如果要那样做的话,势必会模糊一般对外汉语课和商务汉语课的界限。商务汉语课应该是一门具有特定目标、特定内容的对外汉语语言课程。它所提供的是现代汉语中常用的商务词汇的知识以及与此相关的社会、文化知识,培养学生在汉语语言环境中进行商务活动所需要的语言交际技能。作为对外汉语课程中的一种,商务汉语与普通汉语课存在着密切的联系。但是商务汉语课的教学目的显然有别于普通汉语课。其教材与教法也应当具有自己的特色。换句话说,商务汉语课必须在其教学内容上提供普通汉语课无法提供的语言、文化知识,才能真正成为一门独立的、无法替代的课程。

基于上述的想法,我们在《基础实用商务汉语》一书的总体设计和具体编写中做了以下的尝试:

(一) 注重培养学生在实际汉语语言环境中进行商务活动的语言能力。能力语言教学法是近二三十年来在美国外语教学界一再讨论及推行的外语教学理论。能力语言教学法强调培养外语学习者实际的语言交流能力,把从书本上学到的语言知识及时地(即时地)运用在真实的生活情境之中。为了在商务汉语课中达到这一目的,《基础实用商务汉语》的课文选题力求概括最具代表性、最有普遍意义的实际商务活动。课文对话的编写力求真实而生动、实用且不乏风趣,尽可能避免单调的或教科书式的语言。每一课的练习与活动的设计均旨在鼓励学生的主动参与。在帮助学生理解课文内容的同时,尽量利用多种形式,为学生提供在真实语境中熟练掌握乃至灵活运用该课词汇与句型的机会。每课的附录则结合课文的需要,提供相关的中文商业信函、文件、表格等实例,以期帮助学生熟悉实际商务活动中可能接触到的这类材料,取得学以致用的效果。

(二) 重视相关文化背景知识的介绍。将文化背景、风俗民情、社交礼仪乃至思维方式的介绍融入外语教学之中的文化、语言融合教学法也是近年来美国欧美语言教学界讨论的重点之一。这种教学理论的一个明显的好处就是使学习外语的人可以通过语言的学习来了解文化、通过了解文化来提高其外语水平。我们觉得商务汉语教学有必要与文化知识的介绍相结合。了解中国人的思想、行为模式以及在待人接物上的种种习惯,将有助于在实际商务活动中双方的有效沟通与交流,避免某些不必要的误会。基于这样的认识,《基础实用商务汉语》一书在每课的主题对话之外,又安排了一篇阅读短文。其内容是与该课主题对话相关的社会背景、文化背景信息。换言之,本书每一课的主题对话是以具体的商务活动设立单元,而每课的阅读短文则是以介绍文化背景设立单元。在文体上,前者是口语,后者是书面语。这样不但可以同时训练学生的会话和阅读能力,同时也增加了学生的学习兴趣。

(三) 从商务汉语的角度出发,合理挑选课文词汇和句型。在从事对外汉语教学的实践中,我们深深感到课本词汇的合理甄选和使用是非常值得重视的一个问题。编写一本汉语教材,应该仔细审慎地考虑它所准备使用的字、词和词组。在决定哪些字词应该介绍给学生、哪些应该列为必需掌握的生词的时候,编写者应该尽量避免主观性和随意性。对外汉语课本中词汇的取舍标准无疑应该建立在科学统计的基础上。商务汉语课本更不能例外。根据《汉语水平词汇与汉字等级大纲》的统计,对外汉语教学基础阶段的词汇量应当以 3000 词为界标。根据我们的分析,在这 3000 个词中,有可能被收入任何一本商业汉语词典的词大约在百分之一左右。因此,一本理想的商务汉语教材所提供的基本词汇,应当能够最直接地反映出其不同于一般汉语课本的特征。在《基础实用商务汉语》一书的编写中,我们决定以《汉语水平词汇与汉字等级大纲》的甲级词表为界线。甲级词表共收词 1033 个,都是现代汉语中使用频率最高的基本常用词，也是初学者在基础阶段应该首先掌握的词汇。这样一个词汇量正好符合我们为本书使用者设定的汉语水平起点。因此，凡是被收入甲级词表的词汇，在这本教材中均被编者视为学生已经掌握的词汇，不再列入生词部分。必须说明的是，由于我们还缺乏商务汉语词汇使用频率方面的统计资料，因此在选择这方面的词汇的时候，本书可能有不少考虑不周的地方。我们真诚地盼望读者提出批评和建议。

《基础实用商务汉语》一书的内容和体例由关道雄与遇笑容拟定。关道雄负责主题对话、阅读短文、生词表、句型表的编写以及全书的统稿，遇笑容负责每课练习与活动的设计和编写。课文的英文翻译由史香侬(Shannon Lee Du)承担。中国江西财经大学经济文化传播系的熊焰、陈秀平教授审读了本书的初稿，且为本书的附录搜集、提供了一些有用的信息和原始材料。陈毓贤女士(Susan Chan Egan, 原美国 Scudder, Stevens & Clark, Inc. 资深证券分析师)为书中涉及的专业词汇的英汉对译解决了不少难题。在此一表示衷心的感谢。我们还应该特别感谢审读本书的北京大学出版社的郭力女士和徐刚先生。因为他们的关心和帮助，本书才能够得以顺利出版。

本书的初稿曾在圣塔芭芭拉加州大学试用。这使我们有机会在实践中对这本教材做出修改。在此我们也想对我们的学生表示由衷的谢意，正是他们对汉语学习的强烈兴趣和热爱给了我们编写本书的动力。

关道雄、遇笑容
2000 年 5 月于加州大学圣塔芭芭拉分校
东亚语言文化研究系

Preface for the First Edition

In recent years, Business Chinese has drawn increasing attention in the field of overseas Chinese teaching. In the United States, some universities are already offering Business Chinese courses. Others are even considering or planning to offer series of Business Chinese courses at different levels, each placing the emphasis on various aspects. Obviously, Business Chinese is becoming a popular new course in the field of teaching Chinese as a foreign language.

The popularity of Business Chinese is a by-product of China's economy, which has grown rapidly in the last decade. There is no doubt that Business Chinese has a tremendous potential as long as China's economy maintains this positive trend and continues growing. On the other hand, Business Chinese as a newborn course is facing a number of questions that have to be solved without delay. What is most urgent and crucial now is to compile textbooks that properly fit the needs of Business Chinese in the field of teaching Chinese as a foreign language. That was our intention in writing this textbook, *A Practical Business Chinese Reader*.

A Practical Business Chinese Reader is designed for those who have completed at least one year to one and a half years of Chinese study at the college level and have gained a good knowledge of basic grammar in modern Chinese as well as around a 1,000-word vocabulary in Chinese, equivalent to the beginning level in *Guidelines of Chinese Proficiency and the Degree of Difficulty of Chinese Characters*. We believe that Business Chinese should be taught beyond the beginning level. There is no need to teach pronunciation, character writing or beginning level vocabulary and grammar in a Business Chinese course. Although there are similarities and connections between Business Chinese and other Chinese language courses, the goal of Business Chinese certainly is different than other Chinese language courses, and so is its content. Business Chinese courses train students to develop their communication skills both in oral and written forms in order to conduct business in a Chinese language environment. The emphasis is placed on the usage of business terms in modern Chinese and on language proficiency in a business context as well as on business related social-cultural awareness.

By following the progress of an American business delegation in China, *A Practical Business Chinese Reader* has developed sixteen lessons in all to introduce some typical business activities and business related social events in the Chinese business world. The contents of the lessons may be seen in the chronological order of events or as sixteen individual stories so that instructors may adjust their teaching plans according to their own needs. In terms of difficulty, the first eight lessons are more basic while the latter eight lessons are more advanced by comparison. However, these sixteen lessons, should they all be used, are sufficient for one semester or two quarters. Each of the sixteen lessons in the book contains the following sections:

1. Dialogues: The dialogues in each lesson are set at various authentic sites in China. The

scenarios are intended to be typical of those encountered by foreigners conducting business in P. R. China. Authentic language of modern Chinese, which occurs in realistic business contexts, is employed to the greatest extent in order to provide the most efficient examples for students to imitate and eventually enhance their Chinese language proficiency.

2. Reading Passages: The reading passage in each lesson is a short essay, in which the topic of the lesson is further explored. The reading passages are intended to sketch some general pictures of cultural background in Chinese society and its business world. In the terms of language style, the reading passages in the book are in written form while the dialogues present a more lifelike spoken style.

3. Vocabulary and Patterns: The book presumes prior competence or mastery of about a 1000-word vocabulary. The Glossary of Beginning Level in *Guidelines of Chinese Proficiency and the Degree of Difficulty of Chinese Characters*, which has a 1033-word vocabulary of the most frequently used words, has been adopted as the measure to establish the vocabulary glosses for each lesson. The words that are not covered in this 1033-word vocabulary glossary are considered as new words for the book. Due to the fact that there is no supporting data of lexicostatistics in business Chinese, it was very difficult to decide what vocabulary items should be included. In order to better equip students with useful business terms in Chinese, a great effort has been made to select proper vocabulary words from a practical standpoint of conducting business. We therefore would welcome the input of teachers and students alike, so that we can continue to best meet the needs of the changing context of Business Chinese in the classroom. The patterns are another component of this section. Normally eight to ten patterns are presented in each lesson. There are certain important patterns that students may have been exposed to in their prior study but that they might not have mastered. Each pattern heading is followed by two examples. The first one is drawn from either the Dialogues or the Reading passage while the second one serves as an additional example.

4. Exercises and Activities: Exercises and activities are designed to reinforce newly introduced vocabulary and patterns as well as to help students in understanding the content of the dialogues and the reading passage in each lesson. Some questions posed in this section require students to do research in business related topics by using various media sources, including the internet, while some questions are intended to lead students into discussions of cultural differences. Instructors may choose to use these exercises in whole or in part, as written homework or as in-class oral exercises.

5. Appendix: Appendixes in each lesson provide examples of business documents in Chinese as well as other useful information such as a Customs Declaration Form, a Product Catalogue, an Order Sheet, a Letter of Credit, a Letter of Intent, a Contract, and Common Chinese Signs etc. Some of them are duplicates of the originals.

The book has also complied a General Appendix, which contains a complete English translation of all dialogues and reading passages, vocabulary, patterns, useful web sites, a map of China, and a bibliography. There are 1010 new words and 152 sentence patterns introduced in the book. All the texts, vocabulary and patterns are printed in both traditional and simplified characters. Through study of this textbook, students may attain an intermediate level of Chinese or higher.

This book was designed by Daoxiong Guan and Hsiao-jung Yu. Daoxiong Guan wrote the dialogues and the reading passages. He also made vocabulary and pattern glossaries and took the responsibility for finalizing the whole book. Hsiao-jung Yu created the exercises and activities. Shannon Lee Du translated all of the dialogues and the reading passages into English. We want to thank Professor Xiong Yan and Chen Xiuping (Jiangxi Finance and Economy University), who not only provided some valuable materials and examples of business documents but also proofread the first draft of the book. Our gratitude also goes to Mrs. Susan Chan Egan (Chartered Financial Analyst, former Vice President at Scudder, Stevens & Clark, Inc.). Her special knowledge in business solved many problems that we encountered during translating business terms into English. We owe a special thanks to Ms. Guo Li and Mr. Xu Gang (Beijing University Press), who proofread the whole book. It would have been impossible to publish this book without their continuous support. Finally, we want to express our gratitude to our students at University of California, Santa Barbara. It was their love of Chinese that encouraged us to complete this book.

Daoxiong Guan, Hsiao-jung Yu
The Department of East Asian Languages and
Cultural Studies,
University of California,
Santa Barbara
May, 2000

目　录

X

主要人物表

美方：

史强生　　美国国际贸易公司亚洲地区总裁

Johnson Smith, CEO of Asia Region, American International Trading Company

白　琳　　美国国际贸易公司亚洲地区总裁助理

Lynn Petty, Assistant to CEO of Asia Region, American International Trading Company

中方：

王国安　　中国东方进出口公司总经理

Wang Guo'an, President, China Eastern Import & Export Corporation

李信文　　中国东方进出口公司副总经理

Li Xinwen, Vice President, China Eastern Import & Export Corporation

张　红　　中国东方进出口公司公共关系部主任

Zhang Hong, Director of Public Relations, China Eastern Import & Export Corporation

第一课 到达中国

　　史强生先生和白琳小姐是美国国际贸易公司的代表。这次他们来中国做生意。史先生过去在台湾工作过两年。白小姐去年来过北京,跟东方进出口公司的李先生认识。史先生和白小姐说中文说得都很好。

(一) 对话

1. 入境

(在海关)

海关官员：　您好! 您是来旅行的吗?

史强生：　　不,我是来做生意的。这是我的护照。

海关官员：　请打开这个箱子。

史强生：　　好吧。

海关官员：　这些是什么?

史强生：　　这些是样品,这一件是礼物。这些东西需要交税吗?

海关官员：　五百美元以上的礼物要交税,样品可以免税。不过,您还是得填一张海关申报单。

白　琳：　　这是我的护照、入境登记卡和健康申明卡。

海关官员：　你有什么需要申报吗?

白　琳：　　没有。

海关官员：　那是什么?

白　琳：　　那是我的好朋友!

海关官员：　好朋友?

白　琳：　　(笑)是呀,那是我的电脑。我们每天在一起,是最好的朋友!

海关官员：　(笑)你的中文真不错!

白　琳：　　哪里哪里!

2. 见面

（在机场出口）

白　琳：看，那是李先生！李先生，好久不见了，你好！

李信文：你好，你好！白琳小姐，我们又见面了！欢迎，欢迎！

白　琳：我来介绍一下儿。这位就是东方公司的副总经理李先生。这位是我的老板，Mr. Smith。

史强生：您好！我是 Johnson Smith，我的中文名字叫史强生。

李信文：您好！我叫李信文。欢迎您来中国！

史强生：谢谢！

白　琳：太好了！坐了十几个小时的飞机，总算到北京了！李先生，谢谢你来机场接我们。

李信文：不客气，我们是老朋友了。你们的入境手续都办好了吗？

白　琳：都办好了，很顺利！

李信文：好，那我们走吧，车就在外边。

词汇（一）Vocabulary（1）：

1.	到达	dàodá	to arrive
2.	国际	guójì	international
3.	贸易	màoyì	trade
4.	公司	gōngsī	company
5.	生意	shēngyi	business
6.	东方	dōngfāng	east; the East
7.	进出口	jìnchūkǒu	import and export
	进口	jìnkǒu	import; to import; entrance
	出口	chūkǒu	export; to export; exit
8.	入境	rù jìng	to enter a country
9.	海关	hǎiguān	customs
10.	官员	guānyuán	officer; official

2

11.	护照	hùzhào	passport
12.	箱子	xiāngzi	suitcase
13.	打开	dǎkāi	to open
14.	样品	yàngpǐn	sample(e.g. merchandise samples)
15.	交税	jiāo shuì	to pay taxes/customs duties
16.	美元	měiyuán	U.S. dollars
17.	以上	yǐshàng	over; more than; above
18.	免税	miǎn shuì	to exempt from taxation; duty free
19.	填	tián	fill out
20.	申报	shēnbào	declaration; to declare(dutiable goods)
21.	单	dān	list; form; voucher
22.	登记卡	dēngjì kǎ	registration card
	登记 dēngjì		registration; to register; to check in
	卡 kǎ		card
23.	健康申明卡	jiànkāng shēnmíng kǎ	health declaration
24.	电脑	diànnǎo	computer
25.	好久	hǎojiǔ	a long time
26.	副总经理	fù zǒngjīnglǐ	vice president
	副 fù		vice
	总经理 zǒngjīnglǐ		president; general manager
27.	老板	lǎobǎn	boss
28.	总算	zǒngsuàn	finally; at last
29.	手续	shǒuxù	procedure; formalities
	办手续 bàn shǒuxù		go through formalities/procedures
30.	顺利	shùnlì	smooth(ly)

专有名词 Proper Nouns：

1.	史强生	Shǐ Qiángshēng	a name
2.	白 琳	Bái Lín	a name
3.	美国国际贸易公司	Měiguó Guójì Màoyì Gōngsī	American International

| 4. 东方进出口公司 | Dōngfāng Jìnchūkǒu Gōngsī | Trading Company Eastern Import & Export Corporation |
| 5. 李信文 | Lǐ Xìnwén | a name |

句型(一) Sentence patterns(1):

1. 是来/去……的 　　　　(express purpose in coming or going)

我是来旅行的。

他是去做生意的。

2. ……以上 　　　　over; more than; above

五百元以上的礼物需要交税。

七岁以上的小孩儿得买票。

3. ……真不错 　　　　…is not bad; … is very good

您的中文真不错!

她做的中国菜真不错!

4. 就 　　　　(an adverb, serves as an emphatic marker; it is usually stressed in speaking)

这位就是从美国来的白小姐。

机场的出口就在那儿!

5. 总算 　　　　finally; at last

我们总算见面了!

我等了三个小时,她总算来了。

6. 谢谢 + clause 　　　　thank + clause

谢谢你来机场送我们。

谢谢您帮我买机票。

4

（二）阅读短文

在中国,说中文

在中国,说中文,会有很多好处。一句最简单的"你好",常常使事情变得容易。"你好"让严肃的官员对你微笑,让认真的谈判变得轻松。不要担心你说中文说得不好。你会发现,当你说中文的时候,中国人总是非常高兴,也更乐意帮助你。

说中文容易交朋友。有了好朋友,做生意、办事情都会有很多方便。只要你每天都说中文,能说多少就说多少,你的中文就会越来越好。

词汇(二) Vocabulary(2):

1.	使	shǐ	to make; to cause
2.	变得……	biànde	have become; to turn(into)
3.	严肃	yánsù	serious; solemn; stern
4.	微笑	wēixiào	to smile; smile
5.	谈判	tánpàn	negotiations; talks; to negotiate
6.	轻松	qīngsōng	relaxed; light
7.	担心	dānxīn	to worry; to feel anxious
8.	乐意	lèyì	be willing/happy to
9.	交朋友	jiāo péngyou	to make friends
10.	办事情	bàn shìqing	to attend to matters; to handle affairs
11.	只要	zhǐyào	as long as; provided
12.	越来越……	yuèláiyuè	more and more

句型(二) Sentence patterns(2):

1. 使/让   to make; to cause

   这件事使/让我担心。

5

他说的话使/让那位官员很生气。

2. 当……的时候　　when…

当你去外国的时候,不要忘了带护照。

当我到出口的时候,我看见李先生在等我。

3. 只要……,就……　as long as…then…(conclusion/result)

只要我有时间,我就一定去飞机场接你。

只要你喜欢那个电脑,我们就买吧。

4. 越来越 + $\langle$ **Adj.** **V.** 　　more and more Adj.; to V. more and more

现在去中国做生意的人越来越多。

白琳小姐发现她越来越喜欢说中文了。

5. 能 + **Verb** + 多少 + 就 + **Verb** + 多少　　to V. as much/many as one can

(你)能说多少就说多少。

我们能卖多少就卖多少。

(三) 练习与活动

I. 句型练习一 Sentence Pattern Exercises (1):

1. 用"是来/去……的"的句型回答下面的问题:

Answer the following questions by using the pattern of "是来/去……的":

(1) 甲:昨天为什么李经理又去北京了?

乙:_____。

(2) 甲:他是去中国做生意的吗?

乙:不,_____。

(3) 甲:你是来旅行的吗?

乙:不,_____。

(4) 甲:那位海关官员是来做什么的?

乙:_____。

2. 你的朋友第一次去中国,他很想知道下面的这些东西在中国要多少钱。请

6

你用"……以上"的句型回答他的问题。

This is your friend's first visit to China. He really wants to find out how much the following things cost there. Please answer his questions by using the pattern of "……以上":

a.   ￥2.00

问：＿＿＿＿＿＿＿＿＿＿

答：＿＿＿＿＿＿＿＿＿＿

b.   ￥100

问：＿＿＿＿＿＿＿＿＿＿

答：＿＿＿＿＿＿＿＿＿＿

c.   ￥2,500

问：＿＿＿＿＿＿＿＿＿＿

答：＿＿＿＿＿＿＿＿＿＿

d.   ￥10,000

问：＿＿＿＿＿＿＿＿＿＿

答：＿＿＿＿＿＿＿＿＿＿

e.   ￥80,600

问：＿＿＿＿＿＿＿＿＿＿

答：＿＿＿＿＿＿＿＿＿＿

f.   ￥4,789,000

问：＿＿＿＿＿＿＿＿＿＿

答：＿＿＿＿＿＿＿＿＿＿

3. 你刚到中国,觉得每一样东西都很有意思。请用"……真不错"的句型说说你觉得什么东西很好。

You have just arrived in China and feel that everything is interesting (and good). Make some sentences to express your impression by using the pattern of "……真不错".

(1) _____

(2) _____

(3) _____

(4) _____

4. 用"就"的句型 (as an emphatic mark) 回答下面的问题:

Answer the following questions by using the pattern of "就" (as an emphatic mark):

(1) 甲:请问,哪位是贸易公司的李先生?

    乙:_____。

(2) 甲:你的护照和海关申报单在哪儿?

    乙:_____。

(3) 甲:您带的样品在哪儿? 那是样品吗?

    乙:_____。

(4) 甲:那是你的电脑吗?

    乙:对,_____。

5. 请用"总算"的句型改写下面的句子:

Rewrite the following sentences by using the pattern of "总算":

(1) 我们到达中国了。

    _____

(2) 花了不少时间,我找到了我们的箱子。

    _____

(3) 我的中文不太好。海关官员说的话我听了三遍才听懂。

    _____

(4) 这么多入境手续,我们都办好了。

    _____

6. 请用"谢谢 + clause"的句型,对帮助你、关心你的人表示感谢:

Please express your gratitude to those who helped you or were concerned about you. Use the pattern of "谢谢 + clause".

(1) 你的朋友开车到机场接你。你对他说:

_____

(2) 服务员把你的箱子送到你的房间。你说:

_____

(3) 你把电脑还给李经理。你说:

_____

(4) 你病了。朋友来看你,送给你花儿。你说:

_____

II. 句型练习二 Sentence pattern exercises (2):

1. 用"使"或者"让"的句型完成下面的句子:

Complete the following sentences by using either "使"or "让":

(1) 那位严肃的海关官员 _____。

(2) 这次的谈判很容易,_____。

(3) 坐了十几个小时的飞机_____。

(4) 手续都顺利地办好了,_____。

2. 用"只要……就……"的句型,完成下面的对话:

Complete the following dialogues by using the pattern of "只要……就……":

(1) 甲:你说,怎样才能学好中文?

乙:_____。

(2) 甲:明天你能去机场接东方公司的代表吗?

乙:_____。

(3) 甲:这个电脑是我带给朋友的礼物。请问,我应该交税吗?

乙:_____。

(4) 甲:怎样才容易跟中国人交朋友?

乙:_____。

3. 用"能 **V.** 多少就 **V.** 多少"的句型,完成下面的对话:

Complete the following dialogues by using the pattern of "能 **V.** 多少就 **V.** 多少":

(1) 甲：今天的事情太多,我担心办不完了!

   乙：别担心, _____。

(2) 甲：对不起,这次我们只能买这些。

   乙：没关系, _____。

(3) 甲：总经理,这次去中国我应该带几件样品?

   乙： _____。

(4) 甲：这些问题不简单,今天的谈判不可能把它们都解决。

   乙： _____。

4. 用"当……的时候"的句型,问一问这些人在飞机上做什么?

Use "当……的时候" to ask what the people are doing on the airplane.

例如 For example:

问：当王先生喝可口可乐的时候,李先生在做什么?

答：当王先生喝可口可乐的时候,李先生在听音乐。

(1) _____

_____

(2) _____

_____

(3) _____

_____

(4) _____

_____

5. 用"越来越……"的句型看图说话：

Describe the pictures below by using the pattern of "越来越……"：

(a).

两年前　　一年前　　今年

―――――――――――――――――――――――――――――――

(b). 以前　　　　　　　　　现在

―――――――――――――――――――――――――――――――

(c).

―――――――――――――――――――――――――――――――

III. 词汇练习 Vocabulary Exercises：

1. 用下面的词汇填空 Fill in the blanks by using words below：

手续、护照、交税、免税、入境登记卡、健康申明卡、海关申报单

　　　当你到达中国的时候，你总是得办一些_____，例如在海关你应
该准备好_____，_____和_____。做生意的人，应该注意什
么是可以_____，什么得_____，准备好_____。

11

2. 反义词 Antonyms.

例如 For example：上飞机 ←→ 下飞机

1. 入境 ←→ _____

2. 打开 ←→ _____

3. 以上 ←→ _____

4. 出口 ←→ _____

5. 紧张 ←→ _____

6. 担心 ←→ _____

IV. 阅读、写作和讨论 Reading, Writing and Discussion：

1. 根据课文对话回答问题：

Answer the following questions according to the dialogues in this lesson：

(1) 史强生和白琳以前去过中国吗？

_____

(2) 他们这次到中国做什么？

_____

(3) 他们坐了多长时间的飞机？

_____

(4) 史先生带了一些什么东西？

_____

(5) 史先生得交税吗？为什么？

_____

(6) 白琳带了什么？

_____

(7) 为什么海关官员说白小姐的中文很好？

_____

(8) 史强生和白琳谁是老板？

_____

(9) 李信文先生是谁？为什么白琳认识他？

_____

（10）史先生和白小姐的公司名字是什么？

_____

（11）史先生和白小姐入境的时候有什么麻烦吗？

_____

2. 这一课的阅读短文想要告诉你什么？请你谈谈你自己跟中国人说中文的经
   验。

What is the Reading Message in this lesson trying to tell you? Could you please
share your personal experiences of speaking Chinese with your classmates?

3. 根据下面给出的情境，写一段对话。

Based on the situations given, create a dialogue and act it out.

（1）你的公司派你去机场接位客人。

Your company sent you to the airport to pick up some important visitors.

（2）在入境的时候，海关官员请你打开你的箱子。

You just arrived in China. At the customs, the officer asks you to open
your suitcase.

（四）附录

（1）入境登记卡

入境登记卡 ARRIVAL CARD
填写前请认真阅读背面说明
Please read the points for attention on the back before filling

姓 Family Name	名 Given Name

出生日期 Date of Birth	年 Y	月 M	日 D	性别 Sex

国籍 Nationality	护照 证件号码 Passport or Certificate No.

中国签证号 Chinese Visa No.	签发地 Place of Issue

偕行人数 Accompanying number	航班(车次) Flight(Train)No.

职业：Occupation　　1. 行政管理人员 Legislators & Adminstrators

2. 专业技术人员 Professionals & Technical　　3. 办事员 Clerk

4. 商业人员 Commerce　　5. 服务人员 Service　　6. 农民 Farmer

7. 工人 Worker　　8. 其他 Others　　9. 无职业 Jobless

在华地址 Address in China (Hotel)

旅客签名 Signature

官方填写：W U Y D Z X F L G C T M
Official Use Only　　　证件种类

说　　明

一、入、出境中、外籍旅客必须如实填写本登记卡,并随同护照、证件一并交边防检查员检验,登记卡由边防检查员收存。

二、请用中、英、法、西班牙其中一种文字填写,日本人姓名用罗马文拼写,字迹要工整、清晰。

三、请根据自己的职业在职业栏内的一项上划"√"。

四、禁止携带法律规定的危险物品入境,如有,必须向边防检查站报告。

五、入境到达居住地后,须按规定办理住宿登记或居留登记手续。

Description

1. Both Chinese and foreign travelers shall fill in the Arrival Card or Departure Card and hand it in along with their passports and other certificates to officers of the Frontier Defence Inspection for checks. The card will be kept by officers.

2. Fill in the card clearly in the following languages: Chinese, English, French and Spanish. Japanese names shall be filled in Rome alphabet.

3. Please use "√" to show your occupation in the frame.

4. Any dangerous articles are forbidden. Passenger taking dangerous articles must declare to officers.

5. You should go through the registation of stay or residence after arriving your place.

(2) 健康申明卡

健 康 申 明 卡
HEALTH DECLARATION

亲爱的旅客们：

Dear Passengers:

欢迎您来到中华人民共和国,请您按下列项目填写表格：

Welcome to the P. R. of China. Please fill in the blanks according to the items below:

姓名　　　　　性别　　　国　籍

Name _____ Sex _____ Nationality _____

护照号码　　　　在 华 联 系 地 址

Passport No. _____ Contact Address in China _____

_____

《中华人民共和国国境卫生检疫法》规定：入境者如有发烧及患有精神病、艾滋病(含病毒感染者)、性病、肺结核或随身携带生物制品/血液制品,请申明。

According to "The Frontier Health & Quarantine Law of the People's Republic of China": If persons arriving in China have fever or suffered from psychosis, AIDS (Inc. HIV carrier), venereal disease, pulmonery tuberculosis and carried biological products/blood products, please make a declaration.

申 明 内 容

Content of Declaration _____

谢 谢 您 的 合 作
Thank you for your cooperation

(此页交卫生检疫官)

(This page should be submitted to the quarantine official)

中华人民共和国
卫生检疫当局通告

入境人员请注意：

在您抵达中华人民共和国之前,可能在境外不经意地接触到某种危险的传染病,因此,为了您和他人的健康,防止疾病的传播,在您入境后十四天内,若发现以下症状：

如：(1)发烧伴皮疹(2)发烧伴黄疸(3)腹泻或呕吐

请您尽快携此卡前往任何一个就近的卫生检疫局,享受优惠、优质的医疗服务。

(此页留给入境者)

欢 迎 莅 临 中 国
WELCOME TO CHINA
与您共创健康美好的明天
FOR A BETTER & HEALTHIER TOMORROW

(3) 中国海关进出境旅客行李物品申报单

中国海关忠告：虚假申报将导致法律责任

中华人民共和国海关

进出境旅客行李物品申报单

姓　　名		性　　别	男/女
国　　籍		来自/前往	
护照号码		旅行目的	

1. 本申报单背面所列必须向海关办理申报手续的旅客,请详细填报有关物品并签名。填单后交海关验核签章。在设有双通道的现场,务必选择"申报"(红色)通道通关。

2. 上述以外的旅客,无须填写申报单,并可选择"无申报"(绿色)通道通关。如进境后需办理提货券、外汇商品、分运行李等手续,不能一次结清的,请在办理有关手续处填写本单向海关申请。

品名/币种	数量/数额	规格型号	海关记录

我已阅知本申报单背面所列事项,并保证以上申报属实。

申报人签名：　　　　　　　　20　年　月　日

海关记事栏：

经办关员签字：　　　　　20　年　月　日

第二课　在旅馆

李信文为史强生和白琳在长城饭店预订了房间。白琳很喜欢这个旅馆，可是她也有很多问题。

（一）对话

1. 旅客登记

服务员：　您好！

李信文：　您好！今天早上我为这两位美国客人预订了房间。麻烦您查一下儿。

服务员：　您是东方公司的李先生吗？

李信文：　对，我叫李信文。

服务员：　请您的两位客人填一下儿旅客登记表。

李信文：　我为你们预订的是一间标准间，一间套房。标准间一天四百五十块，套房八百块。

白　琳：　哇，比去年贵了不少啊！请问，我可以用英文填表吗？

服务员：　可以。我要看一下儿你们的护照。

李信文：　客人需要先付房间押金吧？

服务员：　对，先付两千五百块押金。可以付现金，也可以用信用卡。

史强生：　我用信用卡吧。

服务员：　你们的房间在十九楼。这是房卡。

白　琳：　十九楼！太好了！那么高，风景一定很好！

2. 旅馆的服务

白　琳：　服务员小姐，请问洗衣房在哪儿？

服务员：　在六楼。不过，您可以把脏衣服放在洗衣袋里交给我，也可以把洗

17

衣袋留在房间里,等一会儿我来拿。

郎可太好了! 请问,你们有"叫早"服务吗?

服务员: 有,您可以打 1237,告诉服务台您需要几点起床。

白　琳: 谢谢。您知道在哪儿可以用因特网吗? 我得查一下儿我的信。

服务员: 二楼的商务中心可以上网。

白　琳: 哪儿可以换人民币?

服务员: 外币兑换就在大厅的服务台。

史强生: 小姐,请问餐厅在几楼? 这位小姐问了这么多问题,肚子一定饿了!

词汇(一) Vocabulary（1）：

√ 1.	旅馆	lǚguǎn	hotel
√ 2.	预订	yùdìng	to reserve; to book
3.	旅客	lǚkè	hotel guest; traveler; passenger
4.	客人	kèrén	guest; visitor
5.	标准间 单间	biāozhǔnjiān	standard room
√ 6.	套房	tàofáng	suite
7.	哇	wā	wow; (expresses surprise)
8.	付	fù	to pay
√ 9.	押金	yājīn	deposit; cash pledge
√ 10.	现金	xiànjīn	cash
√ 11.	信用卡	xìnyòngkǎ	credit card
√ 12.	房卡	fángkǎ	key card; room card
13.	风景	fēngjǐng	scenery; view
14.	洗衣房	xǐyīfáng	laundry room
15.	不过	búguò	but; however
16.	洗衣袋	xǐyīdài	laundry bag
	袋	dài	bag
17.	叫早	jiàozǎo	wake-up call; morning call
18.	服务台	fúwùtái	service desk; front desk
√ 19.	因特网	yīntèwǎng	internet

20.	商务中心	shāngwù zhōngxīn	business center
21.	上网	shàng wǎng	to access the internet
√22.	人民币	rénmínbì	Chinese currency; RMB
23.	外币兑换	wàibì duìhuàn	foreign currency exchange
	外币	wàibì	foreign currency
	兑换	duìhuàn	to exchange; to convert
24.	大厅	dàtīng	lobby
25.	餐厅	cāntīng	restaurant; dining hall
26.	肚子	dùzi	stomach

句型(一) Sentence Patterns (1):

1. A 为 B V. ……　　　A V. … for/on behalf of B

   我为这两位美国客人预订了房间。

   请你为我们换一些人民币。

2. A 比 B Adj. + specific quantity (or rough estimation)　　A is … Adj. than B

   (今年)比去年贵了不少。

   坐飞机比坐火车快十五个小时。

3. 可……了　　　(emphatic adverb)

   那可太好了!

   哇,一天没吃饭,我肚子可饿了!

4. 得　　　　　　have to; must

   我得查一下儿我的信。

   你得填一张海关申报表。

(二) 阅读短文

中国的旅馆

中国的旅馆又叫宾馆、饭店或者酒店。最好的旅馆是五星级旅馆,当然也

是最贵的旅馆。像北京的长城饭店,上海的希尔顿饭店,南京的金陵饭店都是
这样的大旅馆。中国政府规定,只有三星或者三星级以上的旅馆才能够接待
外国人。如果你打算住旅馆,最好请旅行社帮你预订,或者请朋友帮忙。你也
可以自己给旅馆打电话或者上网预订。很多旅馆都有商务中心。在那里,你
可以使用电脑、上网和发传真。打国际电话也很方便。你可以付现金,使用信
用卡或者买一张电话磁卡。

词汇(二) Vocabulary (2):

1. 宾馆	bīnguǎn	hotel; guesthouse
2. 酒店	jiǔdiàn	hotel; wineshop
3. 最好	zuìhǎo	best; had better; it would be best
4. 五星级	wǔxīngjí	five star ranking; five star
级	jí	rank; level; grade
5. 规定	guīdìng	to stipulate; to rule; rules; regulations
6. 只有	zhǐyǒu	only
7. 接待	jiēdài	receive (a guest); to admit; reception
8. 如果	rúguǒ	if
9. 打算	dǎsuàn	to plan; to intend; plan
10. 旅行社	lǚxíngshè	travel agency
11. 帮忙	bāng máng	to help; to give a hand
帮	bāng	to help
12. 使用	shǐyòng	to use
13. 传真	chuánzhēn	fax
发传真	fā chuánzhēn	send a fax
14. 电话磁卡	diànhuà cíkǎ	prepay phone card

专有名词 Proper Nouns:

1. 长城饭店	Chángchéng Fàndiàn	Great Wall Hotel
2. 希尔顿饭馆	Xī'ěrdùn Fàndiàn	Sheraton Hotel

3. 金陵饭店　　　　　Jīnlíng Fàndiàn　　　　　Jinling Hotel

句型（二）Sentence Patterns（2）：

1. 只有……才……　　　　only（if）…（then and only then）…

　　只有三星级以上的旅馆，才能够接待外国旅客。

　　只有会说中文，办事情才方便。

2. 如果　　　　　　　　if

　　如果您要上网，请到二楼商务中心。

　　如果住在十九楼，风景一定很好！

3. 最好　　　　　　　　had better; it would be best

　　您最好使用信用卡。

　　打国际电话，最好买一张电话磁卡。

4. 或者　　　　　　　　or

　　你可以付现金，或者使用信用卡。

　　我想住长城饭店或者东方宾馆。

5. 请 A 帮 B V.……　　ask A help B to do …

　　如果你打算住旅馆，最好请旅行社帮你预订。

　　请您帮我兑换两百美元的人民币。

（三）练习与活动

I. 句型练习一 Sentence Pattern Exercises（1）：

1. 用"A 比 B Adj. + specific quantity（or rough estimation）"的句型造句，回答下面的问题：

Answer the following pictures by using the patterns "A 比 B Adj. + specific quantity（or rough estimation）".

（1）这家旅馆有一百九十位客人，那家旅馆有两百九十位客人。哪家旅馆的客人少？少多少？

（2）标准间贵还是套房贵？贵多少？

_____

（3）史先生兑换了四百美元的人民币，白小姐兑换了两百美元的人民币。
现在谁的人民币多？多多少？

_____

（4）小箱子能放四五件样品，大箱子能放十几件样品。大箱子比小箱子大
多少？

_____

2. 昨天老板告诉你，星期三有两位从一家外国公司来的客人要来参观、访问你
们公司。老板让你负责接待他们。今天是星期二，老板叫你到他的办公
室。他想知道你准备得怎样了。请用"A 为 B V.……"的句型，说出你已经
做了什么，还计划做什么：

Yesterday, your boss told you that two important guests from a foreign
company will visit your corporation this Wednesday. You have been assigned to
arrange everything for this visit and make sure that your guests are happy.
Tuesday, your boss called you to his office. He wants to know what you have
done so far and what you plan to do for their visit. Use the pattern of "A 为 B
V.……" to make your sentences.

（1）_____

（2）_____

（3）_____

（4）_____

（5）_____

3. 完成下面带"可……了"的句子：

Complete the following sentences with "可 …… 了".

（1）_____ 可忙了!

（2）_____ 可好了!

（3）_____ 可贵了!

（4）_____ 可方便了!

(5) _____ 可担心了!

(6) _____ 可容易了!

(7) _____ 可严肃了!

(8) _____ 可顺利了!

4. 今天你非常忙。你有很多事一定得在下午五点钟以前做完。请用"得"的句型写出你要做的事:

You have a very tight schedule today and so many things have to be done by 5:00 p.m.. Use "得" to list those things along with a timetable.

(1) _____

(2) _____

(3) _____

(4) _____

(5) _____

II. 句型练习二 Sentence Pattern Exercises (2):

1. 用"只有……才……"的句型完成下面的对话:

Use the pattern of "只有……才……" to complete the following dialogues.

(1) 甲:在海关,哪些东西可以免税?

乙: _____。

(2) 甲:中国政府规定,什么样的旅馆能够接待外国旅客?

乙: _____。

(3) 甲:你住旅馆的时候,总是用"叫早"服务吗?

乙:不, _____。

(4) 甲:怎样能够学好中文?

乙: _____。

2. 根据下面的要求,用"如果"和"最好"的句型造句:

Use the patterns of "如果"and"最好"to accomplish the following tasks:

(1) 下个月,你的朋友要去中国商务旅行。他想知道他应该怎样准备这次旅行。

你告诉他: _____。

(2) 你朋友打算在北京一个星期。他怎样可以找到一个好旅馆？

你告诉他：_____。

(3) 你朋友想知道他在中国的时候怎样跟你联系最方便。

你告诉他：_____。

(4) 你朋友还想知道怎样才能跟中国人交朋友。

你告诉他：_____。

3. 根据下面的要求，用"或者"的句型造句：

Use the pattern of "或者"to accomplish the following tasks:

(1) 说出两个你计划去的中国城市：

_____

(2) 说出两种预订旅馆的方法：

_____

(3) 说出两个你想住的旅馆：

_____

(4) 说出两种付旅馆押金的办法：

_____

4. 根据下面的要求，用"A 帮 B V. ……"的句型造句：

Use the pattern of "A 帮 B V. ……"to accomplish the following tasks:

(1) 你给旅行社打电话，要预订两张飞机票。（不要忘了告诉旅行社你要去哪儿、哪天去。）

你说：_____。

(2) 你也请旅行社为你预订一个旅馆。（不要忘了告诉旅行社你要星级的旅馆和什么样的房间。）

你说：_____。

(3) 在旅馆的服务台，你想把五百美元兑换成人民币。

你说：_____。

(4) 你告诉服务员小姐你忘了带你的房卡，你请她为你开门。

你说：_____。

III. 词汇练习 Vocabulary Exercises：

1. 用本课学习的生词回答下面的问题：

Answer the following questions based on the vocabulary list for this lesson.

(1) 在中文里，"旅馆"还有什么别的名字？它们的意思都一样吗？

_____

(2) 哪些词汇在住旅馆的时候可能有用？

_____

2. 填空组词 Fill in the blanks to build up words：

例如 for example：_____意 _____意 → 生意 乐意

(1) _____金 _____金 _____金

(2) _____卡 _____卡 _____卡

(3) _____厅 _____厅 _____厅

(4) 旅_____ 旅_____ 旅_____

(5) 洗衣_____ 洗衣_____ 洗衣_____

IV. 阅读、写作和讨论 Reading, Writing and Discussion：

1. 根据课文对话回答问题：

Answer the following questions according to the dialogues in this lesson：

(1) 李先生为史强生和白琳在什么饭店预订了房间？预订了什么样的房间？

_____

(2) 他们的房间多少钱一天？

_____

(3) 住旅馆的时候，客人得办什么手续？

_____

(4) 他们得付多少钱的押金？

_____

(5) 如果客人有脏衣服要洗，他们可以怎么办？

_____

（6）这家旅馆的"叫早"服务的电话是多少？

_____

（7）这家旅馆的商务中心在哪儿？白小姐为什么要去商务中心？

_____

（8）他们可以在哪儿换人民币？

_____

2．根据下面的情境写对话。

Based on the situation given, create a dialogue and act it out.

（1）你给旅行社打电话，告诉他们你的旅行计划，请他们帮你买票、预订旅馆、到飞机场接你，等等。

You are calling a travel agency and asking them to book a flight ticket, make a hotel reservation, and pick you up at the airport, etc..

（2）在旅馆的服务台填旅客登记表、拿房卡、付押金。你也问了很多问题。请参考使用下面的附图写出你和服务台小姐的对话。

You check in at the hotel front desk. You ask a lot of questions too. To create a dialogue, you may use the picture below as a clue.

（四）附录

（1）旅客登记表

江西宾馆
JIANGXI HOTEL
☆　☆　☆　☆

房号：
房价：
抵店时间：
离店时间：

REGISTRATION FORM

账 单 号 ACCOUNT No.	抵店日期 ARRIVAL DATE	离店日期 DEP DATE	抵店时间 ARRIVAL TIME	房间种类 ROOM TYPE	房 价 RM RATE	旅行社/公司代码 T/A, C.

房 号 ROOM No.	加收15%服务费及5元/间天的城建费。The room rate subjects to 15 percent service charge and 5 yuan city construction tax.	人 数 No. of GUEST	定 金 DEPOSIT	担 保 GUARANTEED BY

以下由本人用正楷填写 PLEASE WRITE IN BLOCK LETTERS

先生、夫人、小姐(姓名) MR./MRS./MS.(FULL NAME)	出生年、月、日 DATE OF BIRTH
家庭地址 FULL HOME ADDRESS	
证件名称及号码 NAME OF CERTIFICATE WITH NO.	入境日期 DATE OF ARRIVING CHINA
签证种类及期限 TYPE OF VISA AND VALID DATE	国籍 NATIONALITY
公司名称 COMPANY NAME/TITLE	职业 OCCUPATION
由何处来 FROM:	交通工具 CARRIER:	往 TO:

注意：请将贵重物品存放在大堂收银处，否则
　　　如有损失宾馆恕不负责。另在客房内
　　　备有私人保险箱。

Guest Notice: Our hotel is not liable for any loss
of valuables. There are safety boxes available for
the use of the hotel guests free of charge. All
rooms are equipped with a personal safe.

付款方式：
METHOD OF PAYMENT
☐订房凭单　　☐VISA　　　☐龙卡
　VOUCHER　　　　　　　　　DRAGON
☐公司付款　　☐MASTER　☐金穗卡
　COMPANY　　　　　　　　　JINSHUI
☐现金　　　　☐ANEX　　　☐长城卡
　CASH　　　　　　　　　　　GREAT WALL
☐DINERS　　　☐JCB　　　　☐牡丹卡
　　　　　　　　　　　　　　　PEONY

宾客签名
GUEST SIGNATURE:

收银员
CASHIER:

（中国江西财经大学经济文化传播系提供）

27

(2) 人民币、外币兑换表

人民币基准价(人民币/100 外币)
中国人民银行 2003 年 3 月 15 日

	美元	日元	欧元	港币
人民币	827.7000	7.0012	902.2900	106.0900

中国人民银行外汇汇率
2003 年 3 月 15 日每一百单位外汇币价

货币种类	现汇买入	现钞买入	卖出价
英镑	1322.7100	1291.5800	1326.6800
港币	105.9700	105.3300	106.2900
美元	826.4600	821.4900	828.9400
瑞士法郎	606.8600	593.1700	609.9000
新加坡元	471.6300	460.5300	473.0500
瑞典克朗	96.5500	94.2800	96.8400
丹麦克朗	120.0600	117.2400	120.4200
挪威克朗	113.9300	111.2400	114.2700
日元	6.9629	6.9106	6.9978
加拿大元	556.5200	543.4200	558.1900
澳大利亚元	491.6200	480.5300	494.0900
欧元	892.0400	884.4400	894.7200
澳门元	102.9000	102.2800	103.2000
菲律宾比索	15.0400	14.6900	15.0900
泰国铢	19.3100	18.8600	19.3700
新西兰元	452.2400	441.5900	453.6000

(中国银行网站 2003 年 3 月 15 日资料)

第三课 正式见面

今天是中美双方代表的第一次正式见面。王国安总经理代表东方进出口公司对美方表示欢迎。史强生先生代表美国国际贸易公司向中方说明了这次访问的目的。

(一) 对话

1. 问候和介绍

王国安： 欢迎，欢迎！欢迎光临。

李信文： 让我来介绍一下儿。这位是美国国际贸易公司亚洲地区总裁史强生先生；这位是他的助理，白琳小姐。这位是我们公司的总经理王国安先生；这位是公共关系部主任张红小姐。

史强生： 幸会，幸会！你们好！(握手)这是我的名片，请多指教。 zhǐ jiào

王国安： 不敢当。这是我的名片，以后也请您多多指教！

史强生： 哪里，哪里！

王国安： 我们坐下谈吧。(倒茶)请喝茶。昨天晚上休息得好吗？

史强生： 休息得很好。旅馆很舒服，服务也很周到。谢谢贵公司的安排。

王国安： 别客气。这是我们应该做的。在北京期间，如果你们有什么问题的话，请随时跟我和李先生联系，或者告诉张红小姐。

张　红： 这是我的名片。上边有我的电话号码和手机的号码。

史强生：
白　琳：　谢谢，谢谢！

李信文： 王总，白琳小姐是我们的老朋友了。去年夏天她来北京，也住在长城饭店。

王国安： 太好了！白小姐，欢迎您再次来到中国！

白　琳： 谢谢！上次李先生给了我很多帮助，我们合作得很愉快。我非常喜欢北京。

2．说明访问目的

史强生： 这次我们来中国的目的是想跟贵公司洽谈一下儿今年秋季的新订单和签订代理合同的问题。另外，如果可能的话，我们也想参观几家工厂，看看生产情况。

王国安： 好啊。我们想把第一次会谈安排在明天上午。参观工厂的事儿，李先生正在联系、安排。等一会儿让他给你们介绍一下儿。

白　琳： 要是有时间的话，我们也希望能够去经济特区看看。像深圳、珠海、厦门等等。

李信文： 我想这些都没有问题。今天下午我们就可以讨论一下儿日程安排。

史强生： 好，没问题。

张　红： 今天晚上，王总打算请大家吃饭，欢迎史先生和白小姐。白小姐，晚上六点半我去旅馆接你们，行吗？

白　琳： 行！六点半我们在大厅等您。

美方　中方

词汇（一）Vocabulary（1）：

√1.	正式	zhèngshì	formal(ly)；official(ly)
2.	双方	shuāngfāng	both sides/parties (in negotiations, etc.)
3.	总经理	zǒngjīnglǐ	general manager；president
√4.	目的	mùdì	purpose；objective；goal
5.	问候	wènhòu	greeting
6.	光临	guānglín	presence (of a guest, etc.)；be present
√7.	亚洲	Yàzhōu	Asia
√8.	地区	dìqū	region；area；district
9.	总裁	zǒngcái	chief executive officer；CEO
10.	助理	zhùlǐ	assistant
11.	主任	zhǔrèn	director
12.	幸会	xìnghuì	It's a pleasure to meet you.

30

√13.	名片	míngpiàn	business card; name card
14.	指教	zhǐjiào	to give advice/comments
15.	不敢当	bùgǎndāng	I don't deserve your compliment; you flatter me.
16.	倒	dào	to pour (tea, etc.)
17.	周到	zhōudào	attentive; considerate; thorough
√18.	期间	qījiān	period; time
19.	随时	suíshí	at any time
√20.	号码	hàomǎ	number
21.	手机	shǒujī	cellular phone
√22.	合作	hézuò	to cooperate; to work together; cooperation
23.	洽谈	qiàtán	to talk over with; to negotiate; negotiation
24.	秋季	qiūjì	autumn
√25.	订单	dìngdān	order sheet; order
26.	签订	qiāndìng	to conclude and sign (a contract, etc.)
27.	代理	dàilǐ	agency; representation; to act as agent; agent
√28.	合同	hétong	contract; agreement
29.	会谈	huìtán	talks
30.	等等	děngděng	and so on; etc.
31.	经济特区	jīngjì tèqū	special economic zone
√32.	日程	rìchéng	schedule; itinerary

专有名词 Proper Nouns：

1.	王国安	Wáng Guó'ān	a name
2.	公共关系部	Gōnggòng Guānxì Bù	Department of Public Relations
3.	张红	Zhāng Hóng	a name
4.	深圳	Shēnzhèn	a city name
5.	珠海	Zhūhǎi	a city name
6.	厦门	Xiàmén	a city name
7.	王总	Wáng Zǒng	a short form for President Wang

31

句型(一) Sentence Patterns(1):

1. A 代表 B V.……   A V. …on behalf of B

   王总经理代表东方公司欢迎美国代表。

   他代表美方说明了这次访问的目的。

2. 让 sb. (来)V.   let sb. V./allow sb. to V.（usually provide some sort of service）

   让我来介绍一下儿。

   让李先生安排明天的日程。

3. 在……期间   during (a certain period of time)

   在北京期间,我们合作得很愉快。

   在这次访问期间,美国代表参观了四家工厂。

4. (sb. V.……的)目的是……   the purpose (that sb. V.…) is …

   我们来中国的目的是洽谈明年的订单问题。

   他去深圳的目的是参观经济特区。

5. 如果/要是……的话   if…

   如果可能的话,我们也想参观几家工厂。

   要是能买到飞机票的话,我打算明天去深圳。

6. 像 A, B, C 等等   such as A, B, C and so on

   我们希望去经济特区看看。像深圳、珠海、厦门等等。

   我喜欢喝茶。像红茶、绿茶、花茶等等,我都常喝。

(二) 阅读短文

宾主见面的礼仪

中国人总是习惯用握手来表示欢迎、感谢或者友好。宾主见面的时候,主人应该首先跟客人握手,表示问候。中国人不习惯互相拥抱。即使是老朋友,见面拥抱也会使中国人觉得不舒服。

很多中国人喜欢在初次见面的时候,互相交换名片。别人给你名片的时

32

chū cì

候,你应该用两只手接,表示礼貌。名片既可以帮助你记住对方的姓名,又便于今后互相联系。顺便说一句,有些人喜欢在自己的名片上列出很多头衔。别担心,你只要记住他的第一个头衔就够了。一般说,列在第一的头衔常常是最重要的。

词汇(二) Vocabulary(2):

1.	宾主	bīnzhǔ	guest and host
2.	礼仪	lǐyí	etiquette; rite; protocol
3.	首先	shǒuxiān	first; first of all
4.	拥抱	yōngbào	to hug; to embrace
5.	即使	jíshǐ	even; even if
6.	初次	chūcì	the first time
7.	交换	jiāohuàn	to exchange; to swap
8.	礼貌	lǐmào	courtesy; politeness
9.	既……也……	jì…yě…	both...and...; as well as
10.	对方	duìfāng	the opposite side; the other party
11.	姓名	xìngmíng	full name
12.	便于	biànyú	easy to; convenient for
13.	今后	jīnhòu	from now on; henceforth; in the future
14.	顺便说一句	shùnbiàn shuō yíjù	by the way; incidentally
	顺便	shùnbiàn	conveniently
15.	列	liè	to list
16.	头衔	tóuxián	official title
17.	一般说	yìbānshuō	generally speaking
	一般	yìbān	general(ly); common(ly)

句型(二) Sentence Patterns(2):

1. 习惯 + V.   be used to/accustomed to V.

    中国人见面的时候,不习惯拥抱。

    我习惯每天七点起床。

2. 即使……也……   even (if) …(still) …

    即使是老朋友,见面拥抱也会使中国人觉得不舒服。

    即使你没有东西需要交税,也得填海关申报表。

3. 既……又……   both A and B; A as well as B

    使用因特网既快又方便。

    服务台既收现金,又收信用卡。

4. 便于   easy to; convenient for

    让我们互相交换名片,便于今后联系。

    请早一点儿告诉李先生您的打算,便于他做出日程安排。

5. 一般说(来)   generally speaking

    一般说,列在第一的头衔常常是最重要的。

    一般说来,见面的时候,中国人不习惯互相拥抱。

(三) 练习与活动

I. 句型练习一 Sentence Patterns Exercises(1)

1. 用"A 代表 B + V.……"的句型完成下面的句子。请从本课的附录《常见职称、头衔》中选择合适的头衔,用在你的句子中。

Use the pattern of "A 代表 B + V.……" to complete the following sentences. Please chose proper titles from the list of "Common Job Titles and Official Titles" (see the Appendix in Lesson 3) and apply them in your sentences.

(1) _____ 代表 _____ 欢迎 _____。

(2) _____ 代表 _____ 说明 _____。

(3) _____ 代表 _____ 参加 _____。

34

(4) _____ 代表 _____ 感谢 _____ 。

(5) _____ 代表 _____ 签订 _____ 。

2. 根据下面的要求,用"让 sb.(来)V.……"的句型造句:

Use the pattern of "让 sb.(来)V.……"to accomplish the following tasks:

(1) 在飞机场,你看见一位小姐有很多箱子,你想帮忙。你说:

_____

(2) 你为客人介绍公司的经理、主任和助理。你说:

_____

(3) 你打算告诉中方你这次访问的目的。你说:

_____

(4) 你告诉你的朋友,你愿意为他打电话预订旅馆。你说:

_____

3. 完成下面带"在……期间"句型的句子:

Complete the following sentences that contain the pattern of "在……期间"

(1) 在这次谈判期间, _____ 。

(2) 在中国旅行期间, _____ 。

(3) 在美国代表访问期间, _____ 。

(4) 在参观经济特区期间, _____ 。

4. 用"(sb. V.……的)目的是……"回答下面的问题:

Answer the following questions by using "(sb. V.……的)目的是……":

(1) 请问,您这次为什么来中国访问?

_____

(2) 史先生为什么给李经理发传真?

_____

(3) 下个月王总为什么要去美国?

_____

(4) 你为什么学商务中文?

_____

5. 用"如果/要是……的话"的句型完成下面的对话：

Complete the following dialogues by using the pattern of " 如果/要是……的话"：

(1) A：您希望哪天洽谈明年的订单问题？

B：_____

(2) A：今天我们可以签订合同吗？

B：_____

(3) A：这次您打算去别的城市看看吗？

B：_____

(4) A：张经理，谢谢您这次帮我们解决了一个大问题。以后请您一定要多多指教！

B：不敢当。_____

6. 回答下面的问题，并用"像 A，B，C 等等"的句型举出例子：

Give your answers to the following questions along with examples by using the pattern of "像 A，B，C 等等"：

(1) 你下次到中国打算去哪些地方？

_____

(2) 入境的时候要办哪些手续？

_____

(3) 三星级旅馆一般有哪些服务？

_____

(4) 你喜欢吃中国菜吗？ 你喜欢什么中国菜？

_____

II．句型练习二 Sentence Patterns Exercises(2)：

1. 用 "习惯 + V．"回答下面的问题：

Answer the following questions by using "习惯 + V．"：

(1) 中国人习惯喝茶还是习惯喝咖啡？

_____

(2) 为什么史先生觉得用现金买东西很麻烦？

_____

(3) 宾主初次见面的时候,中国人一般怎样表示对客人的欢迎？

_____

(4) 二十年前,人们洽谈生意的时候一般怎样互相联系？现在呢？

_____

2. 用"即使……也……"的句型说出你的决定：

Use the pattern of "即使……也……"to tell your decisions for the following：

(1) 去中国旅行很有意思,可是得坐十几个小时的飞机。你想去吗？

_____

(2) 那家旅馆的服务很周到,可是有一点儿远,不太方便。你打算住吗？

_____

(3) 这家旅馆非常贵,可是它是最好的五星级旅馆。你愿意住吗？

_____

(4) 明天的日程安排是去参观工厂,可是我听说明天可能下雨。你去不去？

_____

3. 用"既……又……"的句型回答下面的问题：

Answer the following questions by using the pattern of "既……又……"：

(1) 为什么很多人都喜欢用因特网？

_____

(2) 你上次住的那家旅馆怎么样？

_____

(3) 外国人在中国旅行可以使用信用卡吗？

_____

(4) 昨天的洽谈,中美双方谈到了哪些问题？

_____

4. 用"便于"的句型回答下面的问题：

Use the pattern of "便于"to answer the following questions：

(1) 为什么做生意的人在初次见面的时候,常常喜欢互相交换名片？

_____

（2）为什么现在用手机的人越来越多？

_____

（3）为什么去中国做生意应该学会说中文？

_____

（4）为什么应该早一点儿通知中方你的旅行计划？

_____

5. 用"一般说"回答下面的问题：

Answer the following questions by using the pattern of "一般说"：

（1）去外国旅行的时候,应该带哪些东西？

_____

（2）用旅馆的电话便宜还是用电话卡便宜？

_____

（3）一个商务代表的名片常常会列出哪些东西？

_____

（4）在中国,宾主见面的时候有哪些礼仪？

_____

III. 词汇练习 Vocabulary Exercises：

1. 用中文回答下面的问题：

Answer the following questions in Chinese.

（1）在这一课里,你学到了哪些职称和头衔？

_____

（2）初次见面的时候,中国人习惯用一些表示客气的词,说一些表示礼貌的
话。在这一课里,你学到了哪些？ 你还知道哪些吗？

_____

2. 组词 Build upon the following words.

例如 For example：顺利 → 工作顺利、一切顺利

（1）正式 → _____

（2）问候 → _____

（3）周到 → _____

38

(4) 期间 → ＿＿＿＿＿＿＿＿＿ ＿＿＿＿＿＿＿＿＿

(5) 号码 → ＿＿＿＿＿＿＿＿＿ ＿＿＿＿＿＿＿＿＿

(6) 洽谈 → ＿＿＿＿＿＿＿＿＿ ＿＿＿＿＿＿＿＿＿

(7) 签订 → ＿＿＿＿＿＿＿＿＿ ＿＿＿＿＿＿＿＿＿

(8) 交换 → ＿＿＿＿＿＿＿＿＿ ＿＿＿＿＿＿＿＿＿

IV. 阅读、写作 和讨论 Reading, Writing and Discussion：

1. 根据课文对话回答问题：

Answer the following questions according to the dialogues in this lesson：

(1) 中美双方参加今天见面的有哪些人？

＿＿＿＿＿＿＿＿＿＿＿＿＿＿＿＿＿＿＿＿＿＿＿＿＿＿＿＿＿

(2) 双方代表见面的时候,他们互相交换了什么？

＿＿＿＿＿＿＿＿＿＿＿＿＿＿＿＿＿＿＿＿＿＿＿＿＿＿＿＿＿

(3) 史强生的头衔是什么？ 白琳呢？

＿＿＿＿＿＿＿＿＿＿＿＿＿＿＿＿＿＿＿＿＿＿＿＿＿＿＿＿＿

(4) 为什么李先生告诉王总说"白琳小姐是我们的老朋友了"？

＿＿＿＿＿＿＿＿＿＿＿＿＿＿＿＿＿＿＿＿＿＿＿＿＿＿＿＿＿

(5) 谁是张红？ 她的头衔是什么？

＿＿＿＿＿＿＿＿＿＿＿＿＿＿＿＿＿＿＿＿＿＿＿＿＿＿＿＿＿

(6) 美国代表这次来中国的目的是什么？

＿＿＿＿＿＿＿＿＿＿＿＿＿＿＿＿＿＿＿＿＿＿＿＿＿＿＿＿＿

(7) 美方代表还想去哪些地方参观？

＿＿＿＿＿＿＿＿＿＿＿＿＿＿＿＿＿＿＿＿＿＿＿＿＿＿＿＿＿

(8) 今天下午有什么安排？ 今天晚上有什么安排？ 明天上午有什么安排？

＿＿＿＿＿＿＿＿＿＿＿＿＿＿＿＿＿＿＿＿＿＿＿＿＿＿＿＿＿

(9) 美国代表在北京期间,如果需要帮助,可以跟谁联系？ 怎么联系？

＿＿＿＿＿＿＿＿＿＿＿＿＿＿＿＿＿＿＿＿＿＿＿＿＿＿＿＿＿

2. 名片 Business Cards

(1) 根据下面的这张名片回答问题。

Answer the following questions regarding the business card below.

```
┌─────────────────────────────────────────┐
│  长城国际贸易公司总经理                    │
│  北京企业家协会理事                        │
│  世界贸易会会员                            │
│                                           │
│               许 永 金                     │
│                                           │
│              地址：北京长安东路六号         │
│              电话：(010)6645 - 8888        │
│              传真：(010)6645 - 3288        │
│              手机：13301020570             │
└─────────────────────────────────────────┘
```

(a) 从这张名片你可以知道什么？

_____

(b) 许先生有三个头衔。哪个头衔最重要？

_____

(2) 用中文为白琳做一张名片。再为你自己也做一张名片。

```
┌───────────────────┐   ┌───────────────────┐
│                   │   │                   │
│                   │   │                   │
│                   │   │                   │
│                   │   │                   │
│                   │   │                   │
│                   │   │                   │
└───────────────────┘   └───────────────────┘
```

3. 这个星期, 一个外国贸易代表团来东方进出口公司访问。今天是双方代表的第一次正式见面。你为每个人做了介绍, 双方交换了名片, 互相说了一些表示客气的话等等。外国代表也向中方说明了他们来中国的目的。请用以上的内容写一个对话或者短剧。

This week a trading delegation from a foreign county will visit Eastern Import & Export Company. Today both sides are having the first formal meeting. You introduced them to each other, then everyone exchanged business cards. The visitors also gave a brief explanation about their main purpose of this trip. Write a short script about the occasion. Please include a dialogue and other background information related to proper manners, such as shaking hands, etc.

（四）附录

（1）常见职称、头衔 Common Job Titles and Official Titles

工商企业（Industry and Commerce）：

董事长	Dǒngshìzhǎng	Chairman of the Board
常务董事	Chángwù Dǒngshì	Managing Director
董事	Dǒngshì	Director；Trustee
总经理	Zǒngjīnglǐ	President；General Manager
总裁	Zǒngcái	President；CEO
部门经理/部门主管	Bùmén Jīnglǐ/Bùmén Zhǔguǎn	Department Manager
厂长	Chǎngzhǎng	Factory Director；Factory Manager
总工程师	Zǒnggōngchéngshī	Chief Engineer
工程师	Gōngchéngshī	Engineer
审计师	Shěnjìshī	Comptroller
会计师	Kuàijìshī	Accountant

政府部门（Government Departments）：

部长	Bùzhǎng	Minister
司长	Sīzhǎng	Department Director（at the state level）
厅长/局长	Tīngzhǎng/Júzhǎng	Department or Bureau Director（at the provincial level）
处长	Chùzhǎng	Section Chief
办公室主任	Bàngōngshì Zhǔrèn	Office Director
科长	Kēzhǎng	Office Chief

（2）名片实例

广州大三元饮食有限公司

黄兴源 董事长

地址：广州市珠海路 128 号　　　　邮编：510079
电话：(027)3612788　　　　　　手机：13072072142

长江电子工业集团总经理
长江科技发展基金会董事

王志强

地址：上海市西藏北路 159 号　　电话：(021)7813328(办)
邮编：200014　　　　　　　　手机：13072015699
传真：(021)7813329　　　　　电子信箱：wzq@hotmail.com

西北大众报

张宏文
主任记者

广告信息部主任
编辑出版部副主任
大众广告总公司总经理

地址：西安市东大街 10 号　　　电话：(029)47813328
邮编：290114　　　　　　　　传真：(029)41417813
电子信箱：hwzhang@nwnews.com.cn　手机：13805100268

第四课　日程安排

史强生和白琳计划在中国逗留一个星期左右。除了跟中国方面洽谈业务以外，他们也要参观工厂和考察经济特区。因为他们的时间很紧，所以需要一个很好的日程安排。

（一）对话

1. 讨论日程安排

李信文：　史先生、白小姐，现在我们一起来谈谈日程安排，怎么样？

史强生：　好啊。这次来中国，我们要办的事很多，是得好好儿地计划一下。我们打算在中国一共呆八天，您看时间够吗？

李信文：　如果把活动安排得紧一点儿，应该没问题。

白　琳：　李先生安排日程非常有经验。去年我在北京，他把每天都安排得满满的。上午洽谈业务，下午参观，晚上看表演，连给男朋友打电话的时间都没有！（笑）

李信文：　（笑）对不起，白小姐。这次我们一定给你专门留出打电话的时间。

白　琳：　没关系，不用了！反正现在我们已经吹了！

2. 修改日程安排

李信文：　这次的日程，我想这样安排：前面五天在北京；后面三天，两天在上海，一天在深圳。你们觉得怎么样？

史强生：　在深圳只呆一天，时间是不是太短了？听说深圳的几家高科技产品公司很有意思，我很希望能有机会去参观参观。

李信文：　如果是这样的话，我们可以把计划改成在北京四天，上海和深圳各两天。行吗？

白　琳：　我觉得这样比较合适。李先生，请问在北京的活动是怎么安排的？

李信文： 在北京，除了洽谈业务以外，还要参观一家服装厂，一家玩具厂，游览故宫和长城。

史强生： 这样安排很好。李先生，让您费心了！

李信文： 没什么，这是我应该做的。另外，今天晚上七点是欢迎宴会，明天晚上，服装厂的钱厂长想邀请你们两位吃饭，后天晚上我想请你们吃北京烤鸭……

史强生： 李先生，您太客气了！

白　琳： (对史强生说)现在你知道为什么去年我胖了十磅吧？ (笑)

词汇(一) Vocabulary(1)：

1.	逗留	dòuliú	to stay; to stop
2.	左右	zuǒyòu	about; around
3.	业务	yèwù	business; professional work
4.	考察	kǎochá	to observe and study; to inspect
5.	好好儿	hǎohāor	carefully; to the best of one's ability
6.	呆	dāi	to stay
7.	专门	zhuānmén	specially; special; specialized
8.	反正	fǎnzhèng	anyway; anyhow; in any case
9.	吹	chuī	to break up (with boyfriend/girlfriend); to fall through (of plans)
10.	修改	xiūgǎi	to revise; to modify; revision
11.	前面	qiánmian	in front; ahead
12.	后面	hòumian	at the back; behind
13.	高科技	gāokējì	high technology; high-tech
14.	产品	chǎnpǐn	product
15.	服装	fúzhuāng	dress; clothing
16.	玩具	wánjù	toy
17.	游览	yóulǎn	to tour; to visit; sight-seeing
18.	费心	fèixīn	to give a lot of care; to take a lot of trouble
19.	没什么	méishénme	it's nothing; it doesn't matter

20.	另外	lìngwài	in addition; besides
21.	厂长	chǎngzhǎng	directory director/manager
22.	邀请	yāoqǐng	to invite; invitation
23.	后天	hòutiān	day after tomorrow
24.	磅	bàng	pound

专有名词 Proper Nouns：

1.	故宫	Gùgōng	the Imperial Palace
2.	长城	Chángchéng	the Great Wall
3.	北京烤鸭	Běijīng Kǎoyā	Beijing roast duck

句型（一）Sentence Patterns（1）：

1. 除了……以外,也/ 还……　　　　　besides/in addition to…, also…

   除了跟中国方面洽谈业务以外,他们也要参观工厂和经济特区。

   除了样品以外,他还带了几件礼物。

2. 因为……所以……　　　　　because…so/therefore…

   因为他们的时间很紧,所以需要一个很好的日程安排。

   因为她每天都很忙,所以没有时间常给男朋友打电话。

3. 是得/是应该……　　must/should (indicates confirmation or strong intention)

   我们要办的事很多,是得好好儿地计划一下儿。

   那家工厂很有意思,你们是应该去参观参观。

4. 连……都/也……　　　　　even

   她连给男朋友打电话的时间都没有!

   我连电脑也带来了。

5. 反正　　　　　anyway; anyhow; in any case

   反正现在我们已经吹了!

   没有带现金没关系,反正我有信用卡。

（二）阅读短文

吃得好、玩儿得好、生意做得好

中国地大人多，交通繁忙。外国人在中国旅行，不但会有语言的问题，而且常常会遇到一些想不到的麻烦。如果你计划去中国，一定要安排好你的旅行计划。你可以把你的日程表事先寄给中方，或者把想要参观、访问的地方通知你在中国的接待单位，请他们为你安排日程。

无论你是去中国洽谈生意还是私人访问，游览和赴宴都是中国人日程安排中少不了的内容。尤其是频繁的请客吃饭，有时候甚至会成为一种负担。中国人觉得，请客吃饭有助于建立关系、发展友谊。有谁在吃了一顿丰盛的晚饭以后，还能对主人说"不"呢？

词汇（二）Vocabulary（2）：

1. 交通	jiāotōng	traffic; transportation; communications
2. 繁忙	fánmáng	(very) busy; hectic
3. 想不到	xiǎng bu dào	unexpected
4. 事先	shìxiān	in advance; beforehand
5. 接待单位	jiēdài dānwèi	host organization
6. 无论	wúlùn	no matter; regardless
7. 私人	sīrén	private; personal
8. 赴宴	fùyàn	to attend a banquet
9. 少不了	shǎo bu liǎo	cannot do without; indispensable
10. 尤其	yóuqí	especially; particularly; in particular
11. 频繁	pínfán	frequently; incessant
12. 请客	qǐngkè	invite/entertain guests; treat sb. (to a meal)
13. 甚至	shènzhì	even (to the extent that …); to go so far as
14. 成为	chéngwéi	to become; to turn into
15. 负担	fùdān	burden

47

16.	有助于	yǒuzhùyú	be conducive/helpful to
17.	建立	jiànlì	to establish; to build
18.	顿	dùn	a measure word for meals
19.	丰盛	fēngshèng	rich; sumptuous
20.	主人	zhǔrén	host

句型(二) Sentence Patterns(2):

1. 不但……而且……　　　　　　not only…but also…

　　外国人在中国旅行,不但会有语言的问题,而且常常会遇到一些想不到的麻烦。

　　我们今年的旅行不但玩儿得很好而且吃得非常好。

2. 无论……还是……　　　　　　no matter…or…

　　无论你是去中国洽谈生意还是私人访问,都应该把你的日程安排好。

　　无论您要订单间还是套房,我们都有。

3. 尤其是　　　　　　especially; particularly; in particular

　　尤其是频繁的请客吃饭,有时候甚至会成为一种负担。

　　这家旅馆的服务很好,尤其是它的商务中心。

4. A 有助于 B　　　　　　A is conducive/helpful to B

　　中国人觉得,请客吃饭有助于建立关系、发展友谊。

　　会说中文有助于跟中国人交朋友。

(三) 练习与活动

I. 句型练习一 Sentence Patterns Exercises (1):

1. 用"除了……以外,也/还"的句型完成下面的句子。

Complete the following sentences by using the pattern of "除了……以外,也/还":

(1) 除了洽谈订单以外,我们还要_____。

48

(2) 除了参观玩具厂以外,美国代表也打算_____。

(3) 除了预订飞机票以外,李先生还要_____。

(4) 除了签订新合同以外,中美双方也要_____。

(5) 除了_____。

2. 用"因为……所以……"的句型回答下面的问题。

Answer the following questions by using the pattern "因为……所以……":

(1) 请问,为什么外国人不能住这家旅馆?

_____

(2) 张主任,昨天的宴会您怎么没来呀?

_____

(3) 为什么您不打算跟那家公司签订合同了?

_____

(4) 今天为什么大家都很严肃?

_____

3. 用"是得 /是应该……"的句型完成下面的句子。

Complete the following sentences by using the pattern of "是得 /是应该 ……":

(1) 这次访问的时间很紧,要去的地方很多,是得_____。

(2) 北京烤鸭非常有名,你们是应该_____。

(3) 明天的谈判很重要,我们是得_____。

(4) 今天参观了两家工厂,大家都很累,晚上是应该_____。

(5) _____,是得/是应该_____。

4. 用" 连……都……"的句型完成下面的对话。

Complete the following dialogues by using the pattern " 连……都……":

(1) A: 白小姐,你请旅行社预订了去中国的飞机票了吗?

B: 别担心。我连_____都预订好了!

(2) A: 王总,昨天跟美国贸易代表的谈判顺利吗?

B: 非常顺利。我们连_____都签订好了!

(3) A: 哇,这么大的箱子,你一定带了不少东西!

B: 是啊,我连_____都带来了。

(4) A: 李经理, 好几天没有看见您了。您最近忙吧?

B: 忙极了! 这个星期我连＿＿＿＿＿＿＿＿＿＿＿都没有时间!

5. 用"反正"的句型回答下面的问题。

Answer the following questions by using the pattern "反正":

(1) A: 不好, 我忘了带信用卡! 怎么办?

B: ＿＿＿＿＿＿＿＿＿＿＿＿＿＿＿＿＿＿＿＿＿＿

(2) A: 对不起, 今天大概没有时间去那家高科技公司考察了!

B: ＿＿＿＿＿＿＿＿＿＿＿＿＿＿＿＿＿＿＿＿＿＿

(3) A: 谈了一天生意, 今天晚上我们好好儿休息休息, 怎么样?

B: ＿＿＿＿＿＿＿＿＿＿＿＿＿＿＿＿＿＿＿＿＿＿

(4) A: 我们就住这家五星级旅馆吧, 你觉得怎么样?

B: ＿＿＿＿＿＿＿＿＿＿＿＿＿＿＿＿＿＿＿＿＿＿

II. 句型练习二 Sentence Patterns Exercises(2):

1. 根据下面的要求, 用"不但……而且……"的句型造句:

Use the pattern of "不但……而且……" to accomplish the following tasks:

(1) 昨天的欢迎宴会非常丰盛。请用 "不但……而且……" 说一说晚宴上有什么菜?

＿＿＿＿＿＿＿＿＿＿＿＿＿＿＿＿＿＿＿＿＿＿＿＿＿＿＿＿

(2) 在今天的洽谈中, 双方代表谈到了很多问题。请用 "不但……而且……" 说一说他们谈到了哪些问题?

＿＿＿＿＿＿＿＿＿＿＿＿＿＿＿＿＿＿＿＿＿＿＿＿＿＿＿＿

(3) 请用"不但……而且……"说一说为什么美国代表希望在中国多逗留几天?

＿＿＿＿＿＿＿＿＿＿＿＿＿＿＿＿＿＿＿＿＿＿＿＿＿＿＿＿

(4) 外国人到中国做生意, 常常会遇到一些想不到的问题。请用"不但……而且……"说一说他们可能会遇到什么问题。

＿＿＿＿＿＿＿＿＿＿＿＿＿＿＿＿＿＿＿＿＿＿＿＿＿＿＿＿

2. 用"无论……还是……"的句型回答下面的问题。

Answer the following questions by using the pattern "无论……还是……":

(1) 中国人习惯跟新朋友拥抱还是跟老朋友拥抱？

_____

(2) 这件是礼物,那两件是样品,请问我应该填海关申报表吗？

_____

(3) 明天您想参观服装厂还是游览长城？

_____

(4) 你觉得长城饭店的服务好还是希尔顿饭店的服务好？

_____

3. 用"尤其是"的句型回答下面的问题。

Answer the following questions by using the pattern "尤其是"：

(1) 你喜欢吃中国菜吗？ 你最喜欢哪个菜？

_____

(2) 你想去中国的哪些地方？ 最想去哪个地方？

_____

(3) 请问,您这次想看看我们的哪些产品？ 最想看什么产品？

_____

(4) 外国人在中国会遇到一些不习惯的事。你觉得什么事他们最不习惯？

_____

4. 用"A 有助于 B"的句型回答下面的问题。

Answer the following questions by using the pattern "A 有助于 B"：

(1) 会说中文有什么好处？

_____

(2) 交换名片有什么好处？

_____

(3) 为什么做生意的时候,请客吃饭常常是少不了的事？

_____

(4) 为什么来谈生意的外国代表,常常希望参观、考察工厂？

_____

III. 词汇练习 Vocabulary：

1. 组词 Build upon the following words.

例如 For example：正式 → 正式见面、正式访问

顺利 → 工作顺利、一切顺利

(1) 繁忙 → _____ _____

(2) 修改 → _____ _____

(3) 游览 → _____ _____

(4) 左右 → _____ _____

(5) 私人 → _____ _____

(6) 负担 → _____ _____

(7) 建立 → _____ _____

(8) 事先 → _____ _____

(9) 产品 → _____ _____

(10) 考察 → _____ _____

2. 用中文解释下面的词汇, 再造句：

Use Chinese to explain the meaning of the following, then make a sentence：

例如 For example：频繁 :次数很多

李经理频繁地给对方打电话, 总算把事情安排好了。

(1) 逗留：_____

(2) 好好儿：_____

(3) 吹：_____

(4) 费心：_____

(5) 少不了：_____

IV. 阅读、写作与讨论 Reading, Writing and Discussion：

1. 根据课文回答问题：

Answer the following questions according to the dialogues in this lesson：

(1) 史强生和白琳计划这次在中国逗留几天?

_____

（2）李信文觉得他们的时间够不够？

_____

（3）为什么白琳说李信文安排日程非常有经验？

_____

（4）白琳现在有男朋友没有？

_____

（5）史强生希望去深圳参观什么地方？

_____

（6）在北京的时候,除了洽谈业务以外,美国代表还要去哪些地方？

_____

（7）李信文修改了日程安排。现在美国代表在北京呆几天？ 在上海和深圳
呆几天？

_____

（8）李先生计划什么时候请美国客人吃北京烤鸭？

_____

（9）为什么去年白琳胖了十磅？

_____

2. 在安排、接待来洽谈生意的客人时,中国人有哪些习惯？ 在你的国家(文化)
里也有这样的习惯吗？ 请列出三个到五个相同和不同的习惯,跟你的同学
进行讨论。

When it comes to receiving business associates, what do the Chinese usually
do? Are there similar practices in your culture? Please list three or more obser-
vations and discuss with your class.

3. 你正在计划下个月去中国的商务旅行,打算把你的计划用传真发给在中国
的接待单位。请用中文写出你在中国的日程安排。例如,到达中国的时间,
你要去的城市,逗留的时间,你打算参观、考察的工厂和公司,你计划跟哪些
人见面,洽谈什么问题等等。

You are going to Beijing on a business trip, and you want to fax your tentative plans to your host organization in China so they can make the necessary arrangements for you. Write a paragraph about your "日程安排." You might want to include the date that you will arrive at China, what other cities you would like to visit, how long you want to stay in a particular place, what other companies and factories you want to see, who you would like to meet and what kind of business matters you would like to take care of while you're there, and so on. Use new vocabulary and patterns whenever possible.

（四）附录

日程表实例

××贸易代表团访华日程表

一月二日(星期五)

    上午 10时：   抵达北京(外贸公司代表××前往迎接)

          10时30分： 前往北京饭店

          12时：   在饭店进午餐

    下午 2时：   会见纺织品公司××总经理

          2时30分： 与纺织品公司出口处处长××会谈

          6时30分： 宴会(××总经理在国际俱乐部宴请)

一月三日(星期六)

    上午 10时：   继续同出口处处长会谈

          12时：   工作午餐

    下午 1时：   参观百花纺织厂(××处长陪同)

    晚上 7时：   观看京剧演出

一月四日(星期日)

    上午 7时30分： 前往颐和园游览

          12时：   在园中午餐

    下午 2时：   前往故宫参观

    晚上 7时：   告别宴会(北京饭店二楼宴会厅)

一月五日(星期一)

    上午 10时：   离开北京(外贸公司代表××送往机场)

(中国江西财经大学经济文化传播系提供)

第五课　出席宴会

王国安总经理代表东方进出口公司举行宴会,欢迎史强生先生和白琳小姐。外贸局的马局长也出席了宴会。史强生和白琳都觉得宴会非常丰盛。

(一) 对话

1. 请坐,请坐,请上座

(在餐厅)

王国安：　史先生、白小姐,你们到了! 请进,请进!

史强生：　谢谢!

白　琳：　这家餐厅布置得可真漂亮!

张　红：　是啊,这儿是北京最有名的饭店之一,大家都喜欢到这儿来。

王国安：　我来为你们介绍一下儿。这位是外贸局的马局长,这位是美国国际
　　　　　贸易公司的史先生、这位是白小姐。

马局长：　欢迎,欢迎! 欢迎两位来中国! (握手)这两天辛苦了吧!

史强生：　还好,不太累。虽然有一点儿时差,但是昨天休息得很好。王总为
　　　　　我们安排得非常周到。

王国安：　各位请入席吧! 史先生、白小姐,你们是客人,请坐这儿。这儿是上
　　　　　座。马局长,您也请坐这儿!

马局长：　你是主人,你跟客人坐一块儿才合适呀!

王国安：　不,不,不,您是领导,应该和贵宾坐一起。我坐您旁边。来,来,来,
　　　　　大家都请随便坐吧!

2. 干杯,干杯!

王国安：　今天晚上是为史先生、白小姐接风。大家先喝一点儿酒,怎么样?
　　　　　史先生,您要茅台酒还是红葡萄酒?

56

史强生： 我听说茅台酒非常有名，我要茅台酒吧。

王国安： 白小姐，您呢？

白　琳： 我不太会喝酒，我喝葡萄酒吧。

王国安： 来，为欢迎史先生和白小姐，干杯！

（大家干杯）

马局长： 史先生，请吃菜。这些都是冷盘，等会儿还有大菜和汤。来，尝尝这个！（给史强生夹菜）

史强生： 谢谢，谢谢！我自己来吧。

（服务员上菜）

张　红： 今天的菜都是这家饭店的特色菜，白小姐，你试试，喜欢吗？（给白琳夹菜）

白　琳： 嗯，很好吃！

张　红： 既然好吃，就多吃一些！你再尝尝这个。（又给白琳夹菜）

白　琳： （笑）谢谢。桌子上这么多菜，我都吃不过来了！

史强生： 王先生，我也敬您一杯，感谢您和各位的热情招待！

王国安： 好，我们一起干一杯，预祝我们的合作圆满成功！

词汇（一）Vocabulary（1）：

1. 出席	chūxí	to attend; be present (at a banquet, etc.)
2. 举行	jǔxíng	to hold (a meeting, etc.)
3. 局长	júzhǎng	director (of a government office or bureau)
4. 布置	bùzhì	to decorate; to arrange
5. ……之一	…zhīyī	one of …
6. 时差	shíchā	time difference; jet lag
7. 入席	rù xí	to take one's seat (at a ceremony, etc.)
8. 上座	shàngzuò	the seat of honor
9. 贵宾	guìbīn	honored/distinguished guest
10. 随便	suíbiàn	as you like; do as one pleases
11. 干杯	gān bēi	to drink a toast; Cheers! ; Bottoms up!
12. 接风	jiēfēng	to give a welcome reception for visitors from afar

13. 葡萄酒	pútáojiǔ	wine
14. 冷盘	lěngpán	cold dish; hors d'oeuvre
15. 大菜	dàcài	main dish
16. 尝	cháng	to taste
17. 夹菜	jiā cài	to pick up food with chopsticks
18. 上菜	shàng cài	to serve (food); to place dishes on the table
19. 特色菜	tèsè cài	special dish; chef's special
20. 嗯	ǹ	"mmm"; h'm; (express an agreement or satisfaction)
21. 既然	jìrán	since; given the fact that
22. 敬	jìng	to offer politely
23. 招待	zhāodài	to receive/entertain (guests); reception
24. 预祝	yùzhù	to congratulate beforehand
25. 圆满	yuánmǎn	satisfactory; satisfactorily
26. 成功	chénggōng	succeed; success; successful

专有名词 Proper Nouns：

| 1. 外贸局 | Wàimàojú | Foreign Trade Bureau |
| 2. 茅台酒 | Máotáijiǔ | Maotai (liquor) |

句型(一) Sentence Patterns(1)：

1. …… 之一   one of …

   这儿是北京最有名的饭馆之一。

   我们的公司是中国最大的公司之一。

2. 虽然……但是/可是……   although … but/however …

   虽然有一点儿时差,但是昨天休息得很好。

   这家旅馆虽然很贵,可是服务非常好。

3. 既然……就……   given the fact that/since … then …

   既然好吃,就多吃一些!

   既然累了,你就休息休息吧。

58

4. 这么多……（我）都 V. 不过来了   there are so many … that one cannot

V. all of them…

这么多菜,我都吃不过来了!

买了这么多东西,我们都拿不过来了!

（二）阅读短文

中国人的宴会

中国菜闻名世界,吃在中国自然也是一件非常重要的事。中国人的宴会总是非常丰盛。据说著名的满汉全席有一百多道菜。就是普通的宴会,也有十多道菜。在宴会上,贵宾和主人被安排在上座。一般说,面对着门或入口的座位是上座。宴会当然少不了酒。"干杯"的意思是喝完你的杯子里的酒。不过,如果你不想马上就醉,最好不要把酒一口气喝下去。因为中国人习惯先喝酒、吃菜,再吃饭、喝汤,所以上菜的次序是先上冷盘,再上热炒和大菜,最后是米饭、汤和甜点。中国人的另外一个习惯是主人应该给客人夹菜。这既代表真诚,又说明主人好客。如果你不习惯这种做法,你可以对主人说:"谢谢,让我自己来。"

词汇（二）Vocabulary（2）:

1. 闻名	wénmíng	famous; well-known
2. 自然	zìrán	of course; naturally
3. 据说	jùshuō	it is said…
4. 著名	zhùmíng	celebrated; renowned
5. 道	dào	a measure word for dishes; courses
6. 普通	pǔtōng	ordinary; common; average
7. 面对	miànduì	to face
8. 入口	rùkǒu	entrance
9. 座位	zuòwèi	seat

10.	醉	zuì	drunk
11.	一口气	yìkǒuqì	in one breath; at one go; without a break; in one stretch
12.	次序	cìxù	order; sequence
13.	热炒	rèchǎo	a fried dish (stir-fried, etc.)
14.	甜点	tiándiǎn	dessert
15.	真诚	zhēnchéng	sincerity; sincere
16.	好客	hàokè	hospitable

专有名词 Proper Nouns：

| 满汉全席 | Mǎnhànquánxí | the complete Manchu and Chinese banquet |

句型（二）Sentence Patterns（2）：

1. 据说   it is said …

    据说著名的满汉全席有一百多道菜。

    据说美国贸易代表团明天要来这儿参观。

2. 就是……也……   even（if）

    在中国,就是普通的宴会,也有十多道菜。

    就是你很忙,也应该给他打一个电话。

3. 把 Obj. 一口气 V. + complement   do sth. at one go/at a stretch

    你最好不要把酒一口气喝下去。

    我们把这些事一口气做完了再休息,好不好?

4. 先……,再……,最后……   first …, then …, lastly …

    中国人习惯先喝酒、吃菜,再吃饭,最后喝汤。

    明天的日程安排是先参观工厂,再参加宴会,最后看电影。

（三）练习与活动

I. 句型练习一 Sentence pattern exercises（1）：

1. 用"……之一"的句型告诉你朋友下面的事：

Use "……之一" to make sentences about the following：

（1）一个中国最有名的菜

_____

（2）一家最好的中国旅馆

_____

（3）一个最重要的中国节日

_____

（4）中国的一个经济特区

_____

（5）一家中国（或者世界）最大的公司

_____

2. 用"虽然…… 但是……"的句型客气地、礼貌地拒绝以下的邀请：

Use "虽然…… 但是……" to decline an offer or invitation in the following situations, but please be polite.

（1）主人请你喝有名的中国酒。

_____

（2）主人请你再多吃一点儿饭店的特色菜。

_____

（3）开了一天的会以后，主人想请你参观他的工厂。

_____

（4）一家中国公司的总裁要给你接风，可是你不想跟这家公司做生意。

_____

3. 用"既然…… 就……"的句型完成下面的句子：

Complete the following sentences by using "既然…… 就……"：

(1) 既然你觉得有时差，_____

(2) 既然时间很紧，_____

(3) 既然您是贵宾，_____

(4) 既然大家都是老朋友，_____

(5) 既然这种产品这么有名，_____

(6) 既然我们公司请你吃了饭，又游览了长城，_____

4. 用"这么多……（我）都 V.不过来了"的句型完成下面的句子：

Complete the following sentences by using "这么多……（我）都 V.不过来了"：

(1) 这么多工作，我都_____

(2) 这么多电话，白小姐都_____

(3) 这么多问题，李经理都_____

(4) 这么多宴会，马局长都_____

(5) 这么多样品，史先生都_____

II. 句型练习二 Sentence pattern exercises（2）：

1. 用"据说"的句型回答下面的问题：

Answer the following questions by using the pattern of "据说"：

(1) 请问有哪些外国大公司在中国做生意？

_____

(2) 除了长城以外，外国人还喜欢去哪些地方游览？

_____

(3) 你听说过满汉全席吗？你知道满汉全席有多少道菜？

_____

(4) 你知道中国人的宴会上菜的次序吗？

_____

(5) 中国人请客吃饭的时候，有哪些习惯？

_____

2. 用"就是……也……"的句型改写下面的句子：

Rewrite the following sentences by using the pattern of "就是……也……"：

（1）茅台酒非常有名。在美国,很多人都知道。

_____

（2）即使我不太会喝酒,也一定要尝尝。

_____

（3）这个月王总非常忙。连星期六也常常得工作。

_____

（4）明天的洽谈很重要。即使还有时差,也得参加。

_____

3. 用"把 Obj. 一口气 V. + complement"的句型完成下面的句子:

Use the pattern of "把 Obj. 一口气 V. + complement" to accomplish the following tasks:

（1）钱厂长非常饿。他把 _____ 一口气都吃完了。

（2）白小姐醉了。她把 _____ 一口气喝下去了!

（3）今天的会谈很顺利。双方把 _____ 一口气都安排好了。

（4）李经理今天很高兴。因为他把 _____ 一口气都做好了。

4. 用"先……,再……, 最后……"的句型回答下面的问题:

Use the pattern of "先……,再……, 最后……" to answer the following questions:

（1）如果你去中国旅行或者做生意,你打算怎么安排你的日程?

_____

（2）去中国以前,你有哪些事需要准备?

_____

（3）明天史先生要和王总经理会谈。他们要谈些什么?

_____

（4）在你的国家,宴会上菜的次序是什么?

_____

III. 词汇练习 Vocabulary Exercises and Special Expressions:

1. 用中文解释以下词汇的意思,然后造句:

Use Chinese to explain the meaning of the following, then make a sentence for each of them:

例如 For example：频繁 :次数很多

李经理频繁地给对方打电话,总算把事情安排好了。

(1) 时差 _____

(2) 上座 _____

(3) 贵宾 _____

(4) 随便 _____

(5) 好客 _____

(6) 圆满 _____

(7) 闻名 _____

(8) 自然 _____

(9) 真诚 _____

(10) 著名 _____

(11) 闻名 _____

2. 列出本课中跟参加宴会有关的词汇。

Write down any words and expressions in this lesson's vocabulary list associated with eating, drinking and attending a dinner party.

_____

3. 什么是"接风"？中国人什么时候"接风"？

What is the meaning of "接风"? In what situations do Chinese people need to "接风"?

_____

IV. 阅读、写作和讨论 Reading, Writing and Discussion：

1. 根据课文回答问题：

Answer the following questions according to the dialogues in this lesson：

(1) 哪些人参加了宴会？

_____

(2) 谁是这次宴会的主人？谁是主人的贵宾？

_____

(3) 这家饭店怎么样?

_____

(4) 王总请史先生和白小姐坐在什么地方?

_____

(5) 马局长是谁? 他坐在哪儿? 为什么?

_____

(6) 白小姐喝了茅台酒没有? 为什么?

_____

(7) 为什么马局长、张红都要给客人夹菜?

_____

(8) 王总为什么举行这个宴会?

_____

2. 你正在一家中国饭馆请美国客人吃饭。你的客人告诉你他非常喜欢中国菜。你按照中国人请客的习惯,给客人夹菜、敬酒。请写一个小对话。请把下面列出的句型用在对话里。

You are entertaining your American client at a Chinese restaurant, and your client just told you that he really likes Chinese food. As a host, naturally you have to make sure he has plenty of food to eat. Use some of the following patterns to write a short dialogue between you and your client. Make sure that you are a good host and that your client knows how to respond appropriately.

"既然……就……"、"先……,再……,最后……"、"据说"、"都 V. 不过来了"。

3. 李先生和白琳小姐是老朋友了。去年夏天在北京他们合作得很愉快。这次白琳跟她的老板史强生先生一起到中国来,李先生想请他们在白琳最喜欢的全家福饭馆吃饭。李先生还邀请了公共关系部主任张红小姐。全家福饭馆的菜单在第五课的附录里。请你用这个菜单,帮李先生安排一桌 250 元左右的晚餐。

Mr. Li and Miss Lynn Petty are old friends. Last summer they had a pleasant experience working together. This time Miss Lynn Petty and her boss, Mr. Johnson Smith, have come to China. Mr. Li invites them to dinner at Miss Lynn Petty's favorite restaurant Quanjiafu. Mr. Li also invites Miss Zhang Hong, the director of Public Relations, to join them. Please see the menu of Quanjiafu Restaurant in Lesson 5's Appendixes. Could you use this menu to plan a dinner at about 250 yuan for Mr. Li?

4. 根据本课的内容和你自己的经验,比较中国宴会和美国(或者你自己国家)宴会的各自特点。例如,宴会的礼节、习惯、上菜的次序,等等。

Based on this lesson's text and your own experience and knowledge, give a presentation comparing a typical Chinese banquet and a typical American (or Western) banquet. Your presentation may include, but is not limited to, the etiquette and convention at a formal banquet, the general sequences for serving dishes, etc..

（四）附录

（1）菜单

全家福饭馆菜单

冷盘

1. 凉拌黄瓜	8.00		2. 凉拌海蛰	8.00
3. 茶叶卤蛋	8.00		4. 油炸花生	8.00
5. 豆腐拌皮蛋	8.00		6. 金陵鸭肫	10.00
7. 五香牛肉	10.00		8. 四色拼盘	10.00

水产、海鲜类

1. 松子鱼	20.00		2. 糖醋鱼	16.00
3. 三鲜海参	48.00		4. 椒盐虾	30.00
5. 腰果虾仁	35.00		6. 全家福烩海鲜	35.00
7. 酱爆田鸡	35.00		8. 红烧甲鱼	时价
9. 清蒸桂鱼	时价		10. 滑炒鲈鱼	时价
11. 姜葱河蟹	时价		12. 基围虾	时价

禽蛋类

13. 辣子鸡丁	18.00		14. 腰果鸡丁	22.00
15. 炒鸡杂	15.00		16. 三杯鸡	18.00
17. 咖哩鸡片	22.00		18. 宫保鸡丁	18.00
19. 时素炒蛋	15.00		20. 全家福涨蛋	14.00
21. 香酥鸭	30.00		22. 北京烤鸭	56.00

煲仔类

23. 什锦豆腐煲 12.00   24. 香辣牛筋煲   18.00
25. 冬笋腐竹煲 15.00   26. 全家福海鲜煲   28.00

豆腐、蔬菜类

27. 三鲜豆腐   12.00   28. 家常豆腐   8.00
29. 麻婆豆腐   8.00   30. 松仁玉米   18.00
31. 蘑菇菜心   18.00   32. 肉末雪菜   8.00
33. 素什锦   10.00   34. 腰果西芹   20.00

猪、牛肉类

35. 红烧肉   18.00   36. 狮子头   18.00
37. 红烧牛腩   18.00   38. 炒腰花   18.00
39. 回锅肉   15.00   40. 木樨肉   15.00
41. 梅菜扣肉   18.00   42. 鱼香肉丝   15.00
43. 糖醋排骨   15.00   44. 咕老肉   15.00

汤菜类

45. 蛋花汤   3.00   46. 酸辣汤   6.00
47. 三鲜汤   10.00   48. 肉丝汤   10.00
49. 酸辣鱼片汤 14.00   50. 草菇鸡丝汤   14.00

甜点类

51. 拔丝苹果   15.00   52. 脆皮香蕉   15.00
53. 珍珠荔枝   20.00   54. 八宝粥   15.00
55. 玉米羹   10.00   56. 银耳汤   15.00

主食

57. 扬州炒饭	8.00	58. 水饺	8.00
59. 蒸饺	10.00	60. 汤包	12.00
61. 小笼包	12.00	62. 炒面	8.00
63. 米饭	3.00	64. 馒头	3.00

(2) 饮料

果汁、汽水

1. 桔子汁	4.00	2. 鲜橙汁	4.00
3. 椰子汁	4.00	4. 柠檬汁	4.00
5. 矿泉水	3.00	6. 健力宝	3.00
7. 可口可乐	6.00	8. 百事可乐	6.00
9. 雪碧	6.00	10. 七喜	6.00

酒类

11. 红葡萄酒	30.00	12. 白葡萄酒	30.00
13. 青岛啤酒	8.00	14. 百威啤酒	10.00
15. 二锅头	20.00	16. 竹叶青	198.00
17. 五粮液	298.00	18. 茅台酒	398.00

（原始材料由中国江西财经大学经济文化传播系提供，有删改）

第六课　初步洽谈

今天中美两家公司的代表要举行初步洽谈。东方进出口公司为这次洽谈做了很多准备。他们带来了产品目录和一些样品。史强生和白琳对其中的一些新设计特别感兴趣。

(一) 对话

1. 看样品

(在会议室)

王国安：史先生,白小姐,按照日程安排,今天是由李经理向二位介绍产品和价格的情况,你们看怎么样?

史强生：好啊,我们来的目的就是要谈生意的。我很想早点儿知道贵公司今年有哪些新东西。

李信文：这是我们今年的产品目录,请二位过目。

史强生：李先生,这些都是今年的新设计吗?

李信文：百分之八十都是新设计,只有列在最后的是我们保留的传统产品。我还带来了一些样品,也请你们看一看。(拿样品)

白　琳：嗯,真漂亮! 李先生,我非常喜欢这几款设计,尤其是这件毛衣,颜色、式样都很好。

李信文：(笑)这件吗? 这件是听了您上次的建议设计的。白小姐,您忘了吗?

白　琳：(笑)是吗? 这么说,你准备怎么谢我呢?

2. 询问价格

史强生：王总,贵公司今年推出的产品很有吸引力,尤其是这些新设计。请问,在目录上列出的价格是零售价还是批发价?

王国安： 目录上的价格都是零售价。批发价要低百分之十五到百分之二十五。

白　琳： 李先生，我注意到有些产品在目录上没有列出价格。您可以告诉我它们的价格吗？

李信文： 没有列出价格的都是试销品。(指着目录)像这条牛仔裤,这件皮茄克都是厂家试生产的。如果贵公司感兴趣,价格可以参照同类产品另议。

史强生： 据我了解到的情况,贵公司皮茄克的价格似乎比其他几家公司高一点儿,这是为什么？

李信文： 我想我们的价格稍高跟产品的质量和设计有关系。您可以再比较比较。

史强生： 好,我想把这份目录带回去,再仔细看看。

王国安： (看手表)啊,已经十二点多了。我看我们先吃中饭,然后再继续谈吧？

白　琳： (开玩笑)我同意。我的肚子已经在跟我谈判了！

词汇(一) Vocabulary(1)：

1.	初步	chūbù	initial; preliminary
2.	目录	mùlù	catalogue; list
3.	其中	qízhōng	among/in (it/which/them, etc.)
4.	对……感兴趣	duì… gǎn xìngqù	be interested in …
5.	设计	shèjì	design; to design
6.	按照	ànzhào	according to; on the basis of
7.	由	yóu	by; through; via; from
8.	价格	jiàgé	price
9.	过目	guòmù	to look over (a paper/list, etc.); so as to check or approve; to go over
10.	保留	bǎoliú	to retain; to continue to have
11.	传统	chuántǒng	traditional; tradition

71

12. 款	kuǎn	a measure word for the design of certain things (especially clothing); a sum of money; item/clause (in document)
13. 式样	shìyàng	style
14. 建议	jiànyì	suggestion; to suggest
15. 询问	xúnwèn	to ask about; to inquire
16. 推出	tuīchū	to present (to the public); to put out
17. 吸引力	xīyǐnlì	appeal
吸引	xīyǐn	to attract; to draw
18. 零售价	língshòujià	retail price
19. 批发价	pīfājià	wholesale price
20. 百分之……	bǎifēnzhī …	… percent
21. 试销品	shìxiāopǐn	trial items/products
22. 牛仔裤	niúzǎikù	jeans
23. 皮茄克	píjiākè	leather jacket
24. 厂家	chǎngjiā	manufacturer
25. 试生产	shì shēngchǎn	to manufacture on a trial basis; trial production
26. 参照	cānzhào	to refer to; to consult
27. 同类	tónglèi	the same kind; similar
28. 另议	lìngyì	be discussed/negotiated separately
29. 似乎	sìhū	it seems; as if
30. 其他	qítā	other
31. 稍	shāo	a little; a bit; slightly
32. 跟……有关系	gēn… yǒuguānxì	have sth. to do with…; relate to…
33. 质量	zhìliàng	quality
34. 仔细	zǐxì	careful(ly); attentive(ly)

句型(一) Sentence Patterns(1):

1. 对…… 感兴趣　　　　be interested in…

72

我对这些新设计特别感兴趣。

美国代表团对中国的经济特区很感兴趣。

2. 按照 ……   according to; on the basis of

按照日程安排,今天客人们要来参观我们的公司。

按照贵公司的建议,我们保留了几种传统的设计。

3. 由 sb. + V. + sth.   (由 introduces the person in charge of a given task)

今天由李经理向美国代表介绍产品和价格的情况。

明天由张小姐去旅馆接你们。

4. 跟……有关系   have sth. to do with…; related to…

这种产品的价格跟质量和设计有关系。

每天都这么忙跟我们的日程安排有关系。

(二) 阅读短文

货比三家不吃亏

无论是买东西,还是做生意,价格都是买主和卖主最关心的事之一。中国有句老话,叫做"货比三家不吃亏"。意思是如果你想买东西,最好多去几家商店,比较比较它们的价钱。只有这样才不会吃亏上当,才能买到又便宜又满意的好东西。

自从一九七九年实行改革开放政策以后,中国的市场经济有了很大的发展。在商品的价格、质量和品种上,顾客都有了更多的选择。市场竞争一方面带来了更多的机会,一方面也带来了更多的挑战。如果你打算到中国去做生意,一定要事先了解中国的市场行情。《孙子兵法》上说,知己知彼,才能成功。做生意也是这样。

词汇 (二) Vocabulary (2):

1. 货   huò   goods; commodities
2. 吃亏   chīkuī   to suffer loss; to come to grief; to be at a disad-
                     vantage

3. 买主　　　mǎizhǔ　　　buyer

4. 卖主　　　màizhǔ　　　seller; vendor

5. 老话　　　lǎohuà　　　old saying; adage

6. 价钱　　　jiàqián　　　price

7. 上当　　　shàngdàng　　to be fooled/taken in

8. 自从　　　zìcóng　　　since

9. 实行　　　shíxíng　　　to implement; to put into practice; to carry out

10. 改革　　　gǎigé　　　reform; to reform

11. 开放　　　kāifàng　　　to open (to trade/to the public/etc.); to lift a ban

　　　　　　　　　　　　 or restriction

12. 政策　　　zhèngcè　　　policy

13. 市场经济　shìchǎng jīngjì　market economy; market-directed economy

　　　市场　shìchǎng　market

14. 商品　　　shāngpǐn　　merchandise; goods; commodity

15. 品种　　　pǐnzhǒng　　variety; assortment; kind

16. 顾客　　　gùkè　　　customer

17. 选择　　　xuǎnzé　　　choice; to choose

18. 竞争　　　jìngzhēng　　competition; to compete

19. 一方面　　yìfāngmiàn　　one side; on the one hand

20. 挑战　　　tiǎozhàn　　challenge; to challenge

21. 行情　　　hángqíng　　business conditions; market conditions; quotation

22. 知己知彼　zhī jǐ zhī bǐ　to know one's self and know the enemy

专有名词 Proper Nouns：

1. 改革开放政策　Gǎigé Kāifàng Zhèngcè　Reform and Opening to the Outside
　　　　　　　　　　　　　　　　　　　World policy (first implemented in
　　　　　　　　　　　　　　　　　　　1979)

2. 孙子兵法　　　Sūnzǐ Bīngfǎ　　*The Art of War* by Sun Wu, ancient
　　　　　　　　　　　　　　　　　Chinese philosopher during the Chun-
　　　　　　　　　　　　　　　　　qiu period (777 – 476 B.C.).

74

句型(二) Sentence Patterns (2):

1. 又……又……   both…and…

   多去几家商店,比较比较它们的价钱,你才能买到又便宜又满意的好东西。

   他办事情又快又好。

2. 自从……以后   (ever) since…

   自从实行改革开放政策以后,中国的市场经济有了很大的发展。

   自从来中国以后,史先生每天都说中文。

3. 在……上   in terms of…; as far as…

   在商品的价格、质量和品种上,顾客都有了更多的选择。

   在式样上,贵公司今年推出的新设计非常有吸引力。

4. 一方面……一方面……   on the one hand…; on the other hand…

   　　　　　　　　　　　　　for one thing…; for another…

   市场竞争一方面带来了更多的机会,一方面也带来了更多的挑战。

   今年我们一方面保留了一些传统产品,一方面也推出了一些新设计。

(三) 练习与活动

I. 句型练习一 Sentence pattern exercises(1):

1. 用"对……感兴趣"的句型回答下面的问题:

   Answer the following questions by using the pattern "对……感兴趣".

   (1) 这是我们的产品目录,请过目。请问,贵公司对哪些产品感兴趣?

   _____

   (2) 您喜欢这款新设计还是喜欢那款传统的设计?

   _____

   (3) 请问,您这次来中国打算参观游览哪些地方?

   _____

(4) 那位美国贸易代表为什么一定要去深圳考察?

_____

2. 用"按照"的句型完成下面的句子:

Complete the following sentences by using the pattern of "按照":

(1) 按照日程安排,_____

(2) 按照中国宴会的习惯,_____

(3) 按照贵厂的产品目录,_____

(4) 按照贵公司的建议,_____

3. 你正在向一个外国贸易代表团客人说明今后几天的日程安排。请用"由 sb. + V. + sth."的句型告诉你的客人,谁会为他们介绍公司情况和介绍产品、谁会带他们参观工厂、谁会陪他们考察经济特区,谁会陪他们游览风景等等。

You are explaining to your guests, a foreign business delegation, about the itinerary that you made for them. Use the pattern of "由 sb. + V. + sth." to tell the details in Chinese, such as who will give an introduction about the host company and products, who will accompany them to do sight-seeing, who will take them to see the factory, who will arrange a trip to the special economic zone ...

(1) _____

(2) _____

(3) _____

(4) _____

4. 用"跟……有关系"的句型回答下面的问题:

Answer the following questions by using the pattern "跟……有关系".

(1) 为什么白小姐胖了十磅?

_____

(2) 为什么她跟男朋友吹了?

_____

(3) 为什么王总经理这几天特别忙?

_____

(4) 为什么美国公司的那位总裁先生似乎不太高兴？

_____

(5) 贵公司的牛仔裤的批发价比其他公司高了百分之十五。请问为什么？

_____

II. 句型练习二 Sentence pattern exercises(2)：

1. 用"又……又……"的句型回答下面的问题：

Answer the following questions by using the pattern "又……又……"：

(1) 你常去哪家商店买东西？为什么？

_____

(2) 你愿意用哪家公司生产的电脑？为什么？

_____

(3) 你喜欢开车去旅行还是坐飞机去旅行？为什么？

_____

(4) 如果可能的话，你喜欢住哪家旅馆？为什么？

_____

2. 根据下面的要求，用"自从……以后"的句型造句：

Use the pattern "自从……以后" to accomplish the following tasks：

(1) 说一说中国的变化。

_____

(2) 说一说一种服装式样的变化。

_____

(3) 说一说你的国家的经济情况。

_____

(4) 说一说你自己的变化。

_____

3. 你正在介绍今年你的公司的新产品。你相信你们的产品是最好的。请用"在……上"的句型说明你们的产品和其他几家公司的同类产品有什么不同。

You are presenting this year's new products of your company at a news conference. You believe that your products are the best ones. Please use the pattern of "在……上"to tell what makes your products special by comparing with similar products made by other companies.

(1) _____

(2) _____

(3) _____

(4) _____

4. 用"一方面……一方面……"的句型回答下面的问题:

Answer the following questions by using the pattern "一方面……一方面……":

(1) 这次史先生和白小姐去中国有什么计划?

_____

(2) 如果你去中国的话,你打算做什么?

_____

(3) 改革开放政策给中国带来了哪些变化?

_____

(4) 你觉得市场竞争的结果是什么?

_____

(5) "知己知彼"这句话有什么意思?

_____

III. 词汇练习 Vocabulary Exercises and Special Expressions:

1. 用中文解释以下词汇的意思:

Use Chinese to explain the meaning of the following:

例如 For example: 频繁: 次数很多

(1) 顾客: _____

(2) 初步: _____

(3) 过目: _____

(4) 另议: _____

(5) 似乎: _____

78

（6）其他：_____

（7）稍：_____

（8）仔细：_____

（9）吃亏：_____

（10）知己知彼：_____

2. 反义词 Antonyms

（1）零售价：_____

（2）买主：_____

（3）推出：_____

（4）询问：_____

3. 你能用上面的词汇造句吗？

Can you use some of the words above to make sentences?

_____

_____

_____

IV. 阅读、写作和讨论 Reading，Writing and Discussion：

1. 根据课文对话回答问题：

Answer the following questions according to the dialogues in this lesson：

（1）今天中美两家公司的代表要做什么？

_____

（2）今年东方进出口公司的产品有多少是新设计的？

_____

（3）传统产品列在产品目录的什么地方？

_____

（4）白小姐问李先生说："你准备怎么谢我呢？"她为什么这么问？

_____

（5）美方代表对什么产品感兴趣？

_____

（6）零售价高还是批发价高？高多少？

_____

（7）为什么有些产品没有列出价格？这些产品的价格怎么决定？

_____

（8）为什么东方进出口公司的皮茄克比较贵？

_____

2．根据阅读短文回答问题：

Answer the following questions based on the reading passage.

（1）"货比三家不吃亏"这句话是什么意思？你买东西的时候这样做过吗？为什么？

_____

（2）哪本书里说过"知己知彼"这句话？是谁说的？这句话跟做生意有什么关系？

_____

3．你是一家大百货公司(baihuo gongsi, department store)的业务代表。因为冬天快要到了,所以你的老板要你跟几家公司询问一下年轻人的毛衣和皮茄克的批发价。请按照下面的要求分别写一个对话或者一篇小报告：

You are a representative of a major department store. Winter is coming soon, and your boss has asked you to check the wholesale prices of youth sweaters and leather jackets at several companies. Choose from two topics below and write a dialogue or a short memorandum.

（1）你看了几家公司的产品目录,也上网看了他们的产品介绍。你对其中一家公司的产品很感兴趣。所以,你现在给他们打电话⋯⋯

You have checked their catalogers and web sites. Now you are calling a company whose products you are interested in;

（2）你已经得到了你需要的信息（xìnxī, information）。现在你向老板报告询问价格的结果。你也告诉老板你建议买哪家的产品。

You have accomplished your investigation and research. Now you report to your boss the result and present your proposal of purchasing.

（四）附录

产品目录实例

东风服装进出口公司羊毛服装产品目录

品名	生产厂家	品牌	价格/打
羊毛衫	南海迪泰针织毛衫有限公司	迪泰	920.00
羊毛衫	广东省汕头纺织品进出口公司	金凤花	960.00
针织羊绒毛衫	南海迪泰针织毛衫有限公司	迪泰	1200.00
翻领羊绒休闲装	上海爱达针织制衣公司	阿黛尔斯	1200.00
低圆领条纹衫	上海爱达针织制衣公司	阿黛尔斯	1800.00
羊绒大衣	南通三贵时装有限公司	金花	2640.00
羊绒大衣	奉化爱伊美西服公司	爱伊美	2880.00
羊绒大衣	内蒙古雪花绒毛制品有限公司	驼乡	3120.00

（原始材料由中国江西财经大学经济文化传播系提供,有删改）

第七课　参观工厂

中美双方的第一次洽谈结束以后,张红陪史强生和白琳去参观了一家玩具工厂。他们公司上次订购的一批电动玩具就是在这儿制造的。玩具厂的管理水平和生产效率给了他们很深刻的印象。

(一) 对话

1. 在会客室

张　红：陈厂长,您的客人到了!

陈厂长：欢迎,欢迎,欢迎光临本厂! 我来自我介绍一下儿吧。我叫陈大方,是这儿的厂长。您一定就是美国国际贸易公司的史先生了!

史强生：对,我是史强生。这位是我的助理,白琳小姐。

白　琳：您好,陈厂长! 听张小姐说,我们去年订购的一批电动玩具,就是在这儿生产的,是吗?

陈厂长：对、对、对,我记得那批玩具是赶在圣诞节前交货的。史先生、白小姐,贵公司对那批产品满意吗?

史强生：非常满意。我们这次来,一是要对贵厂表示感谢,二是想亲眼看看贵厂的生产情况。

陈厂长：史先生,您太客气了! 这样吧,我陪各位先去车间看看。张小姐,您说怎么样?

张　红：行啊! (对史强生和白琳)咱们可以一边走,一边听陈厂长的介绍。好不好?

史强生：
　　　　好!
白　琳：

83

＊2. 在车间

陈厂长： 这儿是我们厂的组装车间。产品在这儿组装好以后,再送到成品车间通过质量检验。

白　琳： 陈厂长,你们的车间不但管理得很好,而且设备也很先进。

陈厂长： 哪里,哪里。我们去年从国外引进了这两条组装线。现在成本降低了,产量却比两年前增加了三倍。质量也提高了。

史强生： 这些正在组装的卡通玩具是要出口的吗?

陈厂长： 对,这些玩具都是为迪斯尼公司生产的。他们计划在今年秋季投放市场,所以催得很紧。

白　琳： 它们太可爱了! 我想它们一定会很受欢迎!

史强生： 陈厂长,你们的工厂给我的印象非常好。我希望今后我们能有更多的合作。

陈厂长： 那太好了! 我们以后多多联系!

词汇（一）Vocabulary（1）：

1.	陪	péi	to accompany; to keep sb. company
2.	订购	dìnggòu	to order（goods）
3.	批	pī	a measure word for goods; batch; lot
4.	电动	diàndòng	electric; battery-operated
5.	制造	zhìzào	to make; to manufacture
6.	管理	guǎnlǐ	to manage; to run; to administer; management
7.	生产效率	shēngchǎn xiàolǜ	productivity
	效率	xiàolǜ	efficiency
8.	深刻	shēnkè	deep; profound
9.	印象	yìnxiàng	impression
10.	会客室	huìkèshì	reception room
11.	本厂	běn chǎng	one's own factory; this factory
12.	自我	zìwǒ	self; oneself
13.	记得	jìdé	to remember; to recall

84

14.	赶	gǎn	to rush; to hurry; to make dash for
15.	交货	jiāo huò	to deliver goods
16.	亲眼	qīnyǎn	with one's own eyes; personally
17.	车间	chējiān	workshop
18.	组装	zǔzhuāng	to assemble; assembly
19.	成品	chéngpǐn	finished products
20.	检验	jiǎnyàn	inspection; to inspect
21.	设备	shèbèi	equipment; facilities
22.	先进	xiānjìn	advanced; state-of-the-art
23.	国外	guówài	overseas; abroad
24.	引进	yǐnjìn	to introduce from elsewhere; to import
25.	组装线	zǔzhuāngxiàn	assembly line
26.	成本	chéngběn	cost
27.	降低	jiàngdī	to reduce; to lower; to cut down
28.	产量	chǎnliàng	output; yield
29.	卡通	kǎtōng	cartoon
30.	投放	tóufàng	to put on (the market)
31.	催	cuī	to urge; to hasten; to press
32.	可爱	kě'ài	cute; lovable

专有名词 Proper Nouns：

圣诞节	Shèngdàn Jié	Christmas
迪斯尼	Dísīní	Disney

句型（一）Sentence Patterns（1）：

1. A 给 B…… 的印象/A 给 B 的印象 Adj.　A makes…impression on B
   玩具厂的管理水平和生产效率给他们很深刻的印象。
   你们的工厂给我的印象非常好。

85

2. 赶在……前 V.   rush/hurry to V. before …

我记得那批玩具是赶在圣诞节前交货的。

我得赶在十点以前到飞机场。

3. 一是……，二是……   one (of the reasons, etc.) is…, the other is …;

on the one hand…, on the other hand …

我们这次来，一是要对贵厂表示感谢，二是想亲眼看看贵厂的生产情况。

我买东西，一是要质量好，二是要便宜。

4. 一边 V$_1$，一边 V$_2$ (to carry out two actions simultaneously)

咱们可以一边走，一边听陈厂长的介绍。

我们一边看样品，一边谈价格，好不好？

5. A 比 B V. 了 + specific quantity (or rough estimation)   A V. ed…than B

现在成本降低了，产量却比两年前增加了三倍。

今年的质量比去年提高了不少！

（二）阅读短文

中国的企业

中国的企业一般分为国有和私有两种。国有企业由中央政府或当地政府投资并进行管理。因为有国家的支持，国有企业在资金、原料、技术和销售上都有一定的优势，但是也有不少国有企业管理不善、长期亏损。中国的私有企业在最近十多年里得到了迅速的发展，成为国有企业有力的竞争对手。目前，中国政府正在积极推动国有企业的改革，鼓励私有企业承包、租赁、兼并或者购买那些效益不好的国有企业。民营企业就是这种改革中出现的新型股份制企业。

中国政府的经济政策对企业有很大的影响。国有企业也好，私有企业也好，都需要按政府的经济政策调整自己的发展计划。在中国政府开放政策的推动下，许多国有企业和私有企业都在积极寻求与外国企业的合作。这是进入中国市场的一个大好机会。

86

词汇（二）Vocabulary（2）：

1.	企业	qǐyè	enterprise; business
2.	分为	fēnwéi	divide (into)
3.	国有	guóyǒu	state-owned
4.	私有	sīyǒu	privately-owned
5.	中央	zhōngyāng	central (government, etc.)
6.	当地	dāngdì	local
7.	投资	tóuzī	to invest; investment
8.	并	bìng	and
9.	支持	zhīchí	support; to support
10.	资金	zījīn	financial resources; funds
11.	原料	yuánliào	raw material
12.	销售	xiāoshòu	marketing; sales; to sell; to market
13.	优势	yōushì	advantage; superiority; dominant position
14.	不少	bùshǎo	not few; many
15.	不善	bùshàn	not good; bad; not good at
16.	长期	chángqī	over a long period of time; long-term
17.	亏损	kuīsǔn	financial loss; deficit; to suffer a loss
18.	迅速	xùnsù	rapid; swift
19.	有力	yǒulì	strong; powerful
20.	对手	duìshǒu	opponent; adversary; competitors
21.	积极	jījí	positive(ly); active(ly)
22.	推动	tuīdòng	to push forward; to promote; to give impetus to; to spur
23.	鼓励	gǔlì	to encourage; to urge
24.	承包	chéngbāo	to contract
25.	租赁	zūlìn	to rent; to lease; lease
26.	兼并	jiānbìng	to merge; to annex; merger
27.	购买	gòumǎi	to purchase; to buy

28. 效益	xiàoyì	beneficial result; benefit
29. 民营	mínyíng	privately run
30. 新型	xīnxíng	new type/pattern
31. 股份制	gǔfènzhì	joint stock/share system
32. 调整	tiáozhěng	to adjust
33. 寻求	xúnqiú	to seek; to explore
34. 进入	jìnrù	to enter; to get into

句型(二) Sentence Patterns(2):

1. A 分为 ……　　A is divided into …

中国的企业一般分为国有和私有两种。

中国的旅馆分为二星、三星、四星和五星级几种。

2. A 对 B 有影响　　A has an impact on B; A influences B

中国政府的经济政策对企业有很大的影响。

从国外引进的这条组装线,对产品质量有很大的影响。

3. A 也好,B 也好　　no matter whether A or B

　国有企业也好,私有企业也好,都需要按照政府的经济政策调整自己的发展计划。

新设计也好,传统式样也好,我们都生产。

4. 在……推动下　　with the impetus of…; pushed forward by…; driven by…

　目前在中国政府开放政策的推动下,许多企业都在积极寻求与外国企业的合作。

在新贸易合同的推动下,这种产品的出口增加得很快。

(三) 练习与活动

I. 句型练习一 Sentence pattern exercises (1):

1. 用"A 给 B……的印象"或者"A 给 B 的印象 + adj."的句型,并参考下面列出

88

的词汇回答问题。

参考词汇：深、深刻、好、不好、不太好、有意思、可爱、难忘、特别

Answer the following questions by using either "A 给 B……的印象"or "A 给 B 的印象 + adj.". You may use the words listed below in your sentences：

深、深刻、好、不好、不太好、有意思、可爱、难忘、特别

(1) 您觉得那家旅馆怎么样？

_____

(2) 您觉得那家工厂的管理水平怎么样？

_____

(3) 您觉得他们今年的新产品怎么样？

_____

(4) 您觉得刚投放市场的这种卡通玩具怎么样？

_____

2. 用"赶在……前 V."的句型回答下面的问题：

Answer the following questions by using the pattern of "赶在……前 V."：

(1) 请问李经理，这份电传我最好什么时候发出去？

_____

(2) 那批新款毛衣贵公司计划在什么时候投放市场？

_____

(3) 这张订单上的产品我们应该什么时候交货？

_____

(4) 您今天为什么这么忙？

_____

3. 根据下面的要求，用"一是……，一是……"的句型造句：

Use the pattern of "一是……，一是……"to accomplish the following tasks：

(1) 说一说明天谈判的内容。

_____

(2) 说一说为什么你的公司决定引进新的组装线。

_____

(3) 说一说为什么迪斯尼希望订购这家玩具厂的产品。

（4）说一说他们考察那家服装厂的目的。

4. 用"一边 V_1，一边 V_2"的句型完成下面的句子：

Complete the following sentences by using the pattern of "一边 V_1，一边 V_2":

（1）客人们一边参观工厂，一边 _____。

（2）谈判代表们一边看样品，一边 _____。

（3）我们的公司希望一边降低成本，一边 _____。

（4）那家国际贸易公司一边从中国进口玩具，一边 _____。

5. 根据下面的数据，用"A 比 B ＋ V. 了 ＋ specific quantity/rough estimation"的句型比较说明去年和今年的生产情况：

According to the chart below, compare this year's statistics with last year's by using the pattern of "A 比 B ＋ V. 了 ＋ specific quantity/rough estimation".

	去年	今年
成本	1,890,000 元	1,700,000 元
服装产量	320,000 件	640,000 件
质量	💣※💣※	☺☺☺
新设计	12 种	36 种

（1）_____

（2）_____

（3）_____

（4）_____

II. 句型练习二 Sentence pattern exercises（2）：

1. 用"分为……"的句型回答下面的问题：

Answer the following questions by using the pattern of "分为……":

（1）请问，那家玩具厂分为哪几个车间？

_____

（2）请问，这本目录上列出的价格有哪几种？

        _____

（3）一般说，中国的企业有哪几种？

        _____

（4）你知道中国有多少个省吗？

        _____

2. 用"A 对 B 有影响"的句型回答下面的问题：

Answer the following questions by using the pattern of "A 对 B 有影响"：

（1）你觉得什么对产品的价格有影响？

        _____

（2）你觉得什么对产量有影响？

        _____

（3）你觉得什么对一家企业的效益有影响？

        _____

（4）你觉得什么对中国的经济有影响？

        _____

3. 用"A 也好，B 也好"的句型回答下面的问题：

Answer the following questions by using the pattern of "A 也好，B 也好"：

（1）您想看看样品还是参观车间？

        _____

（2）您想知道零售价还是批发价？

        _____

（3）您的公司寻求与国有企业合作还是与 私有企业合作？

        _____

（4）您对租赁那家企业感兴趣还是对兼并那家企业感兴趣？

        _____

4. 用"在……推动下"的句型完成下面的句子：

Complete the following sentences by using the pattern of "在……推动下"：

（1）在双方代表的努力推动下，_____

（2）在新贸易合同的推动下，_____

（3）在国有企业改革政策的推动下，_____

（4）在市场竞争的推动下，_____

III. 词汇练习 Vocabulary Exercises and Special Expressions：

1. 组词 Build upon the following words.

例如 For example：购买 → 购买产品、购买汽车

（1）降低 → _____ _____

（2）引进 → _____ _____

（3）寻求 → _____ _____

（4）长期 → _____ _____

（5）自我 → _____ _____

（6）调整 → _____ _____

（7）推动 → _____ _____

（8）效益 → _____ _____

2. 用下面列出的词填空：

Fill in the blanks by using the following words.

效率、引进、进入、先进、印象、迅速、寻求、亏损、管理、成本

过去，因为我们公司的 管理 不善，所以长期 亏损 。自从公司从最新技术以后，我们的生产 效率 就开始提高了， 成本 也降低了。因为我们给客户的 印象 越来越好了，所以订单也就 迅速 增加了。最近不但有外国公司 寻求 和我们合作的机会，而且我们也成功地 进了 国际市场了。

IV. 阅读、写作和讨论 Reading, Writing and Discussion：

1. 根据课文对话回答问题：

Answer the following questions according to the dialogues in this lesson：

（1）张红陪史先生和白小姐去什么工厂参观？

_____

(2) 这家工厂的厂长叫什么名字?

_____

(3) 史先生的公司和这家工厂做过生意吗?

_____

(4) 美国客人为什么要参观这家工厂?

_____

(5) 厂长说引进的组装线对生产有什么帮助?

_____

(6) 美国客人看到的玩具是为谁生产的?

_____

(7) 美国客人觉得这家工厂怎么样?

_____

2. 根据阅读短文回答问题:

Answer the following questions based on the reading passage.

(1) 中国的国有企业一般由谁投资管理?

_____

(2) 国有企业有哪些优势?

_____

(3) 对那些有问题的国有企业,政府怎样进行改革?

_____

(4) 无论是国有企业还是私有企业,都要怎样调整发展计划?

_____

(5) 为什么现在是进入中国市场的大好机会?

_____

3. 利用图书馆或者上网,找出三到五家做进出口生意的中国企业。把你找到的信息写下来,在课堂上报告。你的报告应该先说明这些企业是国有企业、私有企业还是民营企业,再对其中一个企业做一个简单的介绍。

Using the library and/or the internet (see Appendix), find 3—5 Chinese companies involved in the import or export business. First, identify them as state-owned, privately-owned or privately run under joint-stock system; then, write

93

a short paragraph giving a general introduction to one of these companies, and present it to your class.

4. 利用图书馆或者上网,找出一条中国国有企业改革的新闻或者是私有企业承包、租赁、兼并或购买国有企业的报导。

Using the library and/or the internet, find a news report regarding a privately-owned enterprise that has contracted, leased, merged or purchased a state-owned enterprise in China.

(四) 附录

中国著名企业

(1) 中国重点骨干企业

1. 中国石油化工集团
2. 中国石油化工股份有限公司
3. 中国华北电力集团公司
4. 中国海洋石油有限公司
5. 攀枝花钢铁集团公司
6. 哈尔滨飞机工业集团
7. 中国华能集团公司
8. 中国洪都航空工业集团有限责任公司
9. 中国航空工业第一集团公司
10. 上海宝钢集团公司
11. 中国南方机车车辆工业集团公司
12. 中国长江三峡工程开发总公司
13. 中国移动通信集团公司
14. 大庆油田有限责任公司
15. 东风汽车公司
16. 昌河飞机工业集团有限责任公司
17. 中国国际信托投资公司
18. 中国电子进出口总公司

19. 中国航空技术进出口总公司　　20. 中国普天信息产业集团公司

21. 深圳市国有免税商品集团有限公司　22. 中国第一汽车集团公司

23. 中国电信集团公司　　　　　　24. 哈尔滨东安发动机集团有限公司

25. 中国南方工业集团公司　　　　26. 首钢集团

27. 煤航集团实业发展有限公司　　28. 陕西秦珠水力有限责任公司

（据 2001 年《中国经济年鉴》）

（2）2001 年中国内地企业五十强

排名	公司	收入（亿美元）	利润（亿美元）	市值（亿美元）
1	中国石化	367.675	16.93	314.43
2	中国石油	288.602	56.548	311.124
3	中国移动	121.208	33.844	654.872
4	中国联通	35.509	5.384	138.427
5	宝山钢铁公司	35.241	3.094	59.102
6	联想集团	34.913	1.103	38.284
7	华润集团	31.021	1.545	18.866
8	中国海洋石油总公司	25.152	9.613	77.415
9	上海石化	24.4	0.086	23.566
10	镇海炼化	23.953	0.0561	4.66
11	龙腾科技	23.636	0.187	10.139
12	中信实业	22.117	2.705	48.716
13	南方航空	20.392	0.411	9.735
14	中国铝业	19.315	1.919	18.054
15	华能电力	19.108	4.393	36.16
16	东方航空	15.511	0.161	20.067
17	扬子石化	15.478	0.042	12.132
18	北京首钢	14.517	0.857	19.925
19	吉林化工	14.393	2.178	14.67
20	青岛海尔	13.823	0.746	15.341
21	美的电器	12.715	0.303	5.928
22	TCL 股份	12.32	0.374	4.186

排名	公司	收入(亿美元)	利润(亿美元)	市值(亿美元)
23	马鞍山钢铁	11.535	0.252	18.848
24	四川长虹	11.494	0.107	20.498
25	鞍钢新钢铁	11.465	0.488	9.773
26	中兴通讯	11.274	0.689	15.76
27	神州数码	10.992	0.182	3.744
28	锦州石化	10.436	0.135	5.566
29	华菱管线	10.268	0.572	11.044
30	东方通信	10.146	0.25	11.877
31	唐山钢铁	9.765	0.885	10.713
32	上海建设	9.669	0.224	7.857
33	仪征化纤	9.433	0.206	19.013
34	广东投资	9.323	0.366	4.808
35	攀枝花新钢铁	9.064	0.581	8.654
36	长安汽车	8.857	0.191	6.355
37	邯郸钢铁	8.743	0.81	10.937
38	浦东发展银行	8.68	1.283	45.681
39	山东电力	8.628	1.667	11.255
40	齐鲁石化	8.484	0.026	10.224
41	中国海外投资	8.443	0.528	7.076
42	泰钢不锈钢	8.252	0.359	9.01
43	中国海运	8.173	0.656	7.02
44	康佳集团	8.152	0.845	4.028
45	北京企业股份	7.984	0.74	7.663
46	格力电器	7.959	0.33	6.461
47	中粮国际集团	7.956	0.271	3.099
48	中化国际	7.934	0.109	6.235
49	大唐电力	7.914	1.737	16.55
50	兖州煤炭	7.815	1.209	26.725

转摘自 www.cwrank.com（全球中文排行榜）网站资料：2002 年 9 月 16 日 《财富》杂志中文版"中国内地企业 100 强排名"。

第八课　价格谈判

今天,中美两家公司要就今年秋季的订单进行谈判。其中,进货的价格和数量是双方谈判的关键。今天的谈判也是史强生和白琳这次来中国的主要目的之一。

(一) 对话

1. 谈判成功

史强生：　王总,这两天参观了你们的工厂,也看了不少产品。现在我想听听你们的报盘。

王国安：　好啊! 不知道您对哪些产品感兴趣?

史强生：　我想知道贵公司的毛衣和牛仔裤的价格。

李信文：　毛衣的价格是每打三百六十美元,牛仔裤每打二百四十美元。

史强生：　您说的价格包括运费吗?

李信文：　是的,价格包括成本和运费。

白　琳：　李先生,毛衣的报盘似乎比去年高了百分之十。这是为什么?

李信文：　毛衣是我们的新设计。式样和质量都有很大的改进,成本也比去年高。我们不得不适当提高价格。

白　琳：　即使是这样,三百六十美元一打还是贵了一些。我们是老客户了,能不能低一点儿,给百分之五的折扣?

王国安：　百分之五恐怕不行。不过,如果贵公司订购一千打以上,我们可以给百分之二点五的折扣。

史强生：　嗯,这个价格可以考虑。另外,我认为贵公司的牛仔裤价格也高了一点儿。目前生产牛仔裤的厂家很多,市场竞争很激烈。如果按这个价格进货,我们就没有赚头了!

李信文：　可是我们的产品质量是国际公认的,在市场上是有竞争力的。

97

史强生： 对！正是这个原因，我们才希望从贵公司进货。这样吧，毛衣和牛仔裤我们各订购两千打，都给百分之三的折扣，怎么样？

王国安： 行！这个价格可以接受。我们一言为定！

2. 谈判失败

白　琳： 李先生，请问这种皮茄克的报价是多少？

李信文： 皮茄克是我们今年的试销品。为了打开销路，我们准备按每打一千八百美元的特价出售。

白　琳： 李先生，您大概不太清楚国际市场目前的行情。您的这个价格跟一些世界名牌产品的价格几乎差不多了！

李信文： 白小姐，我相信我们产品的设计和质量不比某些世界名牌产品差。上个月我们和一家日本公司就是按这个价格签订了合同。不过，在没有建立知名度以前，我们愿意适当降低我们的报价。请问，您的还盘是多少呢？

白　琳： 如果每打在一千二百美元，我们可以考虑订购一千打。

李信文： 一千二百美元一打我们太吃亏了！我们最多降两百块，一千六百美元一打，怎么样？

白　琳： 还是太贵了！如果销路不好，我们就要赔本了。我说，咱们双方再各让价两百，一千四百美元一打，好不好？

李信文： 对不起，一千六是我们的底价，不能再低了。

白　琳： 真遗憾！看来我们只好另找货源了。

词汇（一）Vocabulary（1）：

1.	进货	jìn huò	to purchase of merchandise; to replenish stocks
2.	数量	shùliàng	quantity
3.	关键	guānjiàn	key; key point; crux
4.	报盘	bàopán	offer; quoted price; to make an offer
5.	打	dá	dozen
6.	包括	bāokuò	to include; including

7.	运费	yùnfèi	transport fees; freight charge
8.	改进	gǎijìn	to improve; improvement
9.	不得不	bùdébù	have no choice but to; to have to
10.	适当	shìdàng	proper(ly)
11.	客户	kèhù	client; customer
12.	折扣	zhékòu	discount
13.	恐怕	kǒngpà	I am afraid; perhaps
14.	不行	bùxíng	won't do/work; be of no good
15.	考虑	kǎolǜ	to consider; to think over
16.	激烈	jīliè	intense; sharp; fierce
17.	赚头	zhuàntou	profit
18.	公认	gōngrèn	generally recognized; universally acknowledged
19.	竞争力	jìngzhēnglì	competitiveness
20.	接受	jiēshòu	to accept
21.	一言为定	yìyánwéidìng	That's settled then.
22.	失败	shībài	to fail; failure
23.	报价	bào jià	quoted price; offer; to quote (a price)
24.	销路	xiāolù	sales; market
25.	特价	tèjià	special/bargain price
26.	出售	chūshòu	to offer for sale; to sell
27.	名牌	míngpái	famous brand
28.	几乎	jīhū	almost; nearly
29.	差不多	chà bu duō	about the same; similar
30.	某些	mǒuxiē	certain (people/things/etc.); some
	某	mǒu	certain; some
31.	知名度	zhīmíngdù	name recognition; notedness; reputation
32.	还盘	huánpán	counter offer; to make a counter offer
33.	赔本	péiběn	to sustain losses in business
34.	让价	ràngjià	to better one's price
35.	底价	dǐjià	bottom price

| 36. | 遗憾 | yíhàn | regrettable; to regret; to feel sorry |
| 37. | 货源 | huòyuán | source of goods; supply of goods |

句型（一）Sentence Patterns（1）：

1. 就……进行（举行）谈判（会谈）　　　have negotiations（talk）on…

今天，中美两家公司要就今年秋季的订单进行谈判。

中美政府就两国关系举行了会谈。

2. 不得不　　　　　　　　　　　have no choice but to; have to

我们不得不适当提高价格。

你们的报盘太高。我们不得不另找货源。

3. 即使……还是……　　　　　　　even（if）…still…

即使是这样，三百六十美元一打还是贵了一些。

即使有百分之三的折扣，这个价格还是不便宜。

4. 为了……　　　　　　　　　　in order to…; for…

为了打开销路，我们准备按每打一千八百美元的特价出售。

为了提高质量，我们引进了外国的新技术。

（二）阅读短文

讨价还价

做生意、谈买卖总是要讨价还价。"漫天讨价"的说法固然有一点儿夸张，不过它的确说明了中国人的讨价还价的本领。

一场商业谈判的成功，常常取决于细心和耐心。开始谈判以前，认真调查市场行情，细心比较各种商品的价格，做好谈判的一切准备，这些都是取得成功的基本条件。不过，外国人到中国做生意，常常会遇到一些想不到的问题。这不但是因为文化和习惯的不同，也是因为社会制度、经济制度的不同。一个善于谈判的好手，非得有耐心不可。只要你愿意理解对方，耐心地和对方交流、沟通，总是能找到解决问题的办法。你在中国的生意也一定会成功。

100

词汇(二) Vocabulary(2)：

1. 讨价还价	tǎo jià huán jià	to bargain; to haggle
2. 买卖	mǎimài	buying and selling; business
3. 漫天讨价	màn tiān tǎo jià	to quote an exorbitant price
		in anticipation of haggling
4. 说法	shuōfa	way of saying sth.; wording
5. 固然	gùrán	no doubt; it is true; admittedly
6. 夸张	kuāzhāng	to exaggerate; exaggeration
7. 的确	díquè	indeed; really; certainly
8. 本领	běnlǐng	skills; ability; talent
9. 商业	shāngyè	commerce; trade; business
10. 取决于	qǔjué	be decided by; to depend on
11. 细心	xìxīn	carefulness; preciseness; careful(ly)
12. 耐心	nàixīn	patience; patient
13. 调查	diàochá	to investigate
14. 制度	zhìdù	system
15. 善于	shànyú	be good at; be adept in
16. 好手	hǎoshǒu	expert; ace; old pro
17. 非……不可	fēi…bù kě	must…
18. 理解	lǐjiě	to understand
19. 交流	jiāoliú	to exchange (ideas, information, etc.)
20. 沟通	gōutōng	to communicate

句型(二) Sentence Patterns(2)：

1. 固然…… 不过…… it is true that…but…

这种说法固然有一点儿夸张,不过它的确说明了中国人的讨价还价的本领。

您的产品固然不错,不过价格贵了一些。

101

2. 取决于……　　　　　　　　be decided by…; depend on…

　　商业谈判的成功,常常取决于细心和耐心。

　　我们这次能订购多少,完全取决于市场行情。

3. 善于……　　　　　　　　　be good at…

　　一个善于谈判的好手,非得有耐心不可。

　　李经理非常善于跟外国人做生意。

4. 非……不可　　　　　　　(absolutely) must…

　　明天我非要问他这个问题不可!

　　如果你想买到又便宜又好的东西,你非得多看几家商店不可。

(三) 练习与活动

I. 句型练习一 Sentence pattern exercises(1):

1. 用"就……进行 谈判(会谈、洽谈)"的句型回答下面的问题:

Answer the following questions by using the pattern of "就……进行谈判(会谈、洽谈)":

(1) 请问,这次美国贸易代表团来中国的目的是什么?

_____

(2) 经理, 请问今天我们要跟客户谈什么?

_____

(3) 按照日程安排,明天双方代表要做什么?

_____

(4) 按照日程安排,后天双方代表要做什么?

_____

2. 用"不得不"的句型回答下面的问题:

Answer the following questions by using the pattern of "不得不":

(1) 请问,贵厂为什么要调整今年的生产计划?

_____

102

(2) 请问,贵公司的这种产品的报价为什么比上个月高了百分之十五?

_____

(3) 贵公司是我们的老客户了,可是为什么这次决定跟日本公司签订合同?

_____

(4) 做生意要有赚头,可是为什么很多商店愿意给老顾客折扣呢?

_____

3. 用"即使……还是……"的句型回答下面的问题:

Answer the following questions by using the pattern of "即使……还是……":

(1) 如果贵公司愿意订购两千打,我们可以给百分之四的折扣。怎么样?

_____

(2) 如果我方同意让价百分之二十,贵公司能增加进货数量吗?

_____

(3) 我们的产品是世界公认的名牌,您再考虑考虑吧?

_____

(4) 让价这么多,您恐怕没有赚头了吧?

_____

4. 用"为了……"的句型回答下面的问题:

Answer the following questions by using the pattern of "为了……":

(1) 请问,为什么贵厂决定从国外引进这条组装线?

_____

(2) 贵公司为什么愿意让价出售这种产品?

_____

(3) 为什么史先生每年都要去中国访问?

_____

(4) 王总,花这么多钱请客户吃饭,我们会赔本吗?

_____

II. 句型练习二 Sentence pattern exercises(2):

1. 用"固然……不过……"的句型回答下面的问题:

Answer the following questions by using the pattern of "固然……不过……":

(1) 这种产品的式样和质量都有了改进，您愿意进货吗？

_____

(2) 我们的产品是世界名牌，贵公司为什么还要另找货源呢？

_____

(3) 听说李先生非常善于讨价还价，可是为什么没有谈成那笔生意呢？

_____

(4) 那家商店打那么多折扣，不怕赔本吗？

_____

2. 用"取决于……"的句型回答下面的问题：
Answer the following questions by using the pattern of "取决于……"：
(1) 什么是商业谈判成功的关键？

_____

(2) 请问，一种新产品怎样打开销路？

_____

(3) 你认为怎样才能建立产品的知名度？

_____

(4) 你认为外国企业怎样才能在中国取得成功？

_____

3. 用"善于"的句型回答下面的问题：
Answer the following questions by using the pattern of "善于"：
(1) 在生意上，什么样的助手是好助手？

_____

(2) 为什么公司这次让李先生去美国洽谈业务？

_____

(3) 为什么那种新产品能够成功地进入中国市场？

_____

(4) 你最善于做什么？

_____

4. 用"非……不可"的句型回答下面的问题：

Answer the following questions by using the pattern of "非……不可"：

(1) 为什么某些名牌商品有时候也会大打折扣？

_____

(2) 要想让对方多订购一些我们的产品，我们应该怎么办？

_____

(3) 今天李先生为什么好像特别忙？

_____

(4) 在中国做生意怎样才能成功？

_____

III. 词汇练习 Vocabulary Exercises and Special Expressions：

1. 用中文解释以下词汇的意思：

Use Chinese to explain the meaning of the following：

(1) 进货：_____

(2) 客户：_____

(3) 出售：_____

(4) 名牌：_____

(5) 赔本：_____

(6) 好手：_____

(7) 公认：_____

(8) 运费：_____

(9) 货源：_____

(10) 底价：_____

(11) 一言为定：_____

(12) 漫天讨价：_____

2. 用下列的词汇填空：

Fill in the blanks by using the words given below.

让价, 底价, 讨价还价, 报价, 特价

(1) 这些名牌今天都是_____，我们快去买吧。

(2) 有人很会＿＿＿＿＿＿，使商人不得不给他打折扣。

(3) 王经理，我们的＿＿＿＿＿＿已经是我们的＿＿＿＿＿＿了，我们的确不能
再＿＿＿＿＿＿了。请原谅!

IV. 阅读、写作和讨论 Reading，Writing and Discussion：

1. 根据课文对话回答问题：

Answer the following questions according to the dialogues in this lesson：

(1) 这次双方代表谈判的关键是什么?

＿＿＿＿＿＿＿＿＿＿＿＿＿＿＿＿＿＿＿＿＿＿＿＿＿＿＿＿＿＿＿＿＿

(2) 美方对哪些产品感兴趣?

＿＿＿＿＿＿＿＿＿＿＿＿＿＿＿＿＿＿＿＿＿＿＿＿＿＿＿＿＿＿＿＿＿

(3) 牛仔裤的报盘是多少? 这个价格包括运费吗?

＿＿＿＿＿＿＿＿＿＿＿＿＿＿＿＿＿＿＿＿＿＿＿＿＿＿＿＿＿＿＿＿＿

(4) 为什么今年中方提高了毛衣的价格?

＿＿＿＿＿＿＿＿＿＿＿＿＿＿＿＿＿＿＿＿＿＿＿＿＿＿＿＿＿＿＿＿＿

(5) 美方觉得毛衣和牛仔裤的报价怎么样?

＿＿＿＿＿＿＿＿＿＿＿＿＿＿＿＿＿＿＿＿＿＿＿＿＿＿＿＿＿＿＿＿＿

(6) 皮茄克的报价是多少?

＿＿＿＿＿＿＿＿＿＿＿＿＿＿＿＿＿＿＿＿＿＿＿＿＿＿＿＿＿＿＿＿＿

(7) 中方为什么愿意适当降低皮茄克的报价?

＿＿＿＿＿＿＿＿＿＿＿＿＿＿＿＿＿＿＿＿＿＿＿＿＿＿＿＿＿＿＿＿＿

(8) 美方的第一次还盘是多少? 第二次还盘是多少?

＿＿＿＿＿＿＿＿＿＿＿＿＿＿＿＿＿＿＿＿＿＿＿＿＿＿＿＿＿＿＿＿＿

(9) 中方皮茄克的底价是多少?

＿＿＿＿＿＿＿＿＿＿＿＿＿＿＿＿＿＿＿＿＿＿＿＿＿＿＿＿＿＿＿＿＿

(10) 美方最后决定买什么? 买多少? 有折扣没有?

＿＿＿＿＿＿＿＿＿＿＿＿＿＿＿＿＿＿＿＿＿＿＿＿＿＿＿＿＿＿＿＿＿

(11) 美方最后决定不买什么? 为什么?

＿＿＿＿＿＿＿＿＿＿＿＿＿＿＿＿＿＿＿＿＿＿＿＿＿＿＿＿＿＿＿＿＿

2. 根据本课的内容和你自己的经验,谈一谈怎样才能取得商业谈判的成功。

Based on what you learned in this lesson and your own knowledge, talk about what it takes to make a successful business deal.

3. 你和你的谈判对手已经会谈了好几次了。现在是双方谈判价格的时候了。请为你们的价格谈判写一个小对话。

You and your business associate have met several times. Now it's time to negotiate prices. Write a dialogue for such a situation.

谈判

（四）附录

报盘信实例

××电子公司彩色电视机产品报盘

××××公司：

七月二十日来函收悉。感谢贵公司对我电视机产品的良好评价。现按贵方要求报盘如下：

品牌	型号	价格(美元)/台
彩虹	19寸彩色	120.00
彩虹	25寸彩色	170.00
彩虹	27寸彩色	200.00
彩虹	27寸彩色立体声	230.00

付款方式：即期信用证，美元支付。证到后七天内装运。

望以上报盘能为贵方接受，并盼早日收到贵公司的订单。

××电子公司

一九××年七月三十日

第九课　文化异同

　　史强生和白琳到中国已经好几天了。除了洽谈生意以外,他们也抽空逛了商店、买了纪念品,还游览了长城。他们遇到了很多有意思的事。有的让他们很奇怪,有的让他们很感动。

(一) 对话

1. 真奇怪

(在街上)

白　琳： Johnson,你不是要给你太太买礼物吗?我知道附近有一家购物中心,东西又多,价钱又公道。我带你去吧。

史强生： 好啊。不过我想先去银行换一些人民币。你知道哪儿有银行吗?

白　琳： 知道。不远就有一家银行。去年我在那儿换过一次钱。

史强生： 如果顺路的话,我们先去银行吧。

白　琳： 行,没问题!

(在银行外边)

白　琳： 真奇怪!银行为什么关了?

史强生： (看营业时间)夏季营业时间……中午十二点到两点休息。

白　琳： (看手表)现在刚十二点十分。我们该怎么办?

史强生： 算了,我们去商店吧。我还有一些零钱。

(在购物中心)

史强生： 哇,这儿好热闹!(小声对白琳说)白琳,你注意到了吗?在中国,吸烟的人可不少。虽然这儿挂着"请勿吸烟"的牌子,但是还是有人在吸烟。

白　琳： 是啊,我也发现李先生和客户谈生意的时候,总是要请他们吸烟。

大概这也是一种客套吧?

史强生： 对。在台湾也有这种习惯。(突然)不好,我的肚子突然很不舒服。
我得去一下儿厕所。对不起,请等我一下儿。(走开)

(一分钟以后,史走回来。)

白　琳： 怎么样,好些了吗?

史强生： 好多了。不过,我并没有用那儿的厕所。

白　琳： 为什么?

史强生： (苦笑)因为那儿的抽水马桶不是坐的,而是蹲的。真不习惯!

2. 遇到热心人

(在长城下)

张　红： 啊,长城到了。咱们坐缆车上去还是爬上去?

白　琳： 坐缆车省力,不过可能自己爬上去更有意思。

(游客甲、游客乙经过,跟白琳、史强生打招呼)

游客甲： (对白琳)你好! 您的中文真好! 您是从哪儿来的?

白　琳： 我们是从美国来的。

游客甲： 逛长城最好是坐缆车上去,再自己走下来。这样又不累又好玩儿!

白　琳： 这个主意好! 咱们就这么办! 谢谢您!

游客乙： (对史强生)您最好带一件外套上去。长城上边风大,只穿一件 T 恤
衫容易着凉。

史强生： 嗯,您说的有道理。我是应该带一件衣服上去。谢谢您! (看着游
客乙拿着的茄克)这件长城茄克真漂亮。您在哪儿买的?

游客乙： 就在东边的一家礼品店。您也想买一件吗?

史强生： 我应该给我太太买一件。她也非常喜欢长城。

游客乙： (热心地)如果您想要一件的话,我可以陪您一块儿去看看。

史强生： 那太麻烦了。不用了。

游客乙： 不麻烦、不麻烦,就在那边,不远!

史强生： 真的不用了。您太客气了! 谢谢您!

游客甲： (热心地)那边还有卖矿泉水的,便宜,牌子也不错。你们应该买两

瓶带着,热了渴了就有的喝。(指着长城)上边的东西可贵了!

白　琳：你们真好,谢谢你们!

史强生：谢谢!

张　红：(笑)我也提醒大家一句:长城上边没厕所。要是想方便一下儿,最
　　　　好现在就去。

词汇(一) Vocabulary(1)：

1. 异同	yìtóng	differences and similarities
2. 抽空	chōu kòng	to manage to find time
3. 逛	guàng	to stroll; to roam
4. 纪念品	jìniànpǐn	souvenir; memento
	纪念 jìniàn	memento; to remember; to commemorate
5. 奇怪	qíguài	strange
6. 感动	gǎndòng	to move (emotionally); to touch; moved
7. 购物中心	gòuwù zhōngxīn	shopping center
8. 公道	gōngdao	fair; reasonable
9. 顺路	shùnlù	on the way
10. 营业	yíngyè	do business; business operation
11. 夏季	xiàjì	summer
12. 算了	suànle	Forget it. That's enough!
13. 热闹	rènào	lively; buzzing with excitement; bustling with activity
14. 零钱	língqián	small change; pocket money
15. 吸烟	xīyān	to smoke
16. 请勿吸烟	qǐng wù xī yān	Please don't smoke!
17. 牌子	páizi	sign; plaque; brand; trademark
18. 客套	kètào	civilities
19. 厕所	cèsuǒ	toilet; restroom
20. 苦笑	kǔxiào	to force a smile; forced/wry smile
21. 抽水马桶	chōushuǐmǎtǒng	flush toilet

111

22.	蹲	dūn	to squat
23.	热心	rèxīn	enthusiastic; warm-hearted
24.	缆车	lǎnchē	cable car
25.	省力	shěnglì	to save energy/labor
26.	甲	jiǎ	indefinite person/thing; first; first of the ten Heavenly Stems
27.	乙	yǐ	indefinite person/thing; second; second of the ten Heavenly Stems
28.	打招呼	dǎ zhāohu	to greet sb.; to say hello
29.	外套	wàitào	coat; outer garment
30.	T恤衫	tīxùshān	T-shirt
31.	着凉	zháoliáng	to catch a cold
32.	礼品店	lǐpǐndiàn	gift shop
33.	矿泉水	kuàngquánshuǐ	mineral water
34.	提醒	tíxǐng	to remind; to call attention to
35.	方便	fāngbiàn	to use the lavatory; convenient

专有名词 Proper Nouns：

1.	台湾	Táiwān	Taiwan

词汇（一）Vocabulary（1）：

1. 有的……有的……　　some…some…

他们遇到了很多有意思的事。有的让他们很奇怪，有的让他们很感动。

这些产品有的是传统式样，有的是新设计。

2. 不是……吗　　　　（a rhetorical question）

你不是要给你太太买礼物吗？

我们不是已经订购了这种牛仔裤吗？

3. 不是……而是……　　is not…but rather…

那儿的抽水马桶不是坐的，而是蹲的。真不习惯！

112

我说的"好朋友"不是人,而是电脑。

4. 就　　　　right away; immediately (an adverb, emphasizes the urgency or imminent of an action)

要是想方便一下儿,最好现在就去。

明天我就给那家公司发传真。

(二) 阅读短文

入境问俗

　　因为文化的差异和习惯的不同,外国人在中国免不了会遇到一些让他们觉得奇怪的事。在街上,一位你完全不认识的陌生人会热情地为你带路,主动给你出主意、帮助你。可是在拥挤的火车上或者地铁里,有人撞了你一下儿,却没有对你说"对不起"。商店的售货员小姐拼命地向你推销商品,可是你买了不合适的东西以后,却发现有时候很难要求退货。你刚刚认识的中国朋友直截了当地问你一年挣多少钱,让你觉得很不舒服。和中国人一起去吃饭,很少有"各付各的"的时候。每个人都争着要替对方付账,让你不知道该怎么办才好。中国有一句成语叫做"入境问俗",意思是到了一个新地方,应该先问一问当地的风俗习惯。对于第一次到中国的外国人来说,这是一个好主意。

词汇(二) Vocabulary(2):

1. 入境问俗	rù jìng wèn sú	When in Rome, do as the Romans do.	
		On entering a country, inquire about its customs.	
2. 差异	chāyì	difference; divergence; discrepancy	
3. 免不了	miǎn bu liǎo	cannot avoid; unavoidable; unavoidably	
4. 陌生人	mòshēngrén	stranger	
5. 热情	rèqíng	enthusiastic; warm; ardent	
6. 带路	dàilù	to lead the way; to act as a guide	
7. 主动	zhǔdòng	on one's own initiative; initiative	

8. 出主意	chū zhǔyi	to make suggestion; to offer advice
9. 拥挤	yōngjǐ	crowd
10. 地铁	dìtiě	subway
11. 撞	zhuàng	to bump against; to run into
12. 却	què	but; yet
13. 售货员	shòuhuòyuán	shop assistant
14. 拼命	pīnmìng	exerting the utmost strength; make one's best effort; with all one's might
15. 推销	tuīxiāo	to promote sales; to sell
16. 退货	tuìhuò	to return merchandise
17. 直截了当	zhíjiéliǎodàng	straightforward(ly); blunt(ly)
18. 挣	zhèng	to earn (money)
19. 各付各的	gè fù gè de	each person pays his or her own bill; go Dutch
20. 争	zhēng	to contend; to vie; to strive
21. 替	tì	for; on behalf of
22. 付账	fù zhàng	to pay a bill
23. 成语	chéngyǔ	idiom; set phrase
24. 对于	duìyú	to; with regard to; for

句型(二) Sentence Patterns(2):

1. 免不了   cannot avoid; unavoidably

外国人在中国免不了会遇到一些让他们觉得奇怪的事。

做生意免不了讨价还价。

2. ……, 却……   …, yet/but…

有人撞了你一下儿, 却没有对你说"对不起"。

他看了很多样品, 却什么也没买。

3. 替 sb. V.   V. for/on behalf of sb.

每个人都争着要替对方付账。

如果你没有时间, 我可以替你去发传真。

4. 对（于）……来说　　as far as … is concerned; with regard to …

　　对（于）第一次到中国的外国人来说,这是一个好主意。

　　对（于）史先生来说,跟中国人洽谈生意是一件很有意思的事。

（三）练习与活动

I. 句型练习一 Sentence pattern exercises(1)：

1. 用"有的……有的……"的句型回答下面的问题：

Answer the following questions by using the pattern of "有的……有的……"：

(1) 很多人喜欢逛购物中心。人们喜欢去购物中心做什么？

　　_____

(2) 购物中心总是有很多不同的商店。举例说一说这些商店卖什么东西。

　　_____

(3) 现在,去中国的外国人越来越多。他们为什么去中国？

　　_____

(4) 到中国做生意的外国公司也越来越多。举例说一说这些公司做什么生意。

　　_____

2. 用"不是……吗"和"不是……而是"的句型完成下面的对话：

Use "不是……吗" and "不是……而是" to complete the dialogues below：

1. 甲：你不是要买 _____ 吗？

　乙：不,我 _____

2. 甲：你不是想去 _____ 吗？

　乙：不是,我 _____

3. 甲：你不是希望 _____ 吗？

　乙：不对, _____

4. 甲：你不是 _____ 吗？

　乙：_____

115

3. 根据括号中给出的条件,用"就"回答下面的问题:

Base on the given condition in the parentheses, answer the following questions by using "就"

(1) 甲:请问,那家新商店哪天开始营业? （下个星期一）

乙:＿＿＿＿＿＿＿＿＿＿＿＿＿＿＿＿＿＿＿＿

(2) 甲:下一班缆车几点开? （还有一刻钟）

乙:＿＿＿＿＿＿＿＿＿＿＿＿＿＿＿＿＿＿＿＿

(3) 甲:厕所的抽水马桶好像坏了。你能给服务台打个电话吗? （立刻）

乙:＿＿＿＿＿＿＿＿＿＿＿＿＿＿＿＿＿＿＿＿

(4) 甲:你们什么时候去礼品店? 走的时候提醒我一下。我也想去买件纪念品。 （今天中午）

乙:＿＿＿＿＿＿＿＿＿＿＿＿＿＿＿＿＿＿＿＿

II. 句型练习二 Sentence pattern exercises(2):

1. 用"免不了"的句型完成下面的句子:

Complete the following sentences by using the pattern of "免不了":

(1) 外国人在中国 ＿＿＿＿＿＿＿＿＿＿＿＿＿＿＿＿。

(2) 参加中国宴会 ＿＿＿＿＿＿＿＿＿＿＿＿＿＿＿＿。

(3) 做生意 ＿＿＿＿＿＿＿＿＿＿＿＿＿＿＿＿＿＿。

(4) 因为他(她)的习惯跟我不同,＿＿＿＿＿＿＿＿＿＿＿。

2. 用"……,却……"的句型完成下面的句子:

Complete the following sentences by using the pattern of "……,却……":

(1) 他在中国住了三年,＿＿＿＿＿＿＿＿＿＿＿＿＿。

(2) 双方已经谈判了几次,＿＿＿＿＿＿＿＿＿＿＿＿。

(3) 长城上边的风景很好,＿＿＿＿＿＿＿＿＿＿＿＿。

(4) 售货员拼命地向那位游客推销各种商品,＿＿＿＿＿＿＿。

3. 你就要从北京回国了。你打算给你的家人、朋友、同事买一些纪念品。准备一张购物单,用"替 sb. V."的句型把你要买的东西写下来。

You will leave Beijing and go back to your country. You are planning to buy some souvenirs for your family, your friends and colleagues. Make a shopping

116

list by using "替 sb. V.".

(1) _____

(2) _____

(3) _____

(4) _____

4. 根据下面的要求用"对……来说"的句型造句：

Use the pattern of "对……来说"to accomplish the following tasks：

(1) 到中国旅行的外国人常常有不同的目的和不一样的经验。请用"对……来说"的句型举例说明。

Tourists may have different expectations and experiences of traveling in China. Use "对……来说" to describe these differences that people may have regarding traveling in China.

a. _____

b. _____

(2) 到中国做生意的外国公司常常有不同的目的和不一样的经验。请用"对……来说"的句型举例说明。

Different foreign companies may also have different expectations and experiences of going to China. Use "对……来说" to describe these differences that foreign companies may have regarding doing business in China.

a. _____

b. _____

III. 词汇练习 Vocabulary Exercises and Special Expressions：

1. 用本课学到的词汇填空：

Fill in the blanks by using the vocabulary list in this lesson.

(1) 到外国旅行的游客总是要买一些_____带回国。

(2) 在很忙的时候找出一点儿时间来叫做_____。

(3) 到街上或者购物中心随便走走、看看,没有什么目的。这叫做_____。

(4) "李(Lee ®)"是一种有名的牛仔裤的_____。

(5) 饭馆还没关。你看,门上的_____写着"营业中"。

117

(6) 价钱不高也不低可以说价钱_____。

(7) _____就是不认识的人。

(8) 把不合适的东西还给商店或者卖主叫做_____。

2. 用中文解释下面的词,再造句:

Explain the following in Chinese, then make a sentence for each of them:

例如 For example:省力:不用花很多力气,很方便

这件事很省力,一点儿也不麻烦。

(1) 入境问俗:_____

(2) 直截了当:_____

(3) 各付各的:_____

(4) 客套:_____

(5) 方便:_____

IV. 阅读、写作和讨论 Reading, Writing and Discussion:

1. 根据课文对话回答问题:

Answer the following questions according to the dialogues in this lesson:

(1) 他们要去哪儿买礼物? 他们为什么要去那儿买礼物?

_____

(2) 他们为什么要先去银行?

_____

(3) 银行为什么不营业?

_____

(4) 在购物中心可以吸烟吗? 有人在购物中心吸烟吗?

_____

(5) 史先生为什么没有用那儿的厕所?

_____

(6) 他们在长城下边遇到了什么人?

_____

(7) 哪种办法上长城最好?

_____

(8) 史先生为什么打算多带一件衣服上长城？

_____

(9) 要是渴了的话，最好在哪儿买矿泉水？为什么？

_____

(10) 长城上边可以"方便"吗？为什么？ ☺

_____

2. 在本课的对话和阅读短文里，说到了一些外国人可能会觉得有趣或者奇怪的中国文化和习惯。也许你还知道一些别的中国人的文化和习惯。它们跟你自己的文化、习惯有什么不同吗？请你把你的想法写下来，跟你的朋友一起讨论讨论"文化异同"的问题。

This lesson's dialogues and reading passage contain some interesting Chinese customs and cultural conventions that a foreigner may feel strange and even uncomfortable about. You may also know some other strange things about Chinese culture. Please write down what you know about Chinese culture and customs, then compare them with your own culture and share your thoughts with your friends.

3. 看图说话

Describe the following pictures. Try to use some new words and patterns in this lesson.

a.

b.

（四）附录

常见中文标志

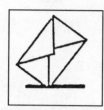
邮箱
Mailbox

商务中心
Business center

邮政
Postal service

国内直拨电话
Domestic direct dial

手续办理
Check-in；Reception

国际直拨电话
International direct dial

问讯
Information

会议室
Conference room

货币兑换
Currency exchange

结账
Settle accounts

 出租车
Taxi

 行李手推车
Luggage trolley

 自行车停放处
Parking for bicycle

 洗衣
Laundry

 失物招领
Lost and found

 干衣
Drying

 行李存放
Left luggage

 饮用水
Drinking water

 卫生间
Toilet

 废物箱
Rubbish receptacle

 中餐
Chinese restaurant

 摄影冲洗
Film developing

 西餐
Restaurant

 电影
Cinema

 快餐
Snack bar

 桑拿浴
Sauna

 酒吧
Bar

 按摩
Massage

 咖啡
Coffee

 理发、美容
Barber

 入口
Way in

 安全保卫
Guard

 出口
Way out

 紧急呼救电话
Emergency call

 紧急出口
Emergency exit

 紧急呼救设施
Emergency signal

 火情警报设施
Fire alarm

 自动扶梯
Escalator

 残疾人设施
Facilities for disabled person

 电梯
Elevator

 保龄球
Bowling

 网球
Tennis

 高尔夫球
Golf

 健身
Gymnasium

 游泳
Swimming

 运动场所
Sporting activities

 舞厅
Dance hall

 安静
Silence

 卡拉 OK
Karaoke bar

 禁止吸烟
No smoking!

（摘自中国国家旅游局 1995 年发布《旅游饭店用公共信息图形符号》）

124

第十课　交货和付款

The US & Chinese reps have kind. worked at the new order over the last couple days of nego.

通过前两天的洽谈，中美双方已经初步商定了新订单。现在，交货时间和
付款方式是他们最关心的问题。今天上午双方要就这些问题举行进一步的会
谈。

Now, the delivery sched. & payment method is the most important concern. This morning the 2 sides are going to hold further talks to address the issue.

(一) 对话

1. 交货时间

史强生： 我想今天我们应该讨论这批订单的交货时间问题。
I think today we should discuss delivery schedule for this order

李信文： 好。不知道您对交货时间有什么具体要求？
OK. I don't know what requirements you have for time of delivery.

史强生： 您知道服装的季节性很强。这次我们向贵公司订购的毛衣和牛仔
裤，都要在今年秋季投放市场。李先生，您能在八月上旬交货吗？
You understand the strong seasonal nature of clothing. This time sweaters & jeans we ordered need to be put on market this fall. Mr. Li, can you deliver w/in the first 10 days of Aug.

李信文： 八月上旬？史先生，您不是开玩笑吧？去年我们是九月才交货的。
我们目前的生产计划已经安排满了。
Mr Smith, you aren't joking are you? Last year we only delivered in Sept. Our current production schedule is already full.

史强生： (认真地)不是开玩笑。九月、十月是毛衣的销售旺季。去年我们的
商品比别人晚进入市场两个星期，结果吃了亏。今年我可不想再错
过机会了。
I'm not joking. Sept, Oct, is peak season for sweaters. Last yr our merch. was put on the market 2 wks later than other @ a disadvantage. This yr, I def. don't want to lose the op. again

李信文： 可是要我们马上调整生产计划、增加产量确实有困难。
But we won't have to adjust production immediately, increasing output would be difficult.

白　琳： 李先生，我知道这个交货时间的确是紧了一些，可是我们也有我们的
难处啊。李先生，咱们是老朋友了，请您帮帮忙、想想办法吧。
Mr.Li, I understand this delivery sched. is pretty tight, but we also have our difficulties. Mr.Li, we are old friends, please help us out, and think of a way

李信文： 白小姐，我是想帮您的忙，也想帮自己的忙，可是要提前一个多月交
货实在不太容易。
Ms Relly, I want to help you and help myself, but to deliver a mnth ahead would really not be easy.

白　琳： 我有一个想法。我们能不能把这些服装分成两次交货？八月上旬交
一半，九月上旬交另外一半。Johnson，你觉得行吗？
I have an idea. Can we divide the clothing into 2 sep. deliveries? half in the first 10 days of Aug, and half in first 10 days of Sept.

史强生： 嗯，这是一个解决的办法。李先生，您说呢？
Hm this is a solution. Mr Li, what do you think

李信文： 让我考虑考虑……我得给王总打个电话。我们先休息一下儿吧？
let me think about it. I have to give Pres. Wang a call. Let's rest first ok

125

史强生： 好！ *OK*

白　琳： 好！

2. 付款方式

李信文： 对不起，让你们久等了。刚才我跟王总联系了一下儿。我们可以接
sorry for making you wait　　*I just got in touch w/ Pres Wang*　　*we can accept*
　　　　　受分两次交货的安排……
the 2 shipments arrangement

史强生： 那太好了！ 谢谢！
Thats great thanks

李信文： 不过，我必须说明我们对付款方式的要求。
However we need to explain our requirements of payment method.

史强生： 当然，我也很关心这个问题。请问，贵公司打算采用哪种方式？
Of curse, I am also very concerned of this matter. What method do you have in mind

李信文： 我们一般采用信用证付款方式。但是这次贵方要求提前交货，这对
we gen. take payment by letter of credit. But you are requesting an early delivery, which will
　　　　　我们的资金周转有一定影响，所以我们要求贵公司预付百分之三十
def. impact our flow of funds, so we request that your co pay 30% in advance
　　　　　的货款，其余的货款采用不可撤销信用证。
& use an irrevocable letter of credit for the remainder of payment

史强生： 百分之三十的预付货款，我可以通过美国花旗银行电汇给您。其余
The remainder
we can have citi bank wire you the 30% advance payment
　　　　　的货款，我们是不是可以采用承兑交单或者其他的分期付款方式？
of payment, can we use a dol against acceptance bill or another type of installment plan

李信文： 很抱歉，我们目前不接受这些付款方式。为了不影响交货时间，请您
I'm sorry, we dont accept these methods at present. So as to not affect the time of delivery, pls
　　　　　务必在装运前三十天开出信用证。
be sure to have the letter of credit 30 day before loading & transport.

白　琳： 李先生，您可真厉害！说到钱，您一点儿情面也不讲！
Mr. Li, you are tough when it comes to $. you show no mercy

李信文： (笑)您没听过这样一句中国话吗？"亲兄弟，明算账"嘛！
You havent heard of the saying? "Even blood brothers keep careful account"

白　琳： (笑)不对！您这是"一手交钱，一手交货"！
NO This is more like no dough no go

词汇(一) Vocabulary(1)：

①.	付款	fù kuǎn	to make payment; payment
2.	商定	shāngdìng	to settle through discussion
③.	方式	fāngshì	manner; mode; way; method
4.	进一步	jìnyíbù	go a step further
5.	具体	jùtǐ	concrete; specific; particular
6.	季节性	jìjiéxìng	seasonal
	季节	jìjié	season
7.	强	qiáng	strong

126

8. 上旬	shàngxún	the first ten days of a month
	旬 xún	a period of ten days
9. 开玩笑	kāi wánxiào	to joke; to make fun of
10. 旺季	wàngjì	peak sales period; busy season
11. 错过	cuòguò	to miss; to let slip by
12. 难处	nánchù	difficulty; problem
13. 提前	tíqián	in advance; beforehand
14. 实在	shízài	really; indeed; truly
15. 想法	xiǎngfǎ	idea; opinion; view
16. 分成	fēnchéng	divide into; split up into
17. 采用	cǎiyòng	to select for use; to employ; to adopt
18. 信用证	xìnyòngzhèng	letter of credit (L/C) (A letter from one bank to another bank, by which a third party, usually a customer, is able to obtain money)
19. 资金周转	zījīnzhōuzhuǎn	capital turnover; flow of funds; circulation of funds
20. 预付	yùfù	to pay in advance
21. 货款	huòkuǎn	payment for goods
22. 其余	qíyú	the rest; the remainder
23. 不可撤销信用证	bùkě chèxiāo xìnyòngzhèng	Irrevocable Letter of Credit (A letter of credit that can only be cancelled with the agreement of the person expecting payment)
24. 电汇	diànhuì	to wire money; telegraphic transfer (T/T)
25. 承兑交单	chéngduìjiāodān	documents against acceptance bill (D/A)(A bill of exchange sent by an exporter with other shipping documents to an agent who will not release the documents until the bill of exchange has been signed/accepted by the person receiving the goods; This is used

127

when the bill of exchange is a period bill and

must be paid by a specified date.)

26. 分期付款   fēnqī fùkuǎn   to pay in installments; payment in installments

27. 抱歉   bàoqiàn   be apologetic; to feel sorry about

28. 务必   wùbì   must; should

29. 装运   zhuāngyùn   to load and transport; to ship

30. 开出   kāichū   to write out; to make out (a check, etc.)

31. 厉害   lìhai   tough; sharp; formidable

32. 说到   shuōdào   to speak of; to mention; when it comes to…

33. 情面   qíngmiàn   feelings; sensibilities; "face"

     不讲情面   to have no consideration for sb.'s feelings

34. 亲兄弟, 明算账   qīnxiōngdì, míngsuànzhàng

       even blood brothers keep careful accounts

35. 一手交钱, 一手交货   yìshǒu jiāoqián, yìshǒu jiāohuò

       literally, "One hand hands over the money;

       one hand hands over the goods"; to deliver

       (only) when the cash is in hand

专有名词 Proper Nouns：

1. 花旗银行   Huāqí Yínháng   Citibank

句型(一) Sentence Patterns(1)：

1. 通过……   by means of; through

   通过前两天的洽谈,中美双方已经初步商定了新订单。

   通过这次访问,史先生交了很多新朋友。

2. (你)对……有什么要求?   What demands/requirements do (you) have

       concerning…?

   您对交货时间有什么具体要求?

   请问,贵公司对我们的产品质量还有什么要求?

3. (你)不是……吧？　　　　(a rhetorical question)

　　您不是开玩笑吧？

　　你们不是上当了吧？

4. A 比 B 早/晚 V. + amount of time　　A V. + amount of time earlier/later
　　　　　　　　　　　　　　　　　　　　　　　　than B

　　去年我们的商品比别人晚进入市场两个星期。

　　对不起,日本公司的报盘比您的报盘早到了几天,我们已经签订了合同。

5. 把 Obj. 分 成 ……　　　divide Obj. into…

　　我们能不能把 这 些服装分成 两次交货？

　　我们可以采用分期付款的方式,把这批货款分成六个月付。

6. 说到……　　　　　when it comes to…; when…is mentioned

　　说到钱,您一点儿情面也不讲!

　　说到那些皮茄克的质量,这位客户变得很生气。

(二) 阅读短文

中国的银行和人民币

　　中国的国家中央银行是中国人民银行。主要商业银行包括中国银行、中国工商银行、中国建设银行,中国农业银行,中国交通银行等等。其中,中国银行是中国最大的外汇专业银行。外国人到中国做生意都会跟这家银行打交道。也许你已经注意到,中国的主要商业银行都是国家银行。政府希望通过国家对银行的直接管理,保证全国财政和金融市场的稳定。

　　中国的法定货币是人民币。它的单位分为元、角、分三种。一元等于十角,一角等于十分。人民币的面值一共有十三种:分为一百元、五十元、二十元、十元、五元、二元、一元、五角、二角、一角、五分、二分和一分。目前,人民币仅限于中国国内流通使用。在对外贸易中,中外双方一般使用美元、日元、欧元等国际通行的硬通货进行结算;使用汇付、托收、信用证等国际通行的方式支付货款。近年来,随着中国经济的迅速发展以及中国加入世界贸易组织,许多外国银行都在中国设立了分行或办事处。外国人在中国做生意将会越来越方便。

129

词汇（二）Vocabulary（2）：

1.	外汇	wàihuì	foreign exchange
2.	专业	zhuānyè	specialty; specialized trade/subject; discipline
3.	打交道	dǎ jiāodào	have dealings with; come into contact with
4.	直接	zhíjiē	direct(ly)
5.	保证	bǎozhèng	to ensure; to guarantee
6.	财政	cáizhèng	finances; financial administration
7.	金融	jīnróng	banking; finance; monetary situation
8.	稳定	wěndìng	stable; steady
9.	法定	fǎdìng	legal; stipulated by law
10.	货币	huòbì	currency; money
11.	单位	dānwèi	unit in measurement or organization
12.	等于	děngyú	be equal to; the same as
13.	面值	miànzhí	face value; denomination
14.	仅	jǐn	only
15.	限于	xiànyú	be limited/confined to
16.	国内	guónèi	interior (of a country); domestic
17.	流通	liútōng	to circulate
18.	对外	duìwài	foreign; external
19.	日元	rìyuán	Japanese yen
20.	欧元	ōuyuán	euro
21.	通行	tōngxíng	of general use; current
22.	硬通货	yìngtōnghuò	hard currency
23.	结算	jiésuàn	to settle/close an account
24.	汇付	huìfù	remittance (e.g. 电汇 T/T, 信汇 M/T, 票汇 D/D)
25.	托收	tuōshōu	collection; to collect (e.g. 承兑交单 D/A, 付款交单 D/P)

26.	支付	zhīfù	to pay (money); defray
27.	近年来	jìnniánlái	in recent years
28.	随着	suízhe	along with; in pace with
29.	以及	yǐjí	as well as; and
30.	加入	jiārù	to join; accede to; add
31.	设立	shèlì	to establish; to found
32.	分行	fēnháng	branch (of a bank)
33.	办事处	bànshìchù	office; agency

专有名词 Proper Nouns：

1.	中国人民银行	Zhōngguó Rénmín Yínháng	People's Bank of China
2.	中国银行	Zhōngguó Yínháng	Bank of China
3.	中国工商银行	Zhōngguó Gōngshāng Yínháng	Industrial and Commercial Bank of China
4.	中国建设银行	Zhōngguó Jiànshè Yínháng	China Construction Bank
5.	中国农业银行	Zhōngguó Nóngyè Yínháng	Agricultural Bank of China
6.	中国交通银行	Zhōngguó Jiāotōng Yínháng	Bank of Communications
7.	世界贸易组织	Shìjiè Màoyì Zǔzhī	World Trade Organization; WTO

句型(二) Sentence Patterns(2)：

1. 跟……打交道　　　come into contact with…; have dealings with…

　　外国人到中国做生意都会跟这家银行打交道。

　　跟这家公司打交道常常让我头疼。

2. 仅限于　　　be limited to…only

　　人民币仅限于中国国内流通使用。

　　这张电话磁卡仅限于打国内电话。

3. 在……中　　　in…; within…

　　在对外贸易中，双方一般使用美元、日元、欧元等国际通行的硬通货进行结算。

在昨天的会谈中,我们讨论了很多问题。

4. 随着   along with; in pace with; as…

近年来,随着中国经济的发展,许多外国银行都在中国设立了分行或办事处。

随着出口的增加,我们公司的生意越来越好。

(三) 练习与活动

I. 句型练习— Sentence pattern exercises(1):

1. 东方电脑公司的李总打算找一位新经理。如果你能用"通过……"的句型很好地回答下面的问题,你当经理一定没问题:

Eastern Computer Company's President Li is looking for a new manager. If you can answer the following questions by using the pattern of "通过……", you certainly are qualified for this job:

(1) 你打算怎样了解市场行情?

_____

(2) 你打算怎样提高产品质量?

_____

(3) 你打算怎样推销产品?

_____

(4) 你打算怎样吸引更多的顾客?

_____

2. 你在跟一位买主洽谈明年的毛衣订单。请用"对……有什么要求"的句型向你的客户询问下面的问题。你的客户会用"说到……"的句型回答你的问题。

A buyer and you are discussing next year's purchase of sweaters. Ask your client the following questions by using the pattern of "对……有什么要求". Your client will answer you by using the pattern of "说到……".

132

(1) 问题一:毛衣的设计或式样

　　你:＿＿＿＿＿＿＿＿＿＿＿＿＿＿＿＿＿＿＿＿＿

　　客户:＿＿＿＿＿＿＿＿＿＿＿＿＿＿＿＿＿＿＿＿＿

(2) 问题二:产品的质量

　　你:＿＿＿＿＿＿＿＿＿＿＿＿＿＿＿＿＿＿＿＿＿

　　客户:＿＿＿＿＿＿＿＿＿＿＿＿＿＿＿＿＿＿＿＿＿

(3) 问题三:交货时间

　　你:＿＿＿＿＿＿＿＿＿＿＿＿＿＿＿＿＿＿＿＿＿

　　客户:＿＿＿＿＿＿＿＿＿＿＿＿＿＿＿＿＿＿＿＿＿

(4) 问题四:付款方式

　　你:＿＿＿＿＿＿＿＿＿＿＿＿＿＿＿＿＿＿＿＿＿

　　客户:＿＿＿＿＿＿＿＿＿＿＿＿＿＿＿＿＿＿＿＿＿

3. 当听到或者遇到一件不能相信的事情的时候,人们常常会用"不是……吧"的句型提出疑问(yíwèn, doubt; question)。你能相信下面这些事情吗? 请用"不是……吧"的句型提出你的疑问。

When people hear or see something unbelievable, they often use the pattern of "不是……吧" to bring up a rhetorical question. Please use this pattern make your questions if you think that the following are really doubtful.

(1) 上个星期陈厂长胖了十磅!

＿＿＿＿＿＿＿＿＿＿＿＿＿＿＿＿＿＿＿＿＿＿＿＿＿

(2) 听说小张当了花旗银行的总裁!

＿＿＿＿＿＿＿＿＿＿＿＿＿＿＿＿＿＿＿＿＿＿＿＿＿

(3) 卖方说,如果我们付现金,一条牛仔裤只要三块钱!

＿＿＿＿＿＿＿＿＿＿＿＿＿＿＿＿＿＿＿＿＿＿＿＿＿

(4) 真奇怪,已经到了会谈的时间了,为什么对方代表还没有来?

＿＿＿＿＿＿＿＿＿＿＿＿＿＿＿＿＿＿＿＿＿＿＿＿＿

4. 用"A 比 B 早/晚 + V. + amount of time"的句型回答下面的问题:

Answer the following questions by using the pattern of "A 比 B 早/晚 + V. + amount of time":

(1) 白小姐昨天已经到达北京了。史先生明天才能到达北京。他们谁先到达北京？早几天？

_____

(2) 我们公司订购的秋季毛衣这个月上旬可以进入市场。他们公司订购的毛衣这个月下旬才能进入市场。哪家公司的毛衣能先进入市场？早多少时间？

_____

(3) 合同要求七月一日交货，可是那家公司到七月十五日才交货。交货时间晚了多少天？

_____

(4) 采用信用证的付款方式，卖方同意立刻装运；采用承兑交单，下个月才能装运。采用信用证的付款方式可以早多少天装运？

_____

4. 根据下面的问题，用"把……分成"的句型造句：

Use the pattern of "把……分成" to accomplish the following tasks：

(1) 怎样用中文告诉中方卖主，你希望"make an installment payment of 1 million dollars over 10 months"？

_____

(2) 怎样用中文通知中方买主，你计划"deliver 20,000 dozens of sweaters in several shipments"？

_____

(3) 怎样用中文说明，你计划"to divide your company into two smaller companies"？

_____

(4) 怎样让中方谈判代表知道，你希望"to discuss this issue in two steps"？

_____

II. 句型练习二 Sentence pattern exercises(2)：

1. 请用"跟……打交道"的句型回答下面的问题：

Answer the following questions by use the pattern of "跟……打交道"：

（1）你喜欢跟什么样的人打交道？

_____

（2）做生意的时候，你喜欢跟什么样的公司打交道？

_____

（3）你不喜欢跟什么样的公司打交道？

_____

（4）到中国做生意的外国人常会跟什么单位打交道？

_____

2．用"仅限于"的句型改写下面的句子：

Rewrite the following sentences by using the pattern of "仅限于"：

（1）今天晚上的招待会只邀请本公司最重要的客户参加。

_____

（2）参加明天会议的人都是局长以上的官员。

_____

（3）这次会谈只讨论交货时间问题。

_____

（4）很抱歉，我们目前接受的支付方式是汇付和信用证。

_____

3．用"在……中"的句型回答下面的问题：

Answer the following questions by using the pattern of "在……中"：

（1）在昨天的会谈中，双方讨论了哪些问题？

_____

（2）在双方讨论的问题中，哪个问题最重要？

_____

（3）在跟你的公司打交道的客户中，哪一位最重要？

_____

（4）在你考察过的城市中，你对投资哪个城市感兴趣？

_____

4．用"随着"的句型完成下面的句子：

Complete the following sentences by using the pattern of "随着"：

(1) 随着_____,
这家公司产品的知名度越来越高。

(2) 随着_____,
这家公司收到的订单越来越多。

(3) 随着_____,
这家公司在中国的业务越来越好。

(4) 随着_____,
经济特区吸引了越来越多的外国公司和厂家。

III. 词汇练习 Vocabulary Exercises and Special Expressions：

1. 用中文回答下面的问题：

Answer the following questions in Chinese：

(1) 你知道哪些商品有季节性？什么时候是它们的销售旺季？

_____

(2) 在中文里，一个月的前十天叫什么？（第二个十天呢？最后十天呢？）

_____

(3) "亲兄弟，明算账"和"一手交钱，一手交货"有什么意思？什么时候可以用 这两句话？

_____

(4) 根据本课的阅读短文，在对外贸易中，中外双方通常使用哪些货币？为什么使用这些货币？

_____

2. 替列在左边的词找出它们的反义词，把每个反义词的号码和英文意思写在括号的空格里。

Match the words on the left with their antonym on the right. Write down the number of the antonym and its English equivalent in the spaces provided.

例子 For example： d. 旺季（2; <u>off season</u>）

a. 对外（　　；_____ ）　　　　1. 下旬

b. 提前（　　；_____ ）　　　　2. 淡季（dànjì）

c. 上旬（　　；_____ ）　　　　3. 收款

136

d. 旺季 (　　　　；＿＿＿＿)　　　4. 间接

e. 直接 (　　　　；＿＿＿＿)　　　5. 对内

f. 付款 (　　　　；＿＿＿＿)　　　6. 推后

IV. 阅读、写作和讨论 Reading, Writing and Discussion：

1. 根据课文对话回答问题：

Answer the following questions according to the dialogues in this lesson：

(1) 今天中美双方要讨论什么问题？

＿＿＿＿＿＿＿＿＿＿＿＿＿＿＿＿＿＿＿＿＿＿＿＿＿＿＿＿

(2) 美方希望中方什么时候交货？为什么？

＿＿＿＿＿＿＿＿＿＿＿＿＿＿＿＿＿＿＿＿＿＿＿＿＿＿＿＿

(3) 中方有什么困难？

＿＿＿＿＿＿＿＿＿＿＿＿＿＿＿＿＿＿＿＿＿＿＿＿＿＿＿＿

(4) 白琳有什么样的解决办法？

＿＿＿＿＿＿＿＿＿＿＿＿＿＿＿＿＿＿＿＿＿＿＿＿＿＿＿＿

(5) 李经理为什么要给王总打电话？中方接受了白琳的建议吗？

＿＿＿＿＿＿＿＿＿＿＿＿＿＿＿＿＿＿＿＿＿＿＿＿＿＿＿＿

(6) 中方要求美方怎样付款？

＿＿＿＿＿＿＿＿＿＿＿＿＿＿＿＿＿＿＿＿＿＿＿＿＿＿＿＿

(7) 中方接受承兑交单的付款方式吗？

＿＿＿＿＿＿＿＿＿＿＿＿＿＿＿＿＿＿＿＿＿＿＿＿＿＿＿＿

(8) 为什么白琳说李先生"可真厉害"？

＿＿＿＿＿＿＿＿＿＿＿＿＿＿＿＿＿＿＿＿＿＿＿＿＿＿＿＿

2. 根据阅读短文回答问题：

Answer the following questions according to the reading passage in this lesson：

(1) 人民币的单位有哪几种？人民币的面值有哪些？

＿＿＿＿＿＿＿＿＿＿＿＿＿＿＿＿＿＿＿＿＿＿＿＿＿＿＿＿

(2) 中国主要的商业银行有哪些？

＿＿＿＿＿＿＿＿＿＿＿＿＿＿＿＿＿＿＿＿＿＿＿＿＿＿＿＿

(3) 本课介绍了哪些付款方式?

_____

3. 你刚跟一家服装厂洽谈订购了一大批夏季服装。现在你们开始讨论交货时间的问题。为了跟别人竞争,你的公司希望能早一点儿把这批服装投放市场。可是服装厂觉得提前交货有困难。请根据这些内容写一个对话。

You are a buyer purchasing summer clothing from another clothing factory. You have just placed a big order. Now, you are discussing the delivery schedule. Your company wants to have these clothes in market earlier due to competition. However, the clothing factory feels that it is difficult for them to deliver the goods beyond their regular schedule. Write a short dialogue describing such a situation.

（四）附录

（1）订货单实例

中国纺织品进出口公司：

贵公司的报盘及样品分别于四月三十日和五月二日收悉。十分感谢贵方对我询盘如此迅速地处理,愿接受贵方报盘。现随函寄去 3009 号订单,谨希按此订单细则发货是盼。

订单：3009 号

1. 商品

品名	编号	颜色	数量
乔其纱	0002	深紫	5,000 米
		淡紫	5,000 米
		石墨蓝	5,000 米
		宝石蓝	5,000 米
双绉	0009	苹果绿	5,000 米
		奶白	5,000 米
		纯白	5,000 米
		火红	5,000 米

2. 价格：（按人民币价）共 28,000,000.00 元

品名	单价(RMB)数量	总额(含佣金 5%)
乔其纱 0002	60.00 元/米×200,000 米	12,000,000.00 元
双绉 0009	80.00 元/米×200,000 米	16,000,000.00 元

3. 包装：

外包装用标准出口纸板箱,内衬防水材料,金属片加固箱角。内包装用挂胶防水棉布打包。

4. 装运：

1994 年 12 月 1 日前装船。起运港:中国天津;目的港:澳大利亚悉尼。由

卖方代保水渍险。保险费按发票金额的 10%。

5. 付款：

信用证付款。1994 年 12 月 23 日前由卖方通过澳大利亚国家银行北京分行开具以中国纺织品进出口公司为收益人的不可撤销的信用证。

澳大利亚××公司

1994 年 11 月 1 日

（引自赵洪琴、吕文珍编《外贸写作》第 164 页至 166 页，北京语言学院出版社 1994 年第一版）

（2）银行信用证

不可撤销跟单信用证

开证行名称：	不可撤销跟单信用证号码：
开证地点和日期：	交单证的到期日期和到期地点：
开证申请人：	信用证受益人：
通知行：	信用证金额：
分批装运允许/不允许：	凭受益人开立以_____行为付款人的汇票,由指定行_____
转运允许/不允许：	* 即期付款
由买方投保：	* 迟期付款（可选项）
装运受 UCP500 节第 46 条约束：	* 承兑
起运港_____到货港_____	* 议付
不迟于___年___月___日	凭以下规定单据,需以_____行为付款人的受益人出具的汇票付款,并随附以下单据：
商业发票正本 1 份,副本 3 份。 联合运输单据制成_____公司来人抬头,注明运费预付,并通知_____公司。 保险凭证按 110% 发票金额,根据伦敦劳埃德保险条款投保,A 险、战争险和罢工险,并背书转让给_____公司。 产地证明：货物产自_____。 装箱单号： 货名：	
单据议付日在装运后 14 天之内有效,但不得迟于信用证有效期。	
我行开立以你方为受益人的不可撤销信用证,受 UCP500 约束, 使我们遵从其条款。汇票上必须注明信用证号和开证日期须在汇票上引用。如果单据被议付,每次议付均需在信用证通知书上背书。	
签署信用证 1 张	

（原件由中国江西财经大学经济文化传播系提供）

第十一课　销售代理

中美双方刚刚就交货时间和付款方式达成了协议。史强生和白琳对此都非常满意。现在双方要就东方公司作为美方在中国的销售代理问题继续进行洽谈。

（一）对话

1. 独家代理

王国安：　史先生、白小姐，李经理告诉我，今天上午你们就今年秋季的新订单达成了协议。我非常高兴。请问，贵公司对此满意吗？

史强生：　我们对此非常满意。尤其是我们双方能够顺利地解决了交货时间的问题，这非常重要。王总经理，谢谢您的关照！

王国安：　您别客气！贵公司是我们的老客户，我们应该尽力满足您的要求。

白　琳：　（笑）王总经理，这次我们公司可是买了您两百多万美元的东西。您打算跟我们买点儿什么呢？

李信文：　（笑）白小姐，我看您才是真厉害。告诉您，王总今天下午来，就是打算谈在中国经销贵公司产品这件事的。

王国安：　是这样的。今年我们东方公司第一次代理销售贵公司的空调、微波炉等家用电器，市场销路很好。我们希望进一步扩大在这方面的合作。

史强生：　好啊，这也是我们这次来中国的目的之一。王先生，您有什么具体的打算？

王国安：　我们希望成为贵公司在中国的独家代理。

史强生：　您知道我们目前跟广东的一家公司也有代理销售空调的协议，把独家代理权给你们恐怕会影响我们跟那家公司的其他生意。

李信文：　史先生，我们公司在国内各地都有很好的销售网点。如果我们有独家代理权，一定会做得更好！

141

史强生： 这样吧，我们可以把微波炉的独家代理权给你们。另外，我们还有一种新型家用洗碗机，打算在中国市场试销。如果你们愿意的话，也想请贵公司独家代理。王先生、李先生，你们看怎么样？

王国安：
李信文： 行！一言为定！

2．资信调查和佣金

史强生： 王先生，既然贵公司将成为我们的独家代理，我们就还需要再了解一下贵公司的资信情况。

王国安： 有关我方的资信情况，您可以向中国银行北京分行查询。

史强生： 您也一定知道，作为独家代理，东方公司必须同意在我们的协议有效期之内不代理其他公司的同类产品。

王国安： 对，这一点我们很清楚。

史强生： 贵方想要提取多少佣金？

王国安： 代理经销外国产品，我们通常提取百分之十的佣金。

史强生： 百分之十太多了！我认为百分之八更合理。

王国安： 如果贵公司愿意分担一半的广告费用，我们可以把佣金减到百分之八。

史强生： 贵公司能保证我们每年有多少出口额？

王国安： 去年微波炉的销售总额是一百四十万。如果独家代理，我们每年至少可以进口贵公司二百八十万美元的微波炉。不过，洗碗机是第一次在中国试销，销路怎么样还不清楚。我们需要先做一个市场调查，然后才能决定。

史强生： 这样吧，我们可以先签订一个一年的独家代理协议，看看我们的产品是不是受欢迎。

白　琳： 我想中国的女士们一定会喜欢用洗碗机。

李信文： (笑)你错了，白小姐！现在在中国洗碗的都是男人！

词汇(一) Vocabulary(1)：

1. 达成 　　　　　　dáchéng　　　　　　to reach (an agreement, etc.)

142

2.	协议	xiéyì	agreement
3.	作为	zuòwéi	as; to act/serve as
4.	独家代理	dújiādàilǐ	sole/exclusive (sales) agent/agency
5.	关照	guānzhào	to look after; to give consideration to; accommodation
6.	尽力	jìn lì	to do all one can; to do one's best
7.	满足	mǎnzú	to satisfy; to meet
8.	百万	bǎiwàn	million
9.	经销	jīngxiāo	to sell/distribute on commission
10.	空调	kōngtiáo	air conditioner
11.	微波炉	wēibōlú	microwave oven
12.	家用电器	jiāyòngdiànqì	household appliances
	电器 diànqì		electrical equipment/appliance
13.	扩大	kuòdà	to expand; to enlarge; to extend
14.	独家代理权	dújiā dàilǐ quán	right of the sole agency
15.	各地	gèdì	various places/localities
16.	销售网点	xiāoshòuwǎngdiǎn	commercial networks
17.	洗碗机	xǐwǎnjī	dishwasher
	洗碗 xǐwǎn		to wash dishes
18.	资信	zīxìn	credit
	资信调查 zīxìndiàochá		credit investigation
19.	佣金	yōngjīn	commission
20.	将	jiāng	be about to
21.	有关	yǒuguān	as regards; concerning; to have sth. to do with
22.	查询	cháxún	to inquire about
23.	有效期	yǒuxiàoqī	term of validity; period of efficacy
24.	通常	tōngcháng	usual(ly); general(ly); normal(ly)
25.	提取	tíqǔ	to draw; to collect
26.	合理	hélǐ	reasonable

27. 分担	fēndān	to share responsibility for (a task/ duty/etc.)
28. 广告	guǎnggào	advertisement; commercial
29. 费用	fèiyòng	cost; expenses
30. 减	jiǎn	to reduce; to cut
31. 出口额	chūkǒu'é	value of exports; export quota
额	é	a specified quantity
32. 销售总额	xiāoshòu zǒng'é	gross sales
33. 至少	zhìshǎo	at (the) least
34. 市场调查	shìchǎngdiàochá	market survey
35. 女士	nǚshì	woman; Ms.; Miss
36. 受欢迎	shòu huānyíng	be well-received; popular
37. 男人	nánrén	man

专有名词 Proper Nouns：

1. 广东	Guǎngdōng	a province in southeast China

句型（一） Sentence Patterns（1）：

1. 就……达成了协议   reach an agreement on…

   中美双方刚刚就交货时间和付款方式达成了协议。

   我们已经就明年的订单达成了协议。

2. 作为   as…；act/serve as…

   今天双方要就东方公司作为美方在中国的销售代理问题进行洽谈。

   作为中方谈判代表，我还有一个问题。

3. 对……（非常）满意   very satisfied with…

   史强生和白琳对此都非常满意。

   我对这个合同很满意。

4. 可是   (emphasizes the tone of the speaker)

   王总经理，这次我们公司可是购买了您两百多万美元的东西。

144

无论您怎么说,这个报盘可是太高了!

5. 有关……的情况　　　　　with regard to (the situation of)…

有关我方的资信情况,建议您向中国银行北京分行查询。

我想向各位介绍一下儿有关这种产品的质量情况。

6. 在……之内　　　　　　within…

东方公司必须同意在我们的协议有效期之内不代理其他公司的同类产品。

我们会在三天之内通知您我们的决定。

(二) 阅读短文

外国货在中国

近年来,随着中外贸易的迅速发展,越来越多的外国产品进入了中国。从衣食住行到高科技产品,中国人对外国货的兴趣正越来越浓。毫无疑问,人口众多的中国是一个非常有潜力的巨大市场。外国厂商正面临着一次难得的商业机会。可是,对于人地生疏的外国公司来说,在中国做生意并不是一件容易的事。进入中国市场的外国货也有不同的命运:有的赚钱,有的赔本,有的还因为当地的非法仿制品而遭受到经济损失。为了在中国市场的竞争中取得成功,许多外国厂商委托资信可靠的中国公司作为代理,销售它们的产品。一般说,代理可分为三种,即总代理、独家代理和普通代理。总代理可以全权代表外国厂商进行各种商业活动。独家代理享有销售某一种产品的专卖权。普通代理有权销售某一种产品,提取佣金,但不能代表厂商,也没有专卖权。销售代理不但可以为外国厂商提供便利的销售网点、保证稳定的销售额,而且有利于建立良好的产品信誉,是一种对双方都有利的商业贸易方式。

词汇(二) Vocabulary(2):

1. 衣食住行　　　yīshízhùxíng　　　clothing, food, shelter and transportation; basic necessities for life

2. 浓	nóng	strong; dense
3. 毫无疑问	háowúyíwèn	without a doubt; undoubtedly
4. 人口众多	rénkǒu zhòngduō	have a very large population
人口	rénkǒu	population
众多	zhòngduō	numerous
5. 潜力	qiánlì	potential
6. 巨大	jùdà	huge; tremendous
7. 厂商	chǎngshāng	manufacturer; firm; commercial corporation
8. 面临	miànlín	to face; be faced with; be up against
9. 难得	nándé	rare; hard to come by; seldom
10. 人地生疏	réndìshēngshū	be unfamiliar with the place and the people; be a complete stranger
11. 并不	bìngbù	not at all, by no means
12. 命运	mìngyùn	fate; destiny
13. 赚钱	zhuànqián	to make money; to make a profit
14. 非法	fēifǎ	illegal
15. 仿制品	fǎngzhìpǐn	imitation
仿制	fǎngzhì	to copy; to manufacture an imitation of sth. already on the market
16. 遭受	zāoshòu	to incur (losses, etc.); to sustain; to suffer
17. 损失	sǔnshī	loss; to lose
18. 委托	wěituō	to entrust
19. 可靠	kěkào	reliable; dependable; trustworthy
20. 即	jí	namely; to be (with emphasis)
21. 总代理	zǒngdàilǐ	general agent/agency
22. 普通代理	pǔtōng dàilǐ	commission agent/agency
普通	pǔtōng	common; ordinary
23. 全权	quánquán	with full authority;

146

		full/plenary powers
24. 享有	xiǎngyǒu	to enjoy（rights/prestige/etc.）
25. 某一种	mǒu yì zhǒng	a certain kind of
26. 专卖权	zhuānmàiquán	exclusive right to sell sth.;
		a monopoly right
27. 有权	yǒuquán	have the right/authority（to）
28. 提供	tígōng	to provide; to supply; to offer
29. 便利	biànlì	convenient
30. 有利于	yǒulìyú	be beneficial to
	有利 yǒulì	beneficial; advantageous
31. 良好	liánghǎo	good; fine; desirable
32. 信誉	xìnyù	reputation; prestige; credit

句型（二）Sentence Patterns（2）：

1. 从……到……   from…to…

从衣食住行到高科技产品,中国人对外国货的兴趣正越来越浓。

从南到北,代表团参观了很多地方。

2. 面临……   to face/be faced with…; be up against

外国厂商正面临着一次难得的商业机会。

我们的产品正面临着新的竞争。

3. 并不   not at all; by no means

在中国做生意并不是一件容易的事。

很抱歉,本公司并不打算签订这个合同。

4. ……即……   namely; to be（with emphasis）

代理可分为三种,即总代理、独家代理和普通代理。

中国的国家中央银行即中国人民银行。

5. A 有利于 B   A is beneficial/helpful to B

这种方式有利于建立良好的产品信誉。

改革开放政策有利于中国经济的发展。

（三）练习与活动

I. 句型练习— Sentence pattern exercises(1)：

1. 请用"就……达成了协议"的句型回答下面的问题：
   Answer the following questions by using the pattern of "就……达成了协议"：
   (1) 在昨天的谈判中,双方就什么问题达成了协议？

   _____

   (2) 长城服装厂的陈厂长跟他的竞争对手就什么达成了协议？

   _____

   (3) 听说广东的一家公司希望作为贵公司在中国的独家代理。你们双方已经洽谈过了吗？
      是啊,_____
   (4) 最近中国跟哪个国家进行过贸易洽谈？谈了一些什么问题？谈得圆满吗？

   _____

2. 请用"作为……"的句型回答下面的问题：
   Answer the following questions by using the pattern of "作为……"：
   (1) 如果请你做我们玩具产品的销售代理,你希望提取多少佣金？

   _____

   (2) 如果你是一家公司的总经理,你打算怎样管理公司的业务？

   _____

   (3) 为什么生产厂家常常要做市场调查？

   _____

   (4) 外国人在中国做生意最大的问题是什么？

   _____

3. 请用"对……(非常)满意"的句型回答下面的问题：
   Answer the following questions by using the pattern of "对……(非常)满意"：
   (1) 你觉得哪个牌子的电脑好用？为什么？

   _____

148

(2) 总裁为什么决定让小张当经理？

_____

(3) 长城服装厂为什么请东方公司作为独家销售代理？

_____

(4) 这次到中国访问，史先生对什么满意？对什么不满意？

_____

4. 把"可是"放进下面的句子中可以加强说话人的语气。想一想把"可是"放在哪儿才合适？（最多可以放入七个"可是"）

Where should you insert the word "可是" into the following sentences to emphasize the tone of the speaker? (insert up to 7 in total)

(1) 那种新型空调真不便宜！

(2) 贵厂生产的洗碗机太方便了！

(3) 甲：百分之十的佣金太高了！

　　乙：可是我觉得很合理。别忘了，我方分担了一半的广告费用呢！

(4) 甲：听说那家公司的销售网点有一些问题。你们别上当啊！

　　乙：不对吧？我们做了资信调查以后，才决定委托他们做我们的独家代理。

5. 在新闻发布会上，史强生总裁宣布了跟中国东方进出口公司的新合同，还用英文回答了提问。请你用"有关……的情况"的句型，写出他的回答。

After he announced a new contract with China Eastern Import & Export Corporation at a news conference, Mr. Smith took some questions from the audience. The following are his answers in English. Please rewrite (not translate) his answers in Chinese by using the pattern of "有关……的情况".

(1) 记者：您能告诉我们贵公司新型洗碗机的价格吗？

　　Mr. Smith：You might look in our product catalogue for the information on wholesale price and retail price.

_____

149

(2) 记者：请问，除了家用电器以外，贵公司还有哪些产品？

Mr. Smith：You can go to our company's web site(i.e. go online) to find the information about our other products.

_____

(3) 记者：请问，贵公司去年的销售总额是多少？

Mr. Smith：I am sorry. I can't tell you the information about the last year's gross sales of our company at this moment.

_____

(4) 记者：您认为东方公司目前的销售网点能满足贵公司的要求吗？

Mr. Smith：It would be better to have Mr. Li, the manger of Eastern Corporation, answer this question.

_____

6. 完成下面带"在……之内"的句型的句子：

Complete the following sentences with the pattern of "在……之内"：

(1) 本厂计划在三年之内_____。

(2) 双方代表将在本星期之内_____。

(3) 在合同有效期之内，_____。

(4) 在产品的质量保证期之内，_____。

II. 句型练习二 Sentence pattern exercises(2)：

1. 用"从……到……"的句型改写下面的句子：

Rewrite the following sentences by using the pattern of "从……到……"：

(1) 李经理这个星期每天都有会谈和宴会。

_____

(2) 进口和出口的生意，那家公司都做。

_____

(3) 这家商店不但代理销售服装、玩具，而且代理销售电脑和汽车。

_____

(4) 昨天的会谈时间非常长。双方代表讨论了交货、付款、总代理权和明年的访问等等问题。

_____

2. 用"面临……"的句型完成下面的句子：

Complete the following sentences by using the pattern of "面临……"：

(1) 因为面临其他厂家的竞争_____。

(2) 虽然那家大型国有企业的改革面临很多困难_____。

(3) 当一家企业的发展面临挑战的时候_____。

(4) 即使面临着这样难得的商业机会_____。

3. 用"并不"的句型回答下面的问题：

Answer the following questions by using the pattern of "并不"：

(1) 在中国家庭里，总是女士洗碗，对吗？

_____

(2) 普通代理可以全权代表厂家和享有产品专卖权,对不对？

_____

(3) 贵公司打算兼并那家国有企业吗？

_____

(4) 听说那家企业的效益不错,信誉也很好。我们跟他们合作吧？

_____

4. 用"……即……"的句型回答下面的问题：

Answer the following questions by using the pattern of "……即……"：

(1) 底价的意思是什么？

_____

(2) 什么是报盘和还盘？

_____

(3) 人民币的单位分为几种？

_____

(4) 请问,什么是"世贸组织"？它的英文是什么？

_____

5. 用"A 有利于 B"的句型回答下面的问题：

Answer the following questions by using the pattern of "A 有利于 B"：

(1) 为什么很多外国厂商委托中国公司作为产品销售代理？

_____

(2) 取得独家代理权对代理商有什么好处？

_____

(3) 到外国去做生意为什么应该入境问俗？

_____

(4) 引进最新的高科技对一个老企业有什么好处？

_____

III. 词汇练习 Vocabulary Exercises and Special Expressions：

1. 组词 Build upon the following words：

例如 For example：提前 → 提前付款   提前交货

(1) 达成 → _____ _____

(2) 满足 → _____ _____

(3) 扩大 → _____ _____

(4) 提取 → _____ _____

(5) 分担 → _____ _____

(6) 面临 → _____ _____

(7) 遭受 → _____ _____

(8) 提供 → _____ _____

2. 用中文解释以下生词的意思并且造句：

Explain the following in Chinese, then make a sentence for each of them：

例如 For example：省力：不用花很多力气，很方便

这件事很省力，一点儿也不麻烦。

(1) 关照 _____

(2) 尽力 _____

(3) 资信 _____

(4) 佣金 _____

152

(5) 查询 _____

(6) 销售总额 _____

(7) 市场调查 _____

(8) 委托_____

(9) 全权 _____

(10) 人地生疏 _____

(11) 人口众多 _____

(12) 毫无疑问 _____

IV. 阅读、写作和讨论 Reading, Writing and Discussion：

1. 根据课文对话回答问题：

Answer the following questions according to the dialogues in this lesson：

(1) 美方对什么非常满意？

_____

(2) 为什么今天下午王总经理也来会谈？

_____

(3) 王总经理希望怎样扩大跟美方的合作？

_____

(4) 为什么美方不想把销售空调的独家代理权给东方公司？

_____

(5) 美方可以向谁查询东方公司的资信情况？

_____

(6) 东方公司希望提取多少佣金？佣金可以减一些吗？

_____

(7) 作为独家代理,东方公司每年能进口多少美元的微波炉？

_____

(8) 东方公司计划做什么产品的市场调查？为什么？

_____

2. 你计划找一个销售代理帮助你在中国销售你的产品。本课介绍了三种不同
的代理,你想用哪一种？为什么？请把你的计划写下来。

You want to start selling your company's products in China and you need a sales agent. What type of agent do you prefer (of the three types mentioned in the reading passage)? Why? Write down your plan.

3. 请上网或者去图书馆,找出两家通过销售代理在中国做生意的外国公司。写出这两家公司的名字、它们使用哪种代理、销售什么产品。如果可能的话,简单介绍一下儿它们的销售网点的情况。

Using the Internet and/or the library, find at least two foreign companies that sell products in China through an agent. Write down the names of the companies, what type of agent they use, and what products they sell. Please also write briefly about these companies' commercial networks if you can find the information.

（四）附录

银行资信证明

银行资信证明书

第 1234 号

××贸易有限公司：

  贵公司一九九九年十一月七日函询北京××实业公司，现将有关情况提供如下：

  该公司建于××××年，与我行已有十二年的账户往来，资信记录良好。其注册资金为人民币××××万元，主要经营成衣及纺织品进出口贸易，目前业务量大约为年××××万元。该公司长期以来经营有方、资金雄厚，跟国内许多零售商都有生意往来，未见客户不满，在同行中信誉很好。

  以上提供的资料仅供参考，我行不负任何责任。

××××银行

（负责人签字 盖章）

一九九九年十一月十六日

（原始材料由中国江西财经大学经济文化传播系提供，有删改）

第十二课　广告促销

在昨天的谈判中，史强生同意由他的公司分担一半的广告费用。现在他急于知道在中国做广告要花多少钱。因为今天下午史强生和白琳就要离开北京去上海了，所以今天一早张红和李信文分别陪他们去电视台和报社的广告部洽谈。

（一）对话

1．在电视台广告部

张　红：我来给两位介绍一下儿。这位是美国国际贸易公司的史先生，这位是电视台广告部的钱经理。钱经理是我的老熟人了，史先生，您有什么问题，尽管问他好了！

史强生：钱经理，我们公司的新型洗碗机即将进入中国市场。为了打开销路，我们打算进行一次促销活动。听张小姐介绍，你们的电视广告做得非常精彩，所以这次想请您帮忙。

钱经理：哪里，哪里，张小姐过奖了！不过，有一点我可以保证，只要看过我们电视广告的人，还没有不买的！（笑）

史强生：（笑）是吗？那么，在您这儿做广告一定不便宜吧？

钱经理：您放心，您是我的新客户，又是张小姐介绍来的，一定会给您最优惠的价格。

史强生：那太好了。钱经理，是否可以请您告诉我具体的收费标准？

钱经理：我们的收费分为两部分，制作费和播出费。制作费根据客户的具体要求决定，播出费以每十五秒三千元人民币计算。不同的时段收费不完全一样。

史强生：请问，您说的"不同时段"是什么？

钱经理：像晚上的播出费比白天的高，周末的播出费比平时的高。在精彩的体育比赛或者文艺演出实况转播时播出广告,一般要高百分之一百。

史强生: 您说的这些都是最优惠的收费标准吗?

钱经理: 没错,我们的收费都是最优惠的!

史强生: (想)嗯……我得先考虑考虑再跟您联系。

2. 在报社广告部

李信文: 周小姐,我给您带来了一位客人。这位是美国来的白小姐,我们的重要客户。白小姐,周小姐是这儿广告部的负责人。

白　琳: 您好!

周小姐: 您好! 您是来洽谈刊登广告的,对吗?

白　琳: 对。我们公司有几种家用电器产品就要投放到中国市场了。为了建立知名度,我带来了一份广告想登在贵报上。请您先看看是否合适。请多多指教。

周小姐: 别客气。嗯,微波炉和洗碗机。这份广告设计得很有吸引力。请问,除了英文的说明以外,您还打算用什么中文广告词呢?

白　琳: 这就得请您帮忙了。当然,我们会按规定付费。

周小姐: 您打算什么时候开始刊登呢?

白　琳: 如果可能的话,最好从十二月中旬开始。一周刊登四次:周一、周三登半版,周五、周六登整版。先登一个月。

周小姐: 好,没问题。这是我们的收费标准,请您看一看。

白　琳: 请问,作为新客户,在价格上有没有优惠呢?

周小姐: 实在抱歉,我们只给常年客户适当的优惠。

李信文: 周小姐,这次的广告费用是美方和我们共同分担的。我们东方公司可是您的常年客户呀。

周小姐: 如果是这样的话,我可以按规定给你们百分之十五的优惠。你们看怎么样?

李信文: 白小姐,您看呢?

白　琳: 那我可是沾了您的光了!

词汇(一) Vocabulary(1):

1. 促销　　　cùxiāo　　　　to promote sales; sales promotion

2. 急于　　　jíyú　　　　　eager to; anxious to

3. 一早　　　yìzǎo　　　　early in the morning

4. 分别　　　fēnbié　　　　separately; respectively

5. 电视台　　diànshìtái　　television station

6. 报社　　　bàoshè　　　newspaper office

7. 广告部　　guǎnggàobù　advertising department

8. 熟人　　　shúrén　　　acquaintance; friend

9. 尽管　　　jǐnguǎn　　　feel free to; not hesitate to

10. 即将　　　jíjiāng　　　be about to; be on the point of

11. 过奖　　　guòjiǎng　　to overpraise; to flatter

12. 优惠　　　yōuhuì　　　preferential; favorable; favorable

　　　　　　　　　　　　　　treatment/price/etc.

13. 是否　　　shìfǒu　　　whether or not

14. 收费　　　shōufèi　　　to collect fees; to charge; fee; charge

15. 标准　　　biāozhǔn　　standard; criterion

16. 制作费　　zhìzuòfèi　　production charge

　　　　制作 zhìzuò　　to produce; to make

17. 播出费　　bōchūfèi　　broadcasting charge

　　　　播出 bōchū　　　to broadcast

18. 以……计算　yǐ… jìsuàn　calculate by …

　　　　计算 jìsuàn　　　to calculate; to count

19. 秒　　　　miǎo　　　　second

20. 时段　　　shíduàn　　period of time

21. 白天　　　báitiān　　　daytime

22. 周末　　　zhōumò　　　weekend

23. 平时　　　píngshí　　　(weekdays); in ordinary times;

　　　　　　　　　　　　　　ordinarily

158

24. 实况转播	shíkuàng zhuǎnbō	live broadcast/telecast	
25. 没错	méi cuò	That's right; You can rest assured; can't go wrong	
26. 负责人	fùzérén	person in charge	
27. 刊登	kāndēng	to publish (in a periodical)	
登	dēng	to publish	
28. 份	fèn	a measure word for copies/ newspapers/etc.	
29. 广告词	guǎnggàocí	advertising slogan	
30. 付费	fù fèi	to make a payment	
31. 中旬	zhōngxún	middle 10 days of the month	
32. 半版	bàn bǎn	half page (of a newspaper)	
版	bǎn	page (of a newspaper); edition	
33. 整版	zhěngbǎn	full page (of a newspaper)	
34. 常年	chángnián	for a very long time; all the year round; year in and year out	
35. 共同	gòngtóng	joint(ly); together; common	
36. 沾光	zhān guāng	to benefit from association with sb. or sth.	

句型(一) Sentence Patterns(1):

1. 急于……　　　　eager to…
   现在他急于知道在中国做广告要花多少钱。
   这家公司正急于推销这种微波炉。

2. 离开 A 去 /回 B　　leave A for/to return to B
   他们就要离开北京去上海了。
   代表团明天将离开中国回美国。

3. 尽管……好了　　"feel free to…"; "don't hesitate to…"
   您有什么问题,尽管问他好了!
   如果你认为价格合适,尽管签订合同好了!

4. 以……计算　　　　　　　　calculate by/in term of…

　　播出费以每十五秒三千元人民币计算。

　　以每打一百美元计算，一千打一共是十万美元。

（二）阅读短文

广告和中国人的心理

　　做生意离不开广告。好广告不但能帮助厂商打开市场销路，而且有利于建立产品的知名度。不过，在中国做生意应该懂得中国人对商品广告的心理。一般说，年轻人喜欢名牌、新潮，中老年人注重物美价廉，这大概是通常的规律。因此，最容易吸引中国消费者的广告总是既能代表现代生活，又能符合中国人的心理。了解中国文化的厂商常常挖空心思，借用中国成语、口头语、甚至古典诗词等等，推陈出新，为外国商品设计出具有中国味儿的广告。例如，雀巢咖啡的广告采用温馨画面和短短的一句话："味道好极了"，制造出一种亲切的生活气氛。可口可乐和百事可乐的名字让喜欢讨吉利的中国人一听就喜欢。"车到山前必有路，有路必有丰田车"则是日本厂商的杰作。值得注意的是，中国人在传统上总觉得产品本身才是最好的广告。"酒香不怕巷子深"，如果你的东西真是非常好，就不用担心没有人买。在中国消费者看来，过分夸张、过分漂亮的广告常常是不可信的。"王婆卖瓜，自卖自夸"，谁不喜欢说自己的产品是最好的呢？

词汇（二）Vocabulary（2）:

1. 心理	xīnlǐ	mentality
2. 离不开	lí bu kāi	cannot do without; unable to separate from
3. 新潮	xīncháo	new trend/fashion
4. 中老年	zhōnglǎonián	middle and old age
	中年 zhōngnián	middle age

160

	老年 lǎonián	old age
5. 注重	zhùzhòng	to attach great importance to; to pay attention to; to lay stress on
6. 物美价廉	wùměijiàlián	(said of merchandise) excellent quality and reasonable price
7. 规律	guīlǜ	law; regular pattern
8. 消费者	xiāofèizhě	consumer
	消费 xiāofèi	to consume
9. 符合	fúhé	to correspond; to match; to accord/tally with
10. 挖空心思	wākōng xīnsī	to rack one's brain
11. 借用	jièyòng	to borrow; to use sth. for another purpose
12. 口头语	kǒutóuyǔ	speech mannerism; commonly-used expression
13. 古典	gǔdiǎn	classical
14. 诗词	shīcí	poetry and song lyrics
15. 推陈出新	tuī chén chū xīn	to find sth. new in what is old; to weed through the old to bring forth the new
16. 味儿	wèir	flavor; taste; smell
17. 温馨	wēnxīn	warm and fragrant (often involving feelings of tenderness/sweetness/etc.)
18. 画面	huàmiàn	general appearance of a picture; screen
19. 味道	wèidào	taste; flavor; smell
20. 亲切	qīnqiè	cordial; warm; intimate
21. 气氛	qìfēn	atmosphere; ambience; mood
22. 讨吉利	tǎo jílì	to seek good fortune (through auspicious sayings, etc.)
	讨 tǎo	to demand; to ask for; to seek
	吉利 jílì	good luck/fortune; auspicious; lucky

23. 一……就	yī… jiù	as soon as
24. 车到山前 必有路	chē dào shān qián bì yǒu lù	When the carriage reaches the mountain, there will surely be a road. Things will take care of themselves when the time comes.
25. 则是	zéshì	then; and so (indicates consequence or result; used in formal writing)
26. 杰作	jiézuò	masterpiece
27. 值得	zhíde	to deserve; be worth
28. 本身	běnshēn	itself; oneself
29. 酒香不怕 巷子深	jiǔ xiāng bú pà xiàngzi shēn	If your wine really tastes good, you don't need to worry about the location of your wineshop, even if it's at the end of a narrow lane. No matter where you are, people will find you if your product is good.
30. 在……看来	zài … kànlái	in one's view/opinion
31. 过分	guòfèn	excessive(ly); over(ly)
32. 不可信	bùkěxìn	cannot be trusted; untrustworthy
33. 王婆卖瓜， 自卖自夸	Wángpó mài guā zì mài zì kuā	When old lady Wang sold melons, she was always overstating her goods. A salesman always says that his products are the best.

专有名词 Proper Nouns：

1. 雀巢咖啡	Quècháo Kāfēi	Nestle coffee
2. 可口可乐	Kěkǒu Kělè	Coca-Cola
3. 百事可乐	Bǎishì Kělè	Pepsi
4. 丰田(车)	Fēngtián (chē)	Toyota (automobile)

句型(二) Sentence Patterns(2)：

1. 一……就……　　　　as soon as; once…then…

   可口可乐的名字让喜欢讨吉利的中国人一听就喜欢。

   一到北京,我们立刻就开车去长城。

2. 值得注意的是 ……　　What is worth noting is…

   值得注意的是,中国人在传统上总觉得产品本身才是最好的广告。

   值得注意的是,我们的产品正面临着新的竞争。

3. 在……看来　　　　in the view of…

   在中国消费者看来,过分夸张的广告常常是不可信的。

   在很多外国厂商看来,到经济特区投资更有吸引力。

4. 谁不 V. …… 呢?　　Who doesn't …?

   谁不喜欢说自己的产品是最好的呢?

   谁不想买到又便宜又好的东西呢?

(三) 练习与活动

I. 句型练习一 Sentence pattern exercises(1)：

1. 完成下面带 "急于……" 的句型的句子：

   Complete the following sentences with the pattern of "急于……"：

   (1) 为了打开销路,本厂急于_____。

   (2) 美方谈判代表急于_____。

   (3) 因为资金周转的问题,这家公司急于_____。

   (4) 我们并不急于_____。

2. 助理白小姐将跟她的老板史强生总裁去中国。白小姐准备了一份日程表。
   现在她需要向史强生说明这次的日程安排,得到他的同意。请用"离开 A
   去/回 B"的句型写出白小姐安排的旅行计划。

   Ms. Lynn Petty is going to accompany her boss, Johnson Smith, on a business
   trip to China, and she has already arranged a preliminary schedule (below).

Now she needs to receive approval from Mr. Smith. Please pretend that you are Lynn Petty and explain the schedule to your boss using the pattern, "离开 A 去/回 B".

China Trip Preliminary Schedule

Date	Departure City	Arrival City
June 30 (Fri)	Los Angeles	Beijing
July 5 (Wed)	Beijing	Shanghai
July 7 (Fri)	Shanghai	Shenzhen
July 9 (Sun)	Shenzhen	Los Angeles

3. 请用"尽管……好了"的句型改写下面的句子:

Rewrite the following questions by using the pattern of "尽管……好了":

(1) 在北京期间,如果您需要什么帮助,请随时给我打电话。

_____

(2) 我是这儿的负责人。如果贵厂想刊登广告,请随时跟我联系。

_____

(3) 如果广告词有不合适的地方,你可以完全按照你的意见修改。

_____

(4) 如果交货时间没有问题,你现在就可以代表公司签订合同!

_____

4. 请用"以……计算"的句型回答下面的问题:

Answer the following questions by using the pattern of "以……计算":

(1) 请问,订购一千打皮茄克的批发价是多少?(一打一千六百美元)

_____

(2) 请问,这种汽车贵厂每年可以制造多少辆?(一个月三千辆)

_____

(3) 刊登三天整版广告多少钱?(一天八百元)

_____

(4) 周末为新产品做三十秒电视广告。播出费怎么计算？(每十秒两千九百元)

_____

II. 句型练习二 Sentence pattern exercises(2)：

1. 白琳在上海呆了一天。她的日程安排得非常紧。她先跟上海进出口贸易公司的张经理见面会谈,接着跟服装厂洽谈明年的订货合同。吃了中饭以后,她去考察家用电器厂,晚上跟张经理、陈厂长吃饭,然后游览外滩 (Wàitān, the Bund),最后给男朋友打电话。请用"一……就"的句型写出她在上海的活动。

Ms. Lynn Petty spent one day in Shanghai. She had a very tight schedule. First, she held a meeting with Manager Zhang from Shanghai Import & Export Trading Company, then had a negotiation with the clothing factory regarding next year's purchase contract. After lunch, she visited a house appliances plant. In the evening, she had dinner with Manager Zhang and Factory Director Chen, then went sightseeing at Shanghai Bund. Finally, she made a phone call to her boyfriend. Please write down her activities in Shanghai by using the pattern of "一……就"：

(1) 白小姐一到上海 _____；

(2) _____；

(3) _____；

(4) _____；

(5) _____；

(6) _____。

2. 根据下面的要求,用"值得注意的是"的句型造句:

Accomplish the following tasks by using the pattern of "值得注意的是"：

(1) 你觉得那家代理公司没有很好的销售网点。请用"值得注意的是"的句型说出你的意见。

_____

（2）你从市场调查发现，越来越多的消费者喜欢外国产品和名牌产品。用"值得注意的是"的句型说出你的发现。

_____

（3）你想告诉你的老板，你觉得在篮球比赛实况转播时播出广告太贵。请用"值得注意的是"的句型说出你的看法。

_____

（4）请用"值得注意的是"的句型提醒中方谈判代表，因为新的经济政策，你的公司不得不调整投资计划。

_____

3. 用"在……看来"的句型完成下面的句子：

Complete the following sentences by using the pattern of "在……看来"：

（1）在消费者看来，_____。

（2）在厂家看来，_____。

（3）在中国政府看来，_____。

（4）在外国投资人看来，_____。

4. 用"谁不 V.……呢?"的句型改写下面的句子；

Rewrite the following sentences by using the pattern of "谁不 V.……呢?"：

（1）做广告的时候，每个人都喜欢说自己的产品好。

_____

（2）人人都喜欢听吉利的话。

_____

（3）物美价廉的商品，大家都愿意买。

_____

（4）做生意的时候，大家都希望赚钱。

_____

5. 你的公司刚刚推出了一款新设计的手表。你打算在电视上为它做广告。所以你去电视台跟广告部负责人洽谈。请用括号中的句型完成下面的对话。

　　Your company has just come out with a new watch design. You want to place an ad on television, so you went to talk to the head of the advertising department at the local TV station. Please complete the following dialogue by using the given patterns in parentheses.

你说：这是我们最新设计、生产的手表。我们＿＿＿＿＿＿＿＿（急于
……），我们想只要广告做得好，＿＿＿＿＿＿＿＿（一……就……）。

广告部负责人：您说得很对。你们的产品质量好，式样新，如果再有广告促
销，＿＿＿＿＿（谁不……呢)？ 您有什么要求＿＿＿＿＿（尽管
…… 好了）。

你说：好的。这是我们第一次在电视上登广告，请问有什么规定吗？

广告部负责人：没有什么特别的规定，只是电视广告的收费标准和在报上刊
登广告不同。＿＿＿＿＿＿＿＿＿（以……计算）。您要不要
看看各个时段的播出费？

你说：好的。您觉得在哪个时段播出我们的广告最好？

广告部负责人：＿＿＿＿＿＿＿＿＿＿(在……看来)

III. 词汇练习 Vocabulary Exercises and Special Expressions：

1. 用中文解释下面的词汇并造句：

Use Chinese to explain the meaning of the following, then make sentences：

例如 For example：周末：一个星期的最后两天;星期六、星期天。

这份广告从下个周末开始刊登。

(1) 促销：＿＿＿＿＿＿＿＿＿＿＿＿＿＿＿＿＿＿

(2) 熟人：＿＿＿＿＿＿＿＿＿＿＿＿＿＿＿＿＿＿

(3) 即将：＿＿＿＿＿＿＿＿＿＿＿＿＿＿＿＿＿＿

(4) 中旬：＿＿＿＿＿＿＿＿＿＿＿＿＿＿＿＿＿＿

(5) 常年：＿＿＿＿＿＿＿＿＿＿＿＿＿＿＿＿＿＿

(6) 新潮：＿＿＿＿＿＿＿＿＿＿＿＿＿＿＿＿＿＿

(7) 杰作：＿＿＿＿＿＿＿＿＿＿＿＿＿＿＿＿＿＿

(8) 共同：＿＿＿＿＿＿＿＿＿＿＿＿＿＿＿＿＿＿

(9) 沾光：＿＿＿＿＿＿＿＿＿＿＿＿＿＿＿＿＿＿

(10) 消费者：＿＿＿＿＿＿＿＿＿＿＿＿＿＿＿＿

(11) 物美价廉：＿＿＿＿＿＿＿＿＿＿＿＿＿＿＿

(12) 挖空心思：＿＿＿＿＿＿＿＿＿＿＿＿＿＿＿

2．请用中文问答下面的问题：

Answer the following questions in Chinese：

(1) 日本的汽车厂商用"车到山前必有路，有路必有丰田车"给他们的丰田汽车做广告。你知道它原来是哪两句话吗？请用你的词典查查看。

_____

(2) 什么时候(什么情况下)可以用"酒香不怕巷子深"这句话？

_____

(3) "王婆卖瓜，自卖自夸"这句话是什么意思？你觉得做广告应该自夸吗？为什么？

_____

IV．阅读、写作和讨论 Reading，Writing and Discussion：

1．根据课文对话回答问题：

Answer the following questions according to the dialogues in this lesson：

(1) 史强生和白琳为什么急于去电视台和报社？

_____

(2) 电视台的钱经理是谁的"老熟人"？

_____

(3) 这家电视台的广告做得好不好？

_____

(4) 为什么钱经理说他一定会给史先生优惠？

_____

(5) 电视广告的播出费怎样计算？

_____

(6) 钱经理说的"不同时段"是什么？

_____

(7) 白琳带到报社的广告有中文广告词吗？

_____

(8) 这份广告要刊登多长时间？一个星期刊登几天？

_____

168

(9) 周小姐同意给白琳优惠吗？给多少？为什么？

_____

(10) 看完课文对话以后，你想史强生和白琳是否会在电视和报纸上做广告？

_____

2. 本课的阅读短文谈到了中国人对广告的心理。在你自己的文化里，人们对商品广告的态度是什么？什么样的广告能够吸引消费者？请写一篇短文，比较不同文化中人们对商品广告的态度。

In the reading passage you learned what points are important to take into consideration in order to make advertisements appealing to Chinese customers. Do you find these points to be valid in your culture as well? Please write a short essay comparing the differences you have noticed in this regard.

3. 找一个广告，说说它的长处和短处。

Find one advertisement as an example to discuss its strong points and shortcomings.

4. 用中文设计一个商品广告。

Use Chinese to design an advertisement.

（四）附录

广告实例

1.

名士手表

让你尽显

出手不凡 的骄傲

工艺精良　　准确可靠

高贵典雅　　传世珍宝

2.

手忙"眼"乱？

明亮眼镜是您最好的选择

明亮眼镜　　世界先进科技制造

让男士更帅

让女性更靓

3.

海内存知己

天涯若比邻

南国传讯

金奖优质产品

手机、寻呼机、无绳电话

让您随时随地与亲朋挚友在一起

4.

　　谁都想十全十美,这是人的天性。

　　　　潇洒衬衫

　　从设计到用料、制作,一切都是最好的!

　　　　潇洒衬衫

*潇洒*的人生,*潇洒*的享受!

为庆祝公司成立三十周年,特别举行三十天七五折酬宾展销活动。

展销日期:六月一日至六月三十日

展销地点:本市各大商场。

展销热线电话:65781788

第十三课　在交易会

在东方公司公共关系部主任张红的陪同下,史强生和白琳从北京坐飞机到了上海。当天,他们去参观了一个国际轻工业品交易会。

(一) 对话

1. 在展览厅

白　琳：啊,这儿真大! 张小姐,听说有几百家厂商参加了这届交易会,是吗?

张　红：是啊,这是今年国内规模最大的交易会之一。不但全国各地都有厂商参加,而且还有不少外国公司参加。史先生、白小姐,这两本小册子上有参加交易会的厂商介绍。

史强生：(看小册子) 嗯……纺织、服装、食品、医药、家庭用品……哦,还有工艺美术品! 参展的商品可真不少! 非常有意思! 张小姐,贵公司这次也参加了吗?

张　红：对,我们公司的展览就在那边。等一会儿我们一块儿过去看看!

白　琳：张小姐,既然这是交易会,如果我们看中什么产品,现在就可以订货吗?

张　红：当然。交易会的好处就是可以当场看样,当场洽谈,当场成交。对买卖双方都很方便。

史强生：张小姐,我有一个问题要向您请教。要是本公司希望参加下一届的交易会,您是否知道应该怎么办手续?

张　红：这很简单。您只要提前向主办单位提出申请、预订展览厅、按规定付费就行了。如果您真有兴趣的话,可以把贵公司的地址留给他们,请他们把有关材料寄给您。

史强生：看起来,参加交易会是进入中国市场的一个好办法。下一次我们一定来!

2. 和参展厂商做生意

一厂商： 张小姐，您好，您好！好久不见了，您也是来参加交易会的吗？

张　红： 不是，我是陪这两位客人来的。这位是美国国际贸易公司亚洲地区
　　　　 总裁史先生，这位是白小姐。他们对您的产品很感兴趣。

厂　商： 史先生、白小姐，幸会，幸会！欢迎光顾，欢迎光顾！

白　琳： 我们刚才看了好几家公司的丝绸产品，可是就数您这儿的最多、最漂
　　　　 亮。

厂　商： 谢谢您的夸奖！实话对您说，我们的丝绸产品是获得国家优质产品
　　　　 金奖的。要是您对中国丝绸感兴趣的话，您算是找对地方了！（拿出
　　　　 两本小册子）这是我们公司的产品目录，请二位过目！

史强生： （看目录）不错，这些产品的确很吸引人，价格也很有竞争力。请问，
　　　　 您的这些产品都有现货供应吗？

厂　商： 保证都有。史先生，如果您打算现在就订货的话，我还可以给您打九
　　　　 五折。

史强生： 今天恐怕不行。我还得再考虑考虑。也许明天我们会再来跟您洽
　　　　 谈。

厂　商： 没关系。做生意嘛，这次不行下次行！欢迎您随时跟我们联系！

张　红： （开玩笑）喂，您不是想把我的客户挖走吧？

厂　商： （笑）哪儿的话！大家在这儿都是做生意嘛！

词汇（一）Vocabulary（1）：

1. 交易会	jiāoyìhuì	trade fair	
	交易	jiāoyì	deal; trade; transaction; to deal; to trade
2. 陪同	péitóng	to accompany	
3. 当天	dàngtiān	the same day; that very day	
4. 轻工业	qīnggōngyè	light industry	
5. 展览厅	zhǎnlǎntīng	exhibition hall	
	展览	zhǎnlǎn	to exhibit; to display; exhibit; display
6. 届	jiè	a measure word for periodic terms or events;

session (of a conference, etc.)

7.	小册子	xiǎocèzi	booklet
8.	纺织	fǎngzhī	textiles
9.	食品	shípǐn	food; foodstuff
10.	医药	yīyào	medicine
11.	家庭用品	jiātíng yòngpǐn	household articles
12.	哦	ò	oh; ah (express a sudden understanding)
13.	工艺美术品	gōngyì měishùpǐn	arts and crafts
14.	参展	cānzhǎn	a short form for 参加展览 (take part in an exhibition)
15.	看中	kànzhòng	to take fancy to; to settle on
16.	订货	dìng huò	to order goods
17.	当场	dāngchǎng	on the spot; then and there
18.	看样	kàn yàng	to view samples
19.	成交	chéngjiāo	to conclude a business transaction; to close a deal
20.	请教	qǐngjiào	to seek advice; to consult
21.	主办	zhǔbàn	to sponsor; to host
22.	提出	tíchū	to put forward; to pose; to raise (a question, etc.); to lodge
23.	申请	shēnqǐng	to apply for; application
24.	地址	dìzhǐ	address
25.	材料	cáiliào	material; data
26.	看起来	kànqilai	it seems; it looks as if
27.	光顾	guānggù	to patronize
28.	丝绸	sīchóu	silk; silk cloth
29.	数	shǔ	to count (as the best, etc.); to be reckoned as exceptionally (good, bad, etc.)
30.	夸奖	kuājiǎng	praise; to praise; to commend
31.	实话	shíhuà	(the) truth

32.	获得	huòdé	to gain; to win; to achieve
33.	优质	yōuzhì	high quality; top quality
34.	金奖	jīnjiǎng	gold medal
35.	算是	suànshì	considered to be
36.	现货	xiànhuò	merchandise on hand; goods in stock
37.	供应	gōngyìng	to supply; supply
38.	九五折	jiǔwǔzhé	5% discount
	打折	dǎzhé	to allow a discount
39.	挖走	wāzǒu	to dig out and take away
	挖	wā	to dig; to scoop

句型(一) Sentence Patterns(1):

1. 在……(的)陪同下　　　　accompanied by

   在张红的陪同下,史强生和白琳从北京坐飞机到了上海。

   在马局长的陪同下,美国代表团昨天参观了高科技交易会。

2. A 的好处就是……　　　　the benefit/advantage of A is…

   交易会的好处就是可以当场看样,当场洽谈,当场成交。

   这种付款方式的好处是不影响资金周转。

3. 只要……就行了　　all you have to do is…; It will be all right as long as…

   您只要提前向主办单位提出申请就行了。

   如果你想知道有关这家公司的情况,只要上网就行了。

4. 看起来　　　　　　"It looks like…"; to appear; to seem

   看起来,参加交易会是进入中国市场的一个好办法。

   这次的谈判看起来很成功。

5. 就数……　　　　　　be reckoned as (the best/worst/etc.)

   我们刚才看了好几家公司的丝绸产品,可是就数您这儿的最多、最漂亮。

   在这届交易会上,就数这家公司的产品最受欢迎。

6. 算是……　　　　　　considered to be…

   要是您对中国丝绸感兴趣的话,您算是找对地方了!

   那家民营企业可以算是一家很大的公司。

(二) 阅读短文

中国的商品交易会

交易会,又叫博览会,是中国的厂商展销产品、交流信息、开展对外贸易和吸引外资的重要方式之一。为了推动经济的发展,每年中国都会定期举行若干国际交易会或者博览会。这些交易会的规模有的大有的小,类型也不完全一样。其中,历史最长、规模最大的是广州出口商品交易会。广州出口商品交易会简称广交会。它一年两次,分别在春季和秋季举行。很多中国厂商都以能够在广交会上展出自己的产品为荣。可以说,广交会是了解中国经济发展的一个窗口。每年九月在厦门举办的中国投资贸易洽谈会,则是近年来中国最重要的国际投资博览会。厦门投洽会以投资洽谈为主题,全面介绍当年的各类招商项目,是投资中国的桥梁。

对于想到中国做生意、投资的外国厂商来说,参加中国的交易会无疑是熟悉中国市场、获得最新商业信息的有效途径。如果你想从中国进口商品,交易会应该是你能买到物美价廉的产品的好地方。由于参展的厂商多,难免竞争激烈。许多厂商往往以降低价格、提供各种优惠条件的办法来吸引买主。你可别错过这样的好机会啊!

词汇(二) Vocabulary(2):

1. 博览会	bólǎnhuì	fair; exhibition
2. 展销	zhǎnxiāo	to exhibit and sell
3. 信息	xìnxī	information; news
4. 开展	kāizhǎn	to develop; to launch; to expand
5. 外资	wàizī	foreign investment
5. 定期	dìngqī	at regular intervals; periodically; regular; periodic
6. 若干	ruògān	a certain number/amount; some; several

7. 类型	lèixíng	type
8. 简称	jiǎnchēng	be called sth. for short; abbreviation
9. 春季	chūnjì	spring
10. 以……为荣	yǐ…wéiróng	consider…as an honor
11. 展出	zhǎnchū	to exhibit; to display
12. 窗口	chuāngkǒu	window
13. 举办	jǔbàn	to conduct; to hold; to run
14. 以……为主题	yǐ…wéizhǔtí	consider…as an subject
主题	zhǔtí	subject; theme
15. 全面	quánmiàn	overall; comprehensive
16. 当年	dàngnián	the same year; that very year
17. 各类	gèlèi	various kinds; various categories
18. 招商	zhāoshāng	inviting investments; investments
19. 项目	xiàngmù	item; project
20. 桥梁	qiáoliáng	bridge
21. 无疑	wúyí	beyond a doubt; undoubtedly
22. 熟悉	shóuxī	to know sth./sb. well; be familiar with
23. 有效	yǒuxiào	effective; valid
24. 途径	tújìng	way; channel
25. 由于	yóuyú	due to; as a result of
26. 难免	nánmiǎn	hard to avoid
27. 往往	wǎngwǎng	often; frequently; more often than not

专有名词 Proper Nouns：

1. 广州	Guǎngzhōu	city name
2. 广州出口商品交易会	Guǎngzhōu Chūkǒu Shāngpǐn Jiāoyìhuì	Guangzhou Export Commodities Fair
3. 广交会	Guǎngjiāohuì	a short form for Guangzhou Export Commodities Fair
4. 中国投资贸易洽谈会	Zhōngguó Tóuzī	China International Fair for

		Màoyì Qiàtánhuì	Investment and Trade
5.	投洽会	Tóuqiàhuì	a short form for China International Fair for Investment and Trade

句型(二) Sentence Patterns(2):

1. 以……为荣/主题　　　　consider/regard…as an honor/a subject

   很多中国厂商都以能够在广交会上展出自己的产品为荣。

   每年九月的厦门投洽会以投资洽谈为主题。

2. 由于……　　　　　　　due to…; as a result of…

   由于竞争激烈,许多厂商往往降低价格。

   由于有了独家代理权,今年我们的销售总额增加了不少。

3. 难免　　　　　　　　　hard to avoid

   由于参加广交会的厂商多,难免竞争激烈。

   如果你不了解市场行情,做生意的时候难免不吃亏上当。

4. 以……的办法　　　　　use the method of…

   厂商往往以提供各种优惠条件的办法来吸引买主。

   这家公司打算以分期付款的办法,引进新的组装线。

(三) 练习与活动

I. 句型练习一 Sentence pattern exercises(1):

1. "在……(的)陪同下"的句型一般用在比较正式的场合。请用这个句型改写下面的句子:

   The pattern of "在……(的)陪同下" usually is only used in a formal situation.

   Please use this pattern to rewrite the following sentences:

   (1) 昨天下午,李经理跟美国贸易代表团一起坐飞机到达了上海。

（2）晚上，上海外贸局马局长邀请美国客人出席了文艺晚会。

_____

（3）今天上午，李经理带美国贸易代表团参观了上海国际纺织交易会。

_____

（4）午饭后，马局长和李经理陪代表团访问了上海丝绸厂。

_____

2. 请用"A 的好处就是……"的句型回答下面的问题：

Answer the following questions by using the pattern of "A 的好处就是……"：

（1）在电视上为产品做广告有什么好处？

_____

（2）获得独家代理权有什么好处？

_____

（3）分期付款有什么好处？

_____

（4）参加大型的交易会有什么好处？

_____

3. 请用"只要……就行了"的句型回答下面的问题：

Answer the following questions by using the pattern of "只要……就行了"：

（1）如果有事怎样跟您联系？

_____

（2）我的公司需要办什么手续才能参加今年的轻工业交易会？

_____

（3）请问，从什么地方可以获得中国医药生产的最新信息？

_____

（4）怎样可以买到质量可靠的丝绸产品？

_____

4. 根据下面的要求，用"看起来"的句型造句：

Use the pattern of "看起来"to accomplish the following tasks：

（1）用"看起来"说一说你对某一种家庭用品的意见。

_____

(2) 用"看起来"说一说你对某一件工艺美术品的意见。

_____

(3) 用"看起来"说一说你觉得这届交易会怎么样?

_____

(4) 你觉得史先生和白小姐对这次访问中国满意吗?

_____

5. 根据下面的要求,用"就数"的句型造句:

Use the pattern of "就数" to accomplish the following tasks:

(1) 用"就数"的句型说出今年最受欢迎的汽车。

_____

(2) 用"就数"的句型说出一家最有名的高科技公司。

_____

(3) 用"就数"的句型说出一家最大的银行。

_____

(4) 用"就数"的句型说出一个中国最大的交易会。

_____

6. 根据下面的要求,用"算是"的句型造句:

Use the pattern of "算是" to accomplish the following tasks:

(1) 史先生打算去中国投资。因为他不太了解中国的情况,所以想听听你的意见。请你用"算是"的句型告诉他在什么地方投资比较好、投资什么比较合适。为什么?

_____

_____

(2) 到了中国以后,史先生想给他的太太买一些纪念品,所以他又跟你请教应该买什么和应该去哪儿买。请你用"算是"的句型告诉他什么东西是值得买的纪念品,哪儿的东西物美价廉。

_____

_____

(3) 听了你的回答以后,史先生非常高兴。他说: "I have finally found the

right person."请你把他的这句话翻译成中文。

_____

II. 句型练习二 Sentence pattern exercises(2):

1. 根据下面的要求,用"以……为荣"或者"以……为主题"的句型造句:
   Use the pattern of "以……为荣"or the pattern of "以……为主题"to accomplish the following tasks:
   (1) 用"以……为荣"的句型说出你们公司最有名的一种产品。

   _____

   (2) 用"以……为荣"的句型说出你最骄傲(jiāo'ào, to be proud)的一件事。

   _____

   (3) 用"以……为主题"的句型说出明天的会谈将要讨论的内容。

   _____

   (4) 用"以……为主题"的句型说出这届国际交易会的重点(zhòngdiǎn, focal point)或者主要目的。

   _____

2. 用"由于……"的句型回答下面的问题:
   Answer the following questions by using the pattern of "由于……":
   (1) 今年贵厂的产品为什么没有参展?

   _____

   (2) 您知道为什么去年他们的丝绸产品没有获得金奖吗?

   _____

   (3) 那笔生意成交了没有?

   _____

   (4) 为什么那家进出口公司没有看中我们的产品?

   _____

3. 用"难免"的句型完成下面的句子:
   Complete the following sentences by using the pattern of "难免":
   (1) 到中国去做生意、投资难免 _____

(2) 推销试销品难免 _____

(3) 给产品做广告难免 _____

(4) 不了解市场行情的厂商难免 _____

4. 用"以……的办法"的句型回答下面的问题：

Answer the following questions by using the pattern of "以……的办法"：

(1) 如果你要在交易会上订货,你打算怎样付款?

_____

(2) 如果你的公司刚生产了一种新产品,你打算怎样打开销路?

_____

(3) 如果你是一家私营企业的总裁,你打算怎样提高你的企业效益?

_____

(4) 如果你的公司有资金周转的问题,你打算怎样解决这个麻烦?

_____

III. 词汇练习 Vocabulary Exercises and Special Expressions：

1. 用中文回答下面的问题：

Answering the following questions in Chinese.

(1) 用中文怎么说 "I want to place an order right here on the spot"?

_____

(2) 在中文里, "the sponsor organization(s)" and "the manufacturers that take part in an exhibition" 是什么(怎么说)?

_____

(3) 在一个大型的轻工业品交易会,一般会展出哪些产品?

_____

2. 用中文解释以下生词的意思并且造句：

Explain the following in Chinese, then make a sentence for each of them：

例如 For example：周末：一个星期的最后两天;星期六、星期天。

这份广告从下个周末开始刊登。

(1) 参展: _____

(2) 简称: _____

182

（3）无疑：_____

（4）成交：_____

（5）实话：_____

（6）获得：_____

（7）展销：_____

（8）食品：_____

Ⅳ. 阅读、写作和讨论 Reading，Writing and Discussion：

1. 根据课文对话回答问题：

Answer the following questions according to the dialogues in this lesson：

（1）这是一个什么交易会？在什么地方？

_____

（2）为什么说这个交易会是"今年国内规模最大的交易会之一"？

_____

（3）张小姐的公司参加了这次交易会吗？

_____

（4）为什么张小姐认为交易会"对买卖双方都很方便"？

_____

（5）如果一个公司想参加交易会,应该怎样办手续？

_____

（6）为什么那位厂商告诉史先生和白小姐"您算是找对地方了"？

_____

（7）你觉得那位厂商善于做生意吗？为什么？

_____

2. 根据阅读短文回答问题：

Answer the following questions based on the reading passage.

（1）中国规模最大的商品交易会是什么？每年的什么时候举行？

_____

（2）为什么说厦门投洽会是"投资中国的桥梁"？

_____

(3) 为什么对跟中国有贸易关系的厂商来说, 参加中国的国际商品交易会是成功的关键之一?

---

3. 利用图书馆或者上网, 找出有关一个在中国(或者在你的国家)举办的国际交易会的信息。然后写一篇短文, 介绍一下这个交易会的情况。请你尽量多用在本课学到的词汇和句型。

Using the library and/or the Internet, find out some information about an international trade fair in China (or your country). Write a short essay giving a general introduction to this fair.

Use as many new words and patterns from this lesson as possible.

（四）附录

（1）广交会申请表

申请参加广交会登记表

有意参加交易会的客商, 请填下述的电子表格, 我们将按您的地址和公司名称寄一份交易会的请柬给您, 您则凭请柬到中国驻贵国的大使馆或领事馆办理入境签证。

姓名

☐

性别

☐

公司所在国(地区)

☐

公司(商号)名称

☐

公司地址

☐

(主要经营范围)(请标注)

☐ 粮油	☐ 食品
☐ 土产	☐ 畜产品
☐ 工艺品	☐ 纺织品
☐ 丝绸	☐ 轻工产品
☐ 机械	☐ 设备
☐ 医药	☐ 保健品
☐ 有色金属	☐ 冶金
☐ 电子	☐ 五金
☐ 矿产	☐ 化工产品
☐ 仪器	☐ 技术
☐ 综合	

登记日期 ☐

| 发送表格 | 清除表格 |

申请参加会的途径

客商可向下列机构申请参加交易会:

1. 向中国出口商品交易会对外联络处联系申请
   地址: 广州市流花路 117 号
   邮编: 510014
   电话: 86 - 20 - 86661664, 86665846
   传真: 86 - 20 - 83335880
   电子信箱: *cecffld @ ciet . cn . net*

2. 向中国驻各国大使馆经商处(室)联系申请;

3. 通过与您有业务关系的中国对外贸易企业提名申请;

4. 通过香港中国旅行社及其海外分社代办申请;

5. 香港地区客商请向香港中华总商会联系申请;
   地址: 香港干诺道中 24 号 9 字楼
   电话: 852 - 25256385
   传真: 852 - 28452610

6. 澳门地区客商请向澳门南光(集团)有限公司联系申请;
   地址: 澳门罗理基博士大马路南光大厦 16 字楼
   电话: 853 - 3911650
   传真: 853 - 330853

7. 台湾地区客商可向"海峡两岸商务协调会"驻台北联络处联系申请;
   地址: 台北市敦化南路二段 98 号蓝天大厦 8 楼之一
   电话: 886 - 2 - 7050888
   传真: 886 - 2 - 7050822

8. 日本客商请向日本国际贸易促进协会申请
   地址: Toranomon, 17th mori
   Bidg., 1 - 26 - 5
   Japan
   电话: 81 - 3 - 3568261
   传真: 81 - 3 - 35068260

申请截止时间为　春交会: 三月三十日　秋交会: 九月三十日

(2) 广交会登录表

首届在线广交会参展企业登录表

Participant Registration Form of the First Online Trade Fair

交易团名称				
所在地区				
参展企业名称				
企业代码				
公司简介 （200 字以内）				
联络方式	地址		邮编	
	电话		传真	
	电子邮件		联系人	

参展商品登录表

Exhibit Registration Form

商品名称		商品类别	
		企业代码	
展出摊位号			
参考单价		供货商	
交货期		包装规格	
产品简介 （200 字以下） 是否附有照片： 是 否			

（摘自中华人民共和国商务部站点：WWW.mofcom.gov.cn）

第十四课　经济特区

　　深圳是史强生和白琳这次中国之行的最后一个城市。从上海到达深圳以后,张红陪他们参观了经济特区和几家中外合资企业,其中包括东方公司在深圳的子公司东方科技发展公司。经济特区的发展、建设和投资环境给他们留下了深刻的印象。

(一) 对话

1. 谈经济特区

白　琳：真想不到这儿发展得这么快!

张　红：是啊,这些年,深圳利用外资发展经济,已经从一个小镇变成了一个现代化的大城市。现在每年都有越来越多的外国厂商到这里来做生意,世界上很多有名的大公司在深圳都有投资。

史强生：张小姐,经济特区是依靠什么来吸引外商投资的呢?

张　红：我想主要是靠良好的投资环境,尤其是完善的基础设施和对外商投资的优惠政策。

史强生：我知道东方科技发展公司也是一家合资企业。请问,它的经济效益怎么样?

张　红：东方科技发展公司是我们和日本一家电脑公司共同投资的,主要生产电脑光盘和数码影碟机,百分之七十五以上的产品外销。因为有完善的管理制度,技术、设备也都很先进,所以效益一直很好。即使在前两年的亚洲金融危机中,我们的正常出口业务也没有受到影响。

白　琳：是吗? 告诉你们,我在美国买的一个影碟机就是中国制造的。说不定就是在这儿生产的呢!

2. 谈三资企业

史强生： 张小姐，在今天的参观中，我常常听到三资企业这个词。请问，这是指三种不同的外商投资企业，对吗？

张　红： 是的。三资企业是指外商独资企业、中外合资企业和中外合作经营企业。在深圳，很多公司都属于三资企业。

史强生： 我对合资企业很感兴趣。但是对具体的规定和申请手续还不太清楚。不知道您是否可以给我做一点儿简单的介绍。

张　红： 据我所知，申请创办合资企业可以分为三步。首先是申请立项，其次是领取各种表格，最后是申请营业执照。哦，对了，我这儿有一本小册子，上面有详细的说明。您需要的话，可以留着看看。

史强生： 那太好了，谢谢您！我回到美国以后，一定仔细研究研究。

白　琳： 张小姐，我听说中国方面往往希望在合资企业中拥有百分之五十以上的控股权，是这样的吗？

张　红： 我想这种说法不准确。拿我们公司来说，投资的比例是由双方协商决定的。中方并不是非要求拥有控股权不可。如果白小姐愿意多出钱的话，我们当然欢迎！（笑）

词汇（一）Vocabulary（1）：

1. ……之行	zhī xíng	the trip of …
2. 合资企业	hézī qǐyè	joint venture enterprise (a business or commercial activity in which two or more people or organizations work together. The investing parties will jointly run the enterprise and be responsible for its profits and losses. Dividends will be distributed between them according to the proportion of shares each of them holds.)
合资	hézī	joint capital
3. 子公司	zǐgōngsī	subsidiary corporation

4. 投资环境	tóuzī huánjìng	investment environment
5. 镇	zhèn	town
6. 现代化	xiàndàihuà	modern; modernized; modernization
7. 依靠	yīkào	to rely on; to depend on
8. 完善	wánshàn	perfect; complete
9. 基础设施	jīchǔ shèshī	infrastructure
10. 经济效益	jīngjì xiàoyì	economic results/benefits/profits
效益	xiàoyì	beneficial result
11. 光盘	guāngpán	CD-ROM
12. 数码影碟机	shùmǎ yǐngdiéjī	DVD player
13. 外销	wàixiāo	to sell abroad; to export
14. 金融危机	jīnróng wēijī	financial crisis
危机	wēijī	crisis
15. 正常	zhèngcháng	normal; regular
16. 说不定	shuō bu dìng	perhaps; maybe
17. 三资企业	sānzī qǐyè	three types of enterprises using foreign investments, i. e. single venture enterprise, joint venture enterprise and cooperative business operation
18. 独资企业	dúzī qǐyè	single venture enterprise that is funded solely by foreign investors
19. 合作经营	hézuò jīngyíng	cooperative business operation (this enterprise is a joint venture by contract. The contract will only regulate what the investments for each party will be, but not calculate how much money each party has invested. The materials, machines, technology, manpower, estates and other properties, jointly invested, will not be worked out in monetary terms or counted as shares. Instead, the investing parties will sign a

189

contract to agree on how they will distribute the products and profits for how many years to come. When the contract period is over, the enterprise will belong to the country where it stands.)

	经营	jīngyíng	to manage; to run
20.	属于	shǔyú	to belong to; to be part of
21.	据我所知	jù wǒ suǒ zhī	as far as I know
22.	创办	chuàngbàn	to establish; to set up
23.	步	bù	step
24.	立项	lìxiàng	a short form for 设立项目（the establishment of a new project/business venture)
25.	其次	qícì	next; secondly; then
26.	领取	lǐngqǔ	to get; to receive; to draw
27.	表格	biǎogé	form; table
28.	营业执照	yíngyè zhízhào	business permit
	执照	zhízhào	license; permit
29.	详细	xiángxì	detailed
30.	拥有	yōngyǒu	to possess; to have; to own
31.	控股权	kònggǔ quán	controlling interest
32.	准确	zhǔnquè	accurate; precise; correct
33.	比例	bǐlì	proportion; scale; ratio
34.	协商	xiéshāng	to consult; to talk things over; consultation
35.	出钱	chūqián	to provide the funds; to invest; to pay

专有名词 Proper Nouns:

1. 东方科技发展公司　Dōngfāng Kējì Fāzhǎn Gōngsī　Eastern Technology Development Company

190

句型(一) Sentence Patterns(1)：

1. 从 A 变成(了)B　　　　change from A into B

   深圳已经从一个小镇变成了一个现代化的大城市。

   在过去的几年中,这家小公司从一家普通代理商变成了一家生产电脑的大公司。

2. (依)靠……来 V.　　　　rely/depend on…to V.

   经济特区是依靠什么来吸引外商投资的呢?

   这家工厂靠引进新技术来提高产品质量。

3. 属于……　　　　belong to…; be a part of…

   在深圳,很多公司都属于三资企业。

   这几家商店都属于同一个销售网。

4. 据我所知　　　　as far as I know…

   据我所知,申请创办合资企业可以分为三步。

   据我所知,那家公司只接受信用证付款方式。

5. 拿……来说　　　　take (or use)…as an example

   拿我们公司来说,投资的比例是由双方协商决定的。

   拿家用电器来说,目前的市场行情并不好。

(二) 阅读短文

中国的经济特区

　　中国的经济特区是中国实行改革开放政策以后开始设立的。它们一般位于沿海地区,便于跟海外交往。一九七九年七月,中国政府决定首先开发四个经济特区。它们分别是广东省的深圳、珠海、汕头和福建省的厦门。这四个经济特区都在中国的东南沿海地区,靠近香港和澳门。

　　中国设立经济特区的目的是为了吸引外国资本、更快地发展本国经济。为了达到这个目的,中国政府决定在特区实行特殊的经济政策,以便创造出一个良好的投资环境。这些特殊政策主要包括税收、进出口、出入境以及土地使用等方面的优惠待遇。例如,合资经营的企业所得税可以获得大幅度的减免。投资额大、资金周转时间长或者是投资在高新科技方面的项目还有更多的优惠措施。到目前为止,经济特区已经成功地吸引了大批外商投资,成为中国经济发展的重要部分。

词汇(二) Vocabulary(2):

1.	位于	wèiyú	be located at/in
2.	沿海	yánhǎi	along the coast; coastal
3.	海外	hǎiwài	overseas; abroad
4.	交往	jiāowǎng	to associate with; to have contact with; association; contact
5.	开发	kāifā	to develop; to exploit; to open up
6.	东南	dōngnán	southeast
7.	靠近	kàojìn	be near/close to
8.	资本	zīběn	capital
9.	本国	běn guó	one's own country
10.	达到	dádào	to achieve; to reach; to attain
11.	特殊	tèshū	special; exceptional; unusual
12.	以便	yǐbiàn	in order to; so that; with the aim of
13.	创造	chuàngzào	to create; to produce
14.	税收	shuìshōu	tax revenue
15.	出入境	chūrùjìng	to leave or enter a country
16.	土地	tǔdì	land
17.	待遇	dàiyù	treatment
18.	所得税	suǒdéshuì	income tax
19.	大幅度	dà fúdù	to a great extent
	幅度 fúdù		range; scope; extent
20.	减免	jiǎnmiǎn	reduction; to reduce or remit (taxation, etc.)
21.	高新科技	gāo xīn kējì	high-tech and new technology
22.	措施	cuòshī	measure; step

23. 到……为止　　dào…wéizhǐ　　until
24. 大批　　　　　dàpī　　　　　large batch of; good deal of

专有名词 Proper Nouns：

1. 汕头　　　Shàntóu　　　a city name
2. 福建省　　Fújiàn Shěng　Fujian Province
3. 香港　　　Xiānggǎng　　Hong Kong
4. 澳门　　　Àomén　　　　Macao

句型（二）Sentence Patterns（2）：

1. 位于……　　　be located at/in…

　　经济特区一般位于中国沿海地区。

　　新国际机场位于上海市西边。

2. 分别是……　　be…respectively(a list of items)

　　首先开发的四个经济特区分别是深圳、珠海、汕头和厦门。

　　本公司今年推出的新产品分别是洗衣机、洗碗机和微波炉。

3. 以便……　　　in order to; so that; with the aim of…

　　中国政府决定在特区实行特殊的经济政策,以便创造出一个良好的投资
　　环境。

　　我们决定播出电视广告,以便打开市场销路。

4. 到……为止　　until…

　　到目前为止,经济特区已经成功地吸引了大批外资。

　　到昨天为止,这两家公司已经签订了三份合同。

(三) 练习与活动

I. 句型练习一 Sentence pattern exercises (1)：

1. 根据下面的要求,用"从 A 变成(了)B"的句型造句：

Use the pattern of "从 A 变成(了)B" to accomplish the following tasks：

(1) 说一说一个人在过去十年中的变化。

_____

(2) 说一说一家公司在最近几年的发展和变化。

_____

(3) 说一说一个地区的发展和变化。

_____

(4) 说一说一个企业在经营、管理上的变化。

_____

2. 完成下面带"(依)靠……来 V."句型的句子：

Complete the following sentences with the pattern of "(依)靠……来 V."：

(1) 他靠_____来赚钱上大学。

(2) 这个地区决定依靠_____来实现现代化。

(3) 王总经理打算依靠_____来提高企业的经济效益。

(4) 在这次金融危机中,这家公司一直依靠_____来保持资金周转正常。

3. 用"属于"的句型改写下面的句子：

Rewrite the following sentences by using the pattern of "属于".

(1) 这些数码影碟机都是本公司的外销产品。

_____

(2) 这个项目是本公司明年投资计划的一部分。

_____

(3) 那家五星级大旅馆也是合资企业。

_____

(4) 这些都是我们需要协商的问题。

_____

4. 请用"据我所知"的句型回答下面的问题：

Answer the following questions by using the pattern of "据我所知".

(1) 请问,什么是三资企业?

_____

(2) 你知道怎样申请创办合资企业吗?

_____

(3) 那家国际贸易公司的信誉怎么样?

_____

(4) 为什么很多外国大企业都愿意到经济特区来投资?

_____

5. 用"拿……来说"的句型改写下面的句子：

Rewrite the following sentences by using the pattern of "拿……来说"：

(1) 在吸引外资上,据说已经有几百家世界著名的公司到深圳投资。

_____

(2) 经济特区有很多特殊政策。例如,在企业所得税上,合资企业可以获得百分之十五的减免。

_____

(3) 那家公司亏损了很多。例如,今年春季的销售就赔了五百万。

_____

(4) 这届的交易会举办得非常成功。例如,有国内外几百家厂商参展,成交总额达到九千万美元。

_____

II. 句型练习二 Sentence pattern exercises(2)：

1. 请用"位于……"的句型改写下面的句子：

Rewrite the following sentences by using the pattern of "位于……"：

(1) 国际商务中心在旅馆的二楼。

_____

（2）家用电器产品展览在交易会大厅入口处的右边。

_____

（3）深圳、珠海和汕头都在广东省的沿海地区。

_____

（4）成品车间在工厂的东边，组装车间的后边。

_____

2. 用"分别是"的句型回答下面的问题：

Answer the following questions by using the pattern of "分别是"：

（1）销售代理商一般分为几种？哪几种？

_____

（2）贵公司今年推出了哪些新产品？

_____

（3）请问，贵公司常打交道的银行有哪几家？

_____

（4）这次中国之行，美国贸易代表团访问了哪几个城市？

_____

3. 用"以便"的句型完成下面的句子：

Complete the following sentences by using the pattern of "以便"：

（1）今年那家工厂调整了生产计划，以便_____

（2）促销期间所有商品都打七折，以便_____

（3）本公司计划采用高新科技，以便_____

（4）当地政府决定对合资企业提供优惠待遇，以便_____

4. 用"到……为止"的句型回答下面的问题：

Answer the following questions by using the pattern of "到……为止"：

（1）这家公司已经开发了多少种高新科技产品？

_____

（2）双方代表就独家代理权问题达成了协议没有？

_____

（3）这届交易会贵公司签订了多少合同？

_____

（4）为什么那位外国投资公司的代表觉得这里的基础设施还不够完善？

_____

III. 词汇练习 Vocabulary Exercises and Special Expressions：

1. 组词 Build upon the following words：

例如 For example：协<u>商</u>　　协<u>议</u>

(1) _____销　　_____销　　_____销　　_____销

(2) 交_____　　交_____　　交_____　　交_____

(3) 资_____　　资_____　　资_____　　资_____

(4) 创_____　　创_____　　创_____　　创_____

例如 For example：提前 → <u>提前付款</u>　<u>提前交货</u>

(5) 达到 → _____　_____

(6) 开发 → _____　_____

(7) 危机 → _____　_____

(8) 执照 → _____　_____

(9) 表格 → _____　_____

(10) 拥有 → _____　_____

(11) 创造 → _____　_____

(12) 减免 → _____　_____

IV. 阅读、写作和讨论 Reading, Writing and Discussion：

1. 根据课文对话回答问题：

Answer the following questions according to the dialogues in this lesson：

(1) 深圳这些年有什么变化？

_____

(2) 深圳依靠什么来吸引外资？

_____

(3) 东方科技发展公司主要生产什么？

_____

(4) 为什么东方科技发展公司的效益很好?

_____

(5) 什么是三资企业?

_____

(6) 怎样申请创办一个合资企业?

_____

(7) 张红说,合资企业的投资比例可以怎样决定?

_____

2. 根据阅读短文回答问题:

Answer the following questions based on the reading passage.

(1) 中国是什么时候开始设立经济特区的?

_____

(2) 设立经济特区的目的是什么?

_____

(3) 中国首先开发的经济特区是哪几个?

_____

(4) 经济特区的特殊政策主要包括哪些方面?

_____

(5) 选择一个经济特区(例如深圳、珠海、汕头、厦门、海南),利用图书馆或者上网,找出有关这个地方的信息和资料。然后写一篇短文,介绍一下这个经济特区的情况。请你尽量多用在本课学到的词汇和句型。

Choose one of the special economic zones in China and gather information about it from the Internet or other sources. Use the vocabulary and patterns you learned in this lesson to write a short essay about the economic growth of the place you have chosen.

（四）附录

（1）招商广告

广东省深圳市福田保税区五万平方米工业用地招商

福田保税区位于全国最大的陆路口岸——皇岗口岸旁,并有一条专用通道与香港连接。我公司——深圳深福保(集团)有限公司,是福田保税区管理局的下属企业。现本公司有五万平方米的工业用地使用权出让、合作或以土地入股举办合资企业。其用途为高科技或高附加值工业项目。如想索取更多的资料,可进入本公司的网站：www.shenfubao.com 或福田保税区的网站：www.fftz-cn.com 。欢迎海内外的商家与我们联系。

地址:中华人民共和国广东省深圳市福田区桂花路三号管理局办公楼 410 室

联系人:李华小姐、黄立春先生、卢铮先生

电话: 086－755－3590279

传真: 086－755－3590277

电子邮件: lihua123@21cn.com

（摘编自 www.chinamarket.com.cn/C/invest/BBS/mess/1402.html）

（2）营业执照

营业执照

（副 本）

字　号

发　　照　　　　　　　　　　　年　月　日

名　　称

地　　址

负 责 人

资 金 数 额

经 济 性 质

经 营 范 围　主营

兼营

经 营 方 式

经 营 期 限

外商投资企业办事机构

注册证

注册号：

该办事机构经审核准予登记注册。
特发此证。

编号：No. 0023901

机构名称（中文）

（外文）

地　　址

负 责 人

业 务 范 围

隶属企业名称

隶属企业地址

本证有效期限自　　　　　　至

中华人民共和国
国家工商行政管理局　局长

年　　　　　　日

（影印件由江西财经大学经济文化传播系提供）

第十五课　签订合同

今天是史强生和白琳在中国的最后一天。中美双方将要正式签订合同。一早,东方公司的副总经理李信文就从北京坐飞机到了深圳。他将代表东方公司参加今天的签字仪式。

(一) 对话

1. 审核合同草案

李信文：　史先生、白小姐,这是我们今天将要签署的两份合同草案,一份是今年秋季的订货合同,另一份是长期协定意向书,请二位审核,尤其是数量、金额、包装要求、交货时间、验收方式和付款方式等条款。如果有任何遗漏或者不合适的地方,请立刻指出,以便修改。

史强生：　好! 白琳,我们一个人看一份。看完一遍以后,再交换看一遍。(史强生、白琳审核合同草案)

白　琳：　李先生,我有一个问题。关于交货时间的条款,合同上只写着在八月初、九月初分两次交货,但是没有指出具体的日期,这似乎还不够清楚。

李信文：　对,我正想跟您再确认一下儿这个问题。根据我们上一次洽谈的结果,双方一致同意的交货时间是八月上旬和九月上旬。如果您不反对的话,我们可以把这一条改成"分别在八月十日和九月十日前交货",您看怎么样?

白　琳：　Johnson,你觉得这样写行吗?

史强生：　我认为可以,这样写符合我们共同商定的交货时间。不过,我希望在合同中补充这样一条:如果因为卖方交货时间的延误,造成买方的经济损失,买方有权提出申诉和索赔。说实话,这批订单的交货时间对我们非常重要,我不想有任何差错。李先生,希望您能理解。

李信文：　重合同、守信用是我们公司的原则，我们一定会按时交货。不过，我完全理解您的要求，我们可以马上把这一条写进去。

史强生：　谢谢！另外，我建议在长期协定中增加这样一句话：今后双方每半年应举行一次会谈，以便随时解决合同执行中可能发生的问题。

李信文：　这一条很必要。我马上加进去。谢谢！

2. 正式签字

李信文：　史先生，这是合同的正本。凡是今天上午提出问题的地方，我们都按你们的意见做了修改。请您再看一遍。希望这次能让我们双方都满意。

史强生：　(看合同)嗯，我认为所有条款都很详细清楚，看不出还有什么地方需要再修改、补充。白琳，你看呢？

白　琳：　我也觉得一切都很好。李先生，您费心了！

李信文：　不客气，这是我应该做的事。请问贵方需要几份副本？

史强生：　麻烦您每份合同给我五份副本。

李信文：　行！如果没有其他问题的话，我想我们可以签字了。史先生，请您在这儿签字吧！

史强生：　好。(签字)李先生，这次我们的合作非常成功。我非常高兴。希望今后跟您、跟贵公司能有更多的合作机会。

李信文：　一定，一定！现在我们有了长期协定，合作的机会一定会越来越多！(倒酒)来，为庆祝我们这次合作的圆满成功，为今后的更多合作，干杯！(大家干杯)

白　琳：　(开玩笑)李先生，看起来今后我会常常来北京麻烦您了。您不会头疼吧？

词汇(一) Vocabulary(1)：

1.	将要	jiāngyào	going to; will
2.	签字	qiānzì	to sign or initial
3.	仪式	yíshì	ceremony; rite

4. 审核	shěnhé	to examine and verify	
5. 草案	cǎo'àn	draft (of a contract/law/etc.) *only document*	
6. 签署	qiānshǔ	to sign (a document)	
7. 协定	xiédìng	agreement	
8. 意向书	yìxiàngshū	letter of intent	
9. 金额	jīn'é	amount/sum of money	
10. 包装	bāozhuāng	packing; packaging; to pack; dress up	
11. 验收	yànshōu	check on delivery; inspection	
12. 遗漏	yílòu	omission; to omit; to miss	
13. 指出	zhǐchū	to point out	
14. 关于	guānyú	about; with regard to; concerning	
15. 条款	tiáokuǎn	clause; article; provision	
16. 初	chū	in the early part of; at the beginning of	
17. 不够	búgòu	not enough; insufficient; inadequate	
18. 确认	quèrèn	to confirm; to identify with certainty	
19. 根据	gēnjù	on the basis of; according to	
20. 一致	yízhì	unanimous(ly); identical; consistent	
21. 补充	bǔchōng	to supplement; to add; to replenish	
22. 延误	yánwù	delay; to incur loss because of delay	
23. 造成	zàochéng	to create; to cause; to result in	
24. 申诉	shēnsù	appeal; to appeal	
25. 索赔	suǒpéi	claim (for damages); to demand compensation	
26. 差错	chācuò	mistake; error	
27. 重合同，守信用	zhòng hétong, shǒu xìnyòng	take one's contract seriously and keep one's word	
28. 原则	yuánzé	principle	
29. 按时	ànshí	on time	
30. 执行	zhíxíng	to carry out; to execute; to implement	
31. 必要	bìyào	necessary; requisite	
32. 正本	zhèngběn	original (of document)	

33. 凡是	fánshì	every; any; all
34. 副本	fùběn	duplicate; copy
35. 庆祝	qìngzhù	to celebrate
36. 头疼	tóuténg	to have a headache; headache

句型（一）Sentence Patterns（1）：

1. 关于……   about; with regard to; concerning

    关于交货时间的条款，合同上写得还不够清楚。

    关于这个问题，我方还需要考虑。

2. 根据……   on the basis of; according to

    根据洽谈的结果，交货时间是八月上旬。

    根据日程安排，明天他们要参观一个交易会。

3. 把 A 改成 B   change A to/into B

    我们可以把交货时间改成九月上旬。

    他们已经把会谈的时间改成明天下午了。

4. sb. 有权 do sth.   sb. has the right/authority to do sth.

    如果因为交货时间的延误造成买方的经济损失，买方有权提出索赔。

    电视台有权决定广告的播出费。

5. 凡是……都……   every; any; all

    凡是有问题的地方，我们都做了修改。

    凡是看了广告的人，都对我们的产品很感兴趣。

（二）阅读短文

中国的涉外经济法规

    为了更好地利用外国资本和先进技术来帮助中国经济的发展，中国政府从一九七九年开始陆续制订了一系列的涉外经济法规。到目前为止，中国已经制订、实施的涉外经济法规主要包括《中外合资经营企业法》、《涉外经济合同法》、《外资企业法》、《中外合作经营企业法》和《外商投资企业和外国企业所

得税法》等等。这些法规在肯定改革开放政策的同时,明确承诺保护外国投资者的合法权益,保证给予来中国投资的外国厂商、公司和个人种种方便和优惠。中国的涉外经济法规强调平等互利的基本原则,同时也规定了解决争议的途径,即协商、调解、仲裁和诉讼等四种不同的方式。为了使争议得到公正合理的解决,中国也接受在第三国仲裁的要求。对于每一个打算到中国投资、做生意的外国人来说,了解这些法规的内容是很有好处的。

中国涉外经济法规的实施明显地改善了中国的投资环境,起到了鼓励外国投资者的作用。今天的中国正在吸引着越来越多的外国投资者的关注。

词汇(二) Vocabulary (2):

1.	涉外	shèwài	involving foreign affairs/nations
2.	法规	fǎguī	law and regulations
3.	陆续	lùxù	one after another; in succession
4.	制订	zhìdìng	to formulate; to draft
5.	一系列	yíxìliè	a series of
6.	实施	shíshī	to put into effect; to implement
7.	同时	tóngshí	at the same time; simultaneously
8.	肯定	kěndìng	to affirm; to approve
9.	明确	míngquè	explicit(ly); clear and definite
10.	承诺	chéngnuò	to promise (to do sth.)
11.	保护	bǎohù	to protect; to safeguard
12.	合法	héfǎ	lawful; legal
13.	权益	quányì	rights and interests
14.	给予	gěiyǔ	to give; to grant
15.	个人	gèrén	the individual (as contrasted with the group)
16.	种种	zhǒngzhǒng	all kinds of; varieties of
17.	强调	qiángdiào	to stress; to emphasize
18.	平等互利	píngděng hùlì	equality and mutual benefit
19.	争议	zhēngyì	dispute; controversy; to dispute

20. 调解	tiáojiě	mediation; to mediate
21. 仲裁	zhòngcái	arbitration; to arbitrate
22. 诉讼	sùsòng	lawsuit; litigation
23. 公正	gōngzhèng	just; fair; impartial
24. 第三国	dìsān guó	a third (and disinterested) country
25. 改善	gǎishàn	to improve
26. 起到……作用	qǐdào…zuòyòng	have the effect of…
作用	zuòyòng	effect; function
27. 关注	guānzhù	attention; interest; to follow with interest; to pay close attention to

专有名词 Proper Nouns：

1. 中外合资经营企业法　　Zhōngwài Hézī Jīngyíng Qǐyè Fǎ
   Law of Joint Ventures Using Chinese and Foreign Investment

2. 涉外经济合同法　　Shèwài Jīngjì Hétong Fǎ
   Foreign Economic Contract Law

3. 外资企业法　　Wàizī Qǐyè Fǎ
   Law of Ventures Using Foreign Investment

4. 中外合作经营企业法　　Zhōngwài Hézuò Jīngyíng Qǐyè Fǎ
   Law of Chinese-Foreign Cooperative Joint Ventures

5. 外商投资企业和外国企业所得税法
   Wàishāng Tóuzī Qǐyè hé Wàiguó Qǐyè Suǒdéshuì Fǎ
   The Income Tax Law for Enterprises with Foreign Investment and Foreign Enterprises

句型（二） Sentence Patterns（2）：

1. 利用 A（来）V.　　　　　use A to V.

206

中国政府希望利用外国资本和先进技术来帮助中国经济发展。

我想利用这个机会,跟贵公司讨论合资企业的问题。

2. 从……开始　　　　　　　start from…

中国从一九七九年开始陆续制订了一系列的涉外经济法规。

这家公司从去年开始生产新型家用电器。

3. 在……(的)同时　　　　　at the same time as…

这些法规在肯定改革开放政策的同时,明确承诺保护外国投资者的合法权益。

在进口中国产品的同时,本公司也计划到中国投资。

4. 起到……作用　　　　　　have the effect of…

中国涉外经济法规的实施,起到了鼓励外国投资者的作用。

这种方法起到了推销产品的作用。

(三) 练习与活动

I. 句型练习— Sentence pattern exercises(1):

1. 请用"关于……"的句型回答下面的问题:

Answer the following questions by using the pattern of "关于……".

(1) 你拿的是一本什么小册子?

_____

(2) 明天要签署的是一份什么样的意向书?

_____

(3) 在学这一课以前, 你听说过中国的涉外经济法规吗?

_____

(4) 审核了协定以后,您认为哪条条款需要修改?

_____

2. 根据下面的要求,用 "根据……"的句型造句:

Use the pattern of "根据……"to accomplish the following tasks:

(1) 说一说在电视上做广告的费用一般是怎么计算的。

_____

(2) 说一说合资企业的投资比例一般是怎么决定的。

_____

(3) 说一说商品的零售价一般是怎么决定的。

_____

(4) 说一说一个工厂的生产计划一般是怎么决定的。

_____

3. 根据下面的要求,用"把 A 改成 B"的句型造句:

Use the pattern of "把 A 改成 B" to accomplish the following tasks:

(1) 告诉电视台,你希望改变广告播出的时间。

_____

(2) 告诉你的客户,因为资金周转的问题,你们希望改变付款方式。

_____

(3) 通知有关厂商,因为销路不好,你们计划降低进货数量。

_____

(4) 通知有关单位,你决定改变投资额。

_____

4. 请用"sb. 有权 do sth."的句型回答下面的问题:

Answer the following questions by using the pattern of "sb. 有权 do sth.".

(1) 谁可以签署这份协定?

_____

(2) 谁可以代表厂家进行促销活动?

_____

(3) 如果延误了交货时间, 买方可以跟卖方提出什么要求?

_____

(4) 消费者买了质量有问题的商品应该怎么办?

_____

5. 请用"凡是……都……"的句型回答下面的问题:

Answer the following questions by using the pattern of "凡是……都……".

(1) 贵公司哪些产品最受欢迎?

_____

208

（2）对做生意的人来说，什么样的事情最让人头疼？

_____

（3）这份意向书有哪些地方需要修改和补充？

_____

（4）这份协定上的哪些条款应该立刻执行？

_____

II. 句型练习二 Sentence pattern exercises（2）:

1. 请用"利用 A 来 V."的句型回答下面的问题：

Answer the following questions by using the pattern of "利用 A 来 V.".

（1）中国政府设立经济特区的目的是什么？

_____

（2）如果你是公司总裁，你打算怎样为你的产品打开中国市场？

_____

（3）如果你是一个代理商，你怎样获得市场信息？

_____

（4）如果一个企业长期亏损，有什么办法可以提高企业效益？

_____

2. 完成下面带"从……开始"句型的句子：

Complete the following sentences with the pattern of "从……开始"：

（1）从去年开始，_____。

（2）从第一次洽谈开始，_____。

（3）从设立经济特区开始，_____。

（4）从制订涉外经济法规开始，_____。

3. 用"在……（的）同时"的句型改写下面的句子：

Rewrite the following sentences by using the pattern of "在……（的）同时"：

（1）除了广告促销以外，还必须提高产品质量，这样才能打开销路。

_____

（2）除了掌握市场行情以外，还必须了解有关的政策和法规，外国公司才能

209

在中国获得成功。

_____

(3) 只有重合同,守信用,努力为消费者提供良好的服务,才能建立起企业
的信誉。

_____

(4) 经济特区不但为外商提供完善的基础设施,还制订了一系列优惠政策。

_____

4. 请用"起到……作用"的句型回答下面的问题:
Answer the following questions by using the pattern of "起到……作用".

(1) 销售旺季为什么还要减价、打折?

_____

(2) 减免三资企业所得税有什么积极的作用?

_____

(3) 在国际贸易中,当买卖双方有了争议,找第三国调解或仲裁有什么好
处?

_____

(4) 这个地区为什么需要进一步改善投资环境?

_____

III. 词汇练习 Vocabulary Exercises and Special Expressions:

1. 组词 Build upon the following words:
例如 For example: 涉外 → 涉外法规   涉外活动

(1) 签署 → _____ _____

(2) 审核 → _____ _____

(3) 执行 → _____ _____

(4) 一致 → _____ _____

(5) 补充 → _____ _____

(6) 造成 → _____ _____

(7) 按时 → _____ _____

(8) 保护 → _____ _____

210

(9) 改善 → _____ _____

(10) 制订 → _____ _____

2. 用中文解释以下生词的意思并造句：

Explain the following in Chinese, then make a sentence for each of them：

例如 For example：周末：一个星期的最后两天；星期六、星期天。

这份广告从下个周末开始刊登。

(1) 关注：_____

(2) 陆续：_____

(3) 承诺：_____

(4) 种种：_____

(5) 平等互利：_____

IV. 阅读、写作和讨论 Reading, Writing and Discussion：

1. 根据课文对话回答问题：

Answer the following questions according to the dialogues in this lesson：

(1) 中美双方将要签署什么？

_____

(2) 美方对哪一条款有问题？双方同意怎样修改这一条款？

_____

(3) 中方同意在合同中补充什么内容？

_____

(4) 美方需要几份合同副本？

_____

(5) 为什么说今后双方一定会有更多的合作机会？

_____

(6) 白琳问李先生："您不会头疼吧？"你想一想白琳的话是什么意思？

_____

2. 根据本课课文对话的内容，写出谈判双方在签署合同时应该注意的事。

Based on the information in the dialogue, write a short paragraph talking about

what issues buyers and sellers need to pay attention to when they are getting ready to sign a contract.

3. 利用图书馆或者上网,查询你的国家制订的有关涉外经济、贸易的法规。用你学到的词汇对这些法规做一个简单的介绍。

Using the Internet or the library, find out what kind of economic regulations your country has with regard to foreign trade. Please write one or two paragraphs using the new words and patterns introduced in this lesson.

4. 写一篇课堂报告,介绍最近中国涉外贸易中成交的一笔生意或者达成的一项协定。你的报告中应该说明这是一笔什么样的生意,双方公司的名称,成交或达成协定的时间、地点、金额,是否签署了什么合同等等。请利用图书馆或者上网找到你需要的信息。

Class presentation: Using the Internet or the library, research a recent business transaction or an agreement between China (or a Chinese company) and a foreign company. Your presentation should provide some details about this deal, including the basic content of this deal, the names of companies involved, when and where this deal was made, the sum of the money involved, what kind of document was signed, etc.

（四）附录

（1）合同实例

中 国 包 装 进 出 口 江 西 公 司

购 货 合 同

合同编号：99AF02
签约日期：99 年 8 月 31 日
签约地点：南昌

供方：**安福金信纸业公司**　　　　　单位法定代码：
地址：　　　　　　　　　　　　　　电话：
　　　　　　　　　　　　　　　　　传真：

需方：中国包装进出口江西公司　　　单位法定代码：15826904—2
地址：南昌市站前路外贸大楼　　　　电话：
　　　　　　　　　　　　　　　　　传真：0791—6224088

兹经双方协商同意，由中国包装进出口江西公司向供方购入下列货物，并按下述条件签订本合同：

一、品名、数量、价款

品　名	商标	规格	单位	数量	单价	金　额	短溢装 ± %	备注
28g 条纹 牛皮纸		70×100cm 35′×47″		80MT	￥5295.00	￥423600.00 广州交货价		

货款总额（大写）　　四十二万三千六百元整

二、货物品质标准：　**出口标准，颜色为偏红色**

三、货物验收办法：　**出口标准**

四、货物包装要求：　70×100cm为500张/令，18元/件，35″×47″为500张/令，14令/件，每令均为蓝色牛皮纸全封闭包装，胶带纸封口固定，外用木夹板及打包铁皮固定。

五、货物的交付：

1. 交货地点(或运输目的地)___广州需方指定仓库___

2. 交货时间：___9月底前交25吨,剩余部分于10月底交清___

3. 交货办法：___供方负责汽车运输至广州需方指定仓库___

4. 运输方式及运费负担：___运费由供方承担___

六、货款结算方式：___货送至广州后,供方凭金额增值税发票及专用缴___款书向需方结算。___

七、违约责任：

1. 供方除人力不可抗拒事故外,超过约定期限未能交货,应向需方偿付未交货物货款总额___10%___的违约金;如因供方延期交货而影响需方销售和出口,需方有权拒收货物。

2. 供方应提供真实的足额增值税发票(出口货物还须提供纳税缴款书)。如因供方提供的增值税发票和专用税票不实而影响需方的进项抵扣和出口退税,由供方赔偿经济损失,并承担法律责任。

3. 供方必须保证交货质量,如因质量问题造成需方的客户索赔,由供方承担经济损失。

4. 需方逾期付款,应承担逾期付款给供方造成的利息损失。

八、合同效力：

1. 本合同一经双方签字盖章即具有法律约束力,任何一方未与对方协商并取得对方书面同意,不得单方擅自变更或解除本合同。

2. 本合同执行完毕,即自行终止。

九、争议的解决：

因履行本合同所发生的争议,应通过双方协商解决,协商不成时,可在签约地/执行地法院提起诉讼。

十、本合同正本一式贰份,供、需双方各执一份。

十一、其他约定事项：___① 供方刷唛头___
___② 具体规格、件数需方提前通知供方___

供　方：　　　　需　方：

法定代表人
或代理人　　　　　　　　　法定代表人
　　　　　　　　　　　　　或代理人：

(影印件由江西财经大学经济文化传播系提供)

(2) 意向书实例

意向书

中国工艺品进出口公司××市分公司,××工艺美术公司所属宇宙金银饰品厂(以下简称甲方)与美国 HARLYN PRODUCTS INC(以下简称乙方)于一九××年×月×日至×日,经双方友好商谈,对合资经营首饰工厂共同拟订意向如下:

1. 合资工厂设立于××,由甲乙双方共同负责生产和推销。

2. 合资工厂的投资金额初步为××万美元,投资比例甲、乙各占百分之五十,盈利亦按双方投资比例分配。

3. 培训工厂的技术人员、安排工厂的布局及工厂制作系统由乙方负责。

4. 甲方提供人员和负责制作,乙方负责制定工厂的基础管理制度。

5. 乙方应尽快提供合资工厂的实施计划。

6. 甲乙双方对合资工厂项目各自向领导和有关部门报告,经获准后双方再进一步洽谈具体的合资协议。

甲方: 中国工艺品进出口公司分公司　　　乙方:HARLYN
　　　××工艺美术公司所属宇宙金银饰品厂　　PRODUCTS INC.
　　　(签字、盖章)　　　　　　　　　　　　(签字、盖章)
　　　　　　　　　　　　　　　　　　　　　　×年×月×日于××

(摘自叶穗编《外经贸常用应用文写作》,上海科学技术文献出版社,1995 年)

第十六课　饯行告别

　　明天史强生和白琳就要回美国了。李信文以东方进出口公司的名义举行晚宴，庆祝中美两家公司这次成功的合作，同时也为史先生和白小姐饯行。

（一）对话

1. 在告别晚宴上

李信文：　史先生、白小姐，今天的晚宴有两个目的。一是庆祝我们两家公司的成功合作，二是为你们二位饯行。请允许我代表东方进出口公司对你们表示感谢。来，让我先敬你们一杯！感谢你们为这次洽谈的圆满成功所做的努力。

（大家干杯）

史强生：　李先生，这次我们来中国的收获很大，我们都非常高兴。我也想借这个机会代表我的公司对您和东方进出口公司表示感谢。感谢东方公司给予我们的热情接待，尤其是感谢您为我们这次访问所做的种种安排。

李信文：　哪里哪里。这次能跟您和白小姐合作，我感到非常愉快。你们这次来中国，不但加强了我们之间的业务联系，而且加深了我们之间的互相理解。我相信有了这样一个良好的基础，我们今后一定会有更多的贸易往来。

史强生：　我完全同意。这次来中国，我亲眼看到了中国的发展。中国已经成为一个重要的经济大国，难怪现在有这么多国家的厂商要到中国来做生意。我敢说在美国一定有很多公司羡慕我们有了东方公司和李先生这样可靠的"关系"。（笑）李先生，今后还要请您多多关照啊！

2. 话别、赠送礼品

白　琳：　时间过得真快！我总觉得好像昨天我才刚到中国似的，可是明天一早我就要飞回美国了！

李信文：　白小姐，如果您真想在中国多呆一些日子，我们非常欢迎。

白　琳：　想倒是想，不过这要看我的老板是不是愿意给我假期了。

李信文：　我有一个办法，也许下一次我们可以把这个问题也列入我们的谈判。史先生，您看怎么样？

史强生：　(笑)对不起，这件事可没有谈判的余地！白琳是我最得力的助手，少了她可不行！

李信文：　(笑)史先生如果也打算来中国度假的话，我们更加欢迎！

史强生：　我倒是想带太太一起来中国旅行，就是总没有时间。她一直说要来看看长城和兵马俑。

李信文：　好啊，您什么时候决定了，请通知我。我负责替您安排。史先生，白小姐，这是我们公司送给你们的礼物，算是你们这次中国之行的纪念吧！

史强生：　谢谢！

白　琳：　我现在就能打开看看吗？

李信文：　当然，请！

白　琳：　啊，景泰蓝花瓶，真漂亮！李先生，谢谢你。

李信文：　不用谢，都是一些小礼物，留个纪念。

史强生：　李先生，我也有一件礼物，想送给您。

李信文：　不敢当，不敢当，您太客气了！

史强生：　请您一定要收下。另外还有两件礼物，想麻烦您带给王总经理和张小姐。

李信文：　好吧。那我就收下了。谢谢！史先生、白小姐，明天我还有一个重要的会，所以不能给你们送行了，很抱歉。不过，张红小姐会送你们去机场的。

史强生：　您陪了我们这么多天，又专门从北京赶到这儿来，我们已经非常感谢了！

李信文： 哪里哪里,不必客气。祝你们一路平安! 希望我们很快会再见!

史强生：
　　　　谢谢,再见!
白　琳：

词汇(一) Vocabulary(1)：

1.	饯行	jiànxíng	to give farewell dinner
2.	告别	gàobié	to part from; to bid farewell
3.	以……的名义	yǐ…de míngyì	in the name of…
	名义	míngyì	name; nominal
4.	晚宴	wǎnyàn	evening banquet
5.	允许	yǔnxǔ	to allow; to permit
6.	所	suǒ	that which
7.	收获	shōuhuò	gains; results
8.	借	jiè	to take advantage of (an opportunity, etc.); to make use of; to borrow; to lend
9.	加强	jiāqiáng	to strengthen; to reinforce
10.	加深	jiāshēn	to deepen
11.	往来	wǎnglái	contact; dealings; intercourse
12.	难怪	nánguài	no wonder
13.	羡慕	xiànmù	to admire; to envy
14.	关系	guānxì	"connections"; relationship; ties
15.	话别	huàbié	to say a few parting words; to say goodbye
16.	赠送	zèngsòng	to present (as a gift); to give
17.	似的	shìde	as if; seem
18.	倒是	dàoshì	actually; really
19.	假期	jiàqī	vacation
20.	列入	lièrù	be included in; be placed on (an agenda, etc.)
21.	余地	yúdì	leeway; margin; room
22.	得力	délì	capable; competent
23.	度假	dùjià	to spend one's vacation

218

24. 更加	gèngjiā	(even) more
25. 太太	tàitai	wife; Mrs.
26. 花瓶	huāpíng	flower vase
27. 送行	sòngxíng	to see sb. off
28. 一路平安	yílù píng'ān	Have a safe journey!

专有名词 Proper Nouns：

| 1. 兵马俑 | Bīngmǎyǒng | terracotta figures of warriors and horses buried in First Emperor（221－206 B.C.）of Qin's mausoleum |
| 2. 景泰蓝 | Jǐngtàilán | cloisonné |

句型（一）Sentence Patterns（1）：

1. 以……的名义　　　　in the name of…

李经理以东方进出口公司的名义举行晚宴。

这次史先生和太太是以参加交易会的名义来中国的。

2. 所＋V.＋的　　　　that which…

感谢你们为这次洽谈的圆满成功所做的努力。

这些都是本公司目前所代理销售的产品。

3. 难怪　　　　no wonder

难怪现在有这么多国家的厂商要到中国来做生意。

史先生已经找到了更便宜的货源,难怪他不想再谈判了。

4. 好像……似的　　　　seem; as if

我觉得好像昨天我才刚到中国似的。

陈厂长带来了很多样品,好像要开一个交易会似的。

5. 倒是……不过/就是……　　actually/really…but…;

actually/really…it's just…/the only thing is…

想倒是想,不过这要看我的老板是不是愿意给我假期了。

我倒是想带太太一起来中国旅行,就是总没有时间。

(二) 阅读短文

建立可靠的长期合作关系

　　说到"关系"这个词，许多在中国做生意的外国人都会立刻想到"走后门"。不可否认，"走后门"常常是能够解决一些问题。可是，"走后门"这种"关系"并不保险。有时候"走后门"不但不能帮你的忙，结果反而耽误了你的正经事，甚至让你上当受骗。对于每一位打算到中国做生意的人来说，与其想办法"走后门"，不如踏踏实实地建立起一种平等互利的合作关系更可靠。

　　中国人重视长期合作关系。如果你是一个有心人，就会利用各种场合，让他们知道你的公司也非常重视这种关系。跟中国人做生意、打交道，你不妨开诚布公，让对方清楚地了解你的立场。在激烈的谈判中，耐心、理解、尊重和友好的态度都是不可缺少的。不要让中国人觉得你是一个只顾眼前利益的生意人。有时候，为了解决双方的争议，你不妨做出适当的妥协。这样做不但让中国人觉得有面子，而且使他们相信你是一个通情达理、值得交往的朋友。

　　签订合同以后，大功告成。这正是你趁热打铁、巩固双方关系的好机会。除了干杯以外，不要忘了代表你的公司表示对今后继续合作的期待。让你的中国朋友相信你的公司确实有保持长期合作关系的诚意。你也不妨借这个机会给你的中国朋友送上一两件有意义的小礼物。中国人常说，"礼轻情义重"。这样做，既表示了你对他们的感谢，又说明了你对双方友谊的重视。

　　总之，多了解一些中国文化，多了解中国人，这对你在中国的生意一定会有帮助。

　　祝你成功!

词汇(二) Vocabulary(2):

| 1. 走后门 | zǒu hòumén | to get in by the back door; to secure advantages through pull or influence |
| 2. 不可否认 | bù kě fǒurèn | can't deny; undeniably |

220

3. 保险	bǎoxiǎn	safe
4. 反而	fǎn'ér	on the contrary; instead
5. 耽误	dānwù	to delay; to hold up; to hinder
6. 正经事	zhèngjing shì	serious matters; reputable affairs
7. 受骗	shòupiàn	be deceived/swindled
8. 与其……不如……	yǔqí…bùrú…	rather than···, it would be better to···
不如	bùrú	not as good as; inferior to; it would be better to
9. 踏实	tāshi	solidly; practical
10. 重视	zhòngshì	to value; to take sth. seriously; to consider important
11. 有心人	yǒuxīnrén	a person with a set purpose
12. 场合	chǎnghé	occasion; situation
13. 不妨	bùfáng	might as well; no harm in (trying, doing, etc.)
14. 开诚布公	kāichéngbùgōng	to speak friendly and sincerely
15. 立场	lìchǎng	position; stand; standpoint
16. 尊重	zūnzhòng	to respect; to value; to esteem
17. 缺少	quēshǎo	to lack; be short of
18. 只顾	zhǐgù	be absorbed in; to be concerned only with
19. 眼前	yǎnqián	at the moment; at present
20. 利益	lìyì	benefit; gain; interest
21. 妥协	tuǒxié	compromise; to compromise; to come to terms
22. 面子	miànzi	"face"; reputation; prestige
23. 通情达理	tōng qíng dá lǐ	sensible; reasonable
24. 大功告成	dà gōng gào chéng	to have finally come to completion; to have been brought to a successful completion

25.	趁热打铁	chèn rè dǎ tiě	to strike while the iron is hot
26.	巩固	gǒnggù	to consolidate; to strengthen; to solidify
27.	期待	qīdài	hope; expectation; to look forward to
28.	保持	bǎochí	to keep; to maintain
29.	诚意	chéngyì	good faith; sincerity
30.	有意义	yǒuyìyì	significant; meaningful
31.	礼轻情义重	lǐ qīng qíngyì zhòng	The gift is trifling, but the feeling is profound. The thoughtfulness is worth far more than the gift itself.
32.	总之	zǒngzhī	in a word; in short

句型(二) Sentence Patterns(2):

1. 不但不……，反而……　　　not only not…but instead…

有时候"走后门"不但不能帮你的忙,结果反而耽误了你的正经事。

王先生不但不肯跟我们合作,反而把销售代理权给了另一家公司。

2. 与其 A 不如 B　　　　　B is a better choice than A; rather than A, it would be better to B

与其想办法"走后门",不如踏踏实实地建立起一种平等互利的合作关系更可靠。

与其每天自己上街推销产品,不如花一些钱在电视上做广告。

3. 不妨 + V.　　　　　　might as well V.

跟中国人做生意、打交道,你不妨开诚布公。

你也不妨借这个机会给你的中国朋友送上一两件有意义的小礼物。

4. 总之　　　　　　　　　in a word; in short

总之,多了解一些中国文化,这对你在中国的生意一定会有帮助。

总之这次中国之行的收获很大。

（三）练习与活动

I. 句型练习一 Sentence pattern exercises(1)：

1. 用"以……的名义"的句型改写下面的句子：

   Rewrite the following sentences by using the pattern of "以……的名义"：

   (1) 李副总经理代表公司总裁向客人赠送纪念品。

   _____

   (2) 马局长代表主办单位举行宴会,欢迎参加交易会的客人们。

   _____

   (3) 王总代表东方进出口公司给史强生先生写信,正式邀请他来访问。

   _____

   (4) 借参加洽谈投资会的机会,美国商务代表团考察、访问了沿海地区的几个城市。

   _____

2. 根据下面的要求,用"所 + V. + 的"的句型造句：

   Use the pattern of "所 + V. + 的"to accomplish the following tasks：

   (1) 指出哪种家用电器产品的牌子是你喜欢的。

   _____

   (2) 说一说哪些产品是你的公司希望立刻进货的。

   _____

   (3) 说出一个你羡慕的成功企业家。

   _____

   (4) 说出一个你想去度假的地方。

   _____

3. 用"难怪"的句型完成下面的句子：

   Complete the following sentences by using the pattern of "难怪"：

   (1) 这次的生意又赔本了,难怪_____。

   (2) 白小姐刚刚跟好朋友话别,难怪_____。

(3) 交货日期已经到了,可是货还没有收到。难怪_____。

(4) 李经理刚度假回来,难怪_____。

4. 根据下面的问题,用"好像……似的"的句型造句:

Use the pattern of "好像……似的"to accomplish the following tasks:

(1) 怎样关心地提醒你的朋友,你觉得他应该注意身体?

_____

(2) 怎样礼貌地告诉对方,你认为合同草案中的某一条条款需要修改补充?

_____

(3) 怎样小心地(礼貌地)让你的老板知道,你觉得你的佣金太低了?

_____

(4) 怎样用开玩笑的办法提醒你的朋友,这次在中国他买的东西已经太多了、不应该再买了?

_____

5. 用"倒是……不过/就是"的句型改写下面的句子:

Rewrite the following sentences by using the pattern of "倒是……不过/就是":

(1) 昨天的饯行晚宴的确很丰盛,就是那家饭馆布置得不够漂亮。

_____

(2) 这次谈判的收获很大,不过获得这些成功真不容易。

_____

(3) 这件毛衣的式样张小姐很喜欢,就是觉得价格贵了一点儿。

_____

(4) 王总很愿意把销售电脑的独家代理权交给长城公司,不过他已经跟另一家公司有了合作协定。

_____

II. 句型练习二 Sentence pattern exercises(2):

1. 用"不但不……反而……"的句型回答下面的问题:

Answer the following questions by using the pattern of "不但不……反而……":

(1) 为什么买了这种洗碗机的顾客都要求退货?

_____

（2）为什么你不要那家电视台为产品做广告了？

_____

（3）为什么你不愿意给总经理当助理了？

_____

（4）为什么你不想再跟那家公司合作了？

_____

2. 你和李经理在很多问题上都有不同的意见。请用"与其……不如……"的句型完成下面的对话：

You differ in opinion with Manager Li on many issues. Complete the following dialogues by using the pattern of "与其……不如……"：

（1）李：为了打开市场销路，我打算在当地报纸上刊登一个星期的广告。你觉得怎么样？

你：_____

（2）李：我打算赠送给每位客户一件小礼物，表示我们的感谢。你觉得怎么样？

你：_____

（3）李：你觉得我们应该先跟对方签订一份意向书还是签署一份长期合同？

你：_____

（4）李：这家公司的丝绸产品并不是最好的。不过他们的张经理是我们的老熟人。你说我们这次买不买他们的产品？

你：_____

3. 用"不妨 + V."的句型完成下面的对话：

Complete the following dialogues by using the pattern of "不妨 + V."：

（1）甲：这次在中国，李先生给了我们很多帮助。你说我们应该怎样谢谢他？

乙：_____

（2）甲：我们这次代理销售的产品倒是价廉物美，就是知名度不高。

乙：_____

（3）甲：对方说他们的生产计划已经安排满了，没有增加产量的余地了。怎么办？

乙：_____

(4) 甲:你觉得我们公司怎样才能在中国建立一些可靠的合作关系?

乙:_____

4. 用"总之"的句型说出你对以下问题的看法和结论 (jiélùn, conclusion):

Give your opinions and conclusions for the questions below. Please use the pattern of "总之" in your sentences.

(1) 到了一个人地生疏的地方应该注意什么?

_____

(2) 跟中国人做生意、打交道的时候应该注意什么?

_____

(3) 找产品销售代理的时候应该注意什么?

_____

(4) 怎样才能获得商务谈判的成功?

_____

III. 词汇练习 Vocabulary Exercises and Special Expressions:

1. 用中文回答下面的问题:

Answering the following questions in Chinese.

(1) "一路平安"在英文里面有什么意思? 什么时候你可以说:"一路平安"?

What is the meaning of "一路平安" in English? When can one use this expression?

_____

(2) "礼轻情意重"在英文里面有什么意思? 什么时候可以说:"礼轻情意重"?

What is the meaning of "礼轻情意重"in English? When can one use this expression?

_____

(3) 什么样的人是"有心人"?

What kind of person has been called "有心人" in Chinese?

_____

(4) 什么是"通情达理"? 在谈判中,什么样的态度是"通情达理"的态度?

What is "通情达理"? What attitude is considered "通情达理" during a

226

negotiation?

_____

（5）"开诚布公"的意思是什么？什么时候应该"开诚布公"？

What is the meaning of "开诚布公"? When should one be "开诚布公"?

_____

（6）"趁热打铁"和"大功告成"的意思有什么不同？

What is the difference between the meanings of "趁热打铁"和"大功告成"?

_____

IV. 阅读、写作和讨论 Reading, Writing and Discussion：

1. 根据课文对话回答问题：

Answer the following questions according to the dialogues in this lesson：

（1）今天的晚宴是谁举行的？

_____

（2）今天的晚宴有什么目的？

_____

（3）史先生为什么感谢李先生？

_____

（4）谁给谁送了礼物？

_____

（5）谁想来中国度假？白小姐？史先生？还是史先生的太太？

_____

（6）谁会送史先生和白小姐去机场？

_____

2. 根据阅读短文回答问题：

Answer the following questions based on the reading passage.

（1）什么是"走后门"？"走后门"是做生意的好办法吗？为什么？

What does "走后门" mean? Is it a good way to be successful in business? Why?

_____

（2）怎样才能成功地跟一个中国企业建立起良好、可靠的关系？

What is the best way to establish a successful business relationship with a Chinese company?

___

(3) 对中国人来说,什么是"面子"? 你能举一个例子吗? 在中国做生意遇到"面子"的问题的时候,你应该怎么办?

What does "面子" mean to the Chinese? Do you have any example of it? How can one prepare to deal with this subtle concept of the Chinese when doing business in China?

___

3. 你跟中国商务代表团刚刚签署了一份很重要的合同。中国代表团明天就要回国了。所以你特别举行了一个正式的晚宴,庆祝这次的成功合作并给中国代表饯行。根据以上情境写一个对话。

You and a Chinese business delegation have just signed a major contract. The Chinese delegation is going to leave tomorrow. You hosted a formal party to celebrate the signing of the contract and also to bid farewell to your Chinese associate. Write a short dialogue for such a situation. (You may include people other than yourself and your partner in the dialogue.)

（四）附录

（1）出境登记卡

出 境 登 记 卡　DEPARTURE CARD
填写前请认真阅读背面说明
Please read the points for attention on the back before filling

姓 Family Name	名 Given Name		
出生日期 Date of Birth	年　　月　　日 Y　　M　　D		性别 Sex
国籍 Nationality	护照证件号码 Passport or Certificate No.		
中国签证号 Chinese Visa No.	签发地 Place of Issue		
偕行人数 Accompanying number	航班(车次) Flight(Train)No.		

职业: Occupation　　1. 行政管理人员 Legislators & Adminstrators

2. 专业技术人员 Professionals & Technical　　3. 办事员 Clerk

4. 商业人员 Commerce　　5. 服务人员 Service　　6. 农民 Farmer

7. 工人 Worker　　8. 其他 Others　　9. 无职业 Jobless

在 华 地 址 Address in China (Hotel)

旅客签名 Signature

官方填写: W U Y D Z X F L G C T M　　证件种类
Official Use Only

（2）感谢信

张经理:

　　您好! 我已于本月十日回国。这次在贵国洽谈业务期间,承蒙您的热情帮助,使我顺利地完成了任务。为此,谨向您表示最真诚的谢意!

　　我在贵国期间,您除了在业务上给予我很大的支持与帮助外,在生活上还给予我无微不至的关怀与照顾。特别是您在百忙中陪同我参观了工厂、游览了北京的名胜古迹。临行前,尊夫人又为我准备了丰盛的晚餐。为此,我再次向您及尊夫人表示由衷的感谢!

　　希望以后加强联系,欢迎您有机会到我们国家来,盼望有一天能在这儿接待您。

　　顺致

敬礼!

　　　　　　　　　　　　　　　　　　　布莱恩
　　　　　　　　　　　　　　　　1994 年 10 月 21 日

（摘引自赵洪琴、吕文珍编《外贸写作》,北京语言学院出版社 1994 年）

总附录

（一）课文英译
English Translation of the Text

Lesson One: Arrival in China

Mr. Johnson Smith and Miss Lynn Petty are representatives of the American International Trading Company. They have come to China on business. Mr. Smith previously worked in Taiwan for two years. Last year Miss Petty came to Beijing and became acquainted with Mr. Li of the Eastern Import & Export Corporation. Mr. Smith and Miss Petty both speak Chinese very well.

Dialogue

1. Entry

(at customs)

Customs Officer:	Hello! Are you here to travel?
Johnson Smith:	No, I'm here on business. Here's my passport.
Customs Officer:	Please open this suitcase.
Johnson Smith:	Okay.
Customs Officer:	What are these?
Johnson Smith:	These are samples. This one is a gift. Are these things subject to duty?
Customs Officer:	Gifts above 500 U.S. dollars are dutiable; samples are duty-free. But you still have to fill out a customs declaration form.
Lynn Petty:	Here are my passport, arrival card and health certificate.
Customs Officer:	Do you have anything to declare?
Lynn Petty:	No.
Customs Officer:	What is that?
Lynn Petty:	That's my good friend!
Customs Officer:	Good friend?
Lynn Petty:	(smiling) That's right—that's my computer. We're together everyday, and we're the best of friends!
Customs Officer:	(smiling) Your Chinese is really good!

233

Lynn Petty:	[modestly declining compliment] You're too kind!

2. Meeting

(at airport exit)

Lynn Petty:	Look, there's Mr. Li! Mr. Li, it's been a long time. Hello!
Li Xinwen:	Hello! We meet again, Miss Petty! Welcome!
Lynn Petty:	I'll make the introductions. This is Mr. Li of the Eastern Corporation. This is my boss, Mr. Smith.
Johnson Smith:	How do you do! I'm Johnson Smith. My Chinese name is Shi Qiangsheng.
Li Xinwen:	How do you do! My name is Li Xinwen. Welcome to China!
Johnson Smith:	Thank you!
Lynn Petty:	This is great! After over ten hours on an airplane, we've finally arrived in Beijing! Mr. Li, thank you for coming to the airport to meet us.
Li Xinwen:	Not at all—we're old friends. Are you finished with all the entry formalities?
Lynn Petty:	Yes. Everything went smoothly!
Li Xinwen:	Good. Let's go then. The car is right outside.

Reading Passage

When in China, Speak Chinese

There are a lot of advantages of speaking Chinese when you are in China. The simplest "Ni hao" often makes matters easier. "Ni hao" [can] make a stern official smile at you; it [can also] lighten up serious negotiations. Don't worry that your Chinese is not very good. You will find that when you speak Chinese, Chinese people will always be very pleased, and more than willing to help you.

It's easy to make friends when you speak Chinese; and once you have good friends, you will enjoy a lot of conveniences when doing business and taking care of [various other] matters. As long as you speak Chinese every day—[just] saying as much as you can—your Chinese will get better and better.

Lesson Two   At the Hotel

Li Xinwen reserved rooms for Johnson Smith and Lynn Petty at the Great Wall Hotel. Lynn Petty likes this hotel very much, but she has a lot of questions.

Dialogue

1. Checking In

Front Desk Clerk: Hello!

Li Xinwen: Hello! This morning I made a reservation for these two American guests. Would you please look it up?

Front Desk Clerk: Are you Mr. Li of the Eastern Corporation?

Li Xinwen: Yes, my name is Li Xinwen.

Front Desk Clerk: Please have your two guests fill out the hotel guest registration form.

Li Xinwen: I reserved one standard room and one suite for you. The standard room is 450 yuan per day; the suite is 800 yuan.

Lynn Petty: Wow. That's a lot more expensive than last year! Excuse me. Can I fill out the form in English?

Front Desk Clerk: That's fine. I need to take a look at your passports.

Li Xinwen: Guests have to put down a room deposit first, right?

Front Desk Clerk: Yes, they [must] first pay a 2500 yuan deposit using [either] cash [or] a credit card.

Johnson Smith: I think I'll use a credit card.

Front Desk Clerk: Your rooms are on the nineteenth floor. Here are the room cards.

Lynn Petty: The nineteenth floor! Wonderful! The view must be great that high up!

2. Hotel Services

Lynn Petty: Excuse me, miss. Could you please tell me where I can find the laundry room?

Hotel Maid: It's on the sixth floor. However, [if you'd like] you can put the dirty clothes in a laundry bag and give them to me [or just] leave the laundry bag in the room, and I'll come pick it up in a little while.

Lynn Petty: That's fantastic! May I ask if you have a wake-up call service?

Hotel Maid:	Yes, we do. You can dial 1-2-3-7 and tell the front desk what time you need to get up.
Lynn Petty:	Thank you. Do you know where I can use the internet? I have to check my messages.
Hotel Maid:	You can access the internet at the business center on the second floor.
Lynn Petty:	Where can I change [dollars into] Renminbi?
Hotel Maid:	Foreign currency exchange is done right at the service desk in the lobby.
Johnson Smith:	Miss, could you please tell me what floor the restaurant is on? After asking so many questions, this young lady must be hungry!

Reading Passage

Chinese Hotels

Chinese hotels [can] also be called *binguan*, *fandian* or *jiudian*. The best hotels are five-star hotels, and naturally they are also the most expensive. The Great Wall Hotel in Beijing, the Hilton Hotel in Shanghai, and the Jinling Hotel in Nanjing are all great hotels of this kind. The Chinese government stipulates that only hotels with a three-star or higher ranking can admit foreigners. If you intend to stay in a hotel, it would be best to have a travel agency make reservations for you or to ask a friend to help. You can also call the hotel yourself or make a reservation over the internet. Many hotels have a business center [where] you can use a computer, access the internet and send faxes. Making international calls is also very convenient. You can pay cash, use a credit card or buy a prepaid phone card.

Lesson Three Formal Meeting

Today was the first formal meeting between the Chinese and American representatives. President Wang Guo'an welcomed the Americans on behalf of the Eastern Import & Export Corporation. Mr. Johnson Smith explained the objectives of this visit to the Chinese party on behalf of the American International Trading Company.

Dialogue

1. Greetings and Introductions

Wang Guo'an: Welcome, welcome! We're honored to have you here.

Li Xinwen: Let me make introductions. This is the CEO of Asia for the American International Trading Company, Mr. Johnson Smith. This is his assistant, Miss Lynn Petty. This is the president of our company, Mr. Wang Guo'an. This is the director of the Department of Public Relations, Miss Zhang Hong.

Johnson Smith: It's a pleasure to meet you! Hello! (shaking hands) Here's my business card. I welcome any advice.

Wang Guo'an: You flatter us. Here's my business card. We hope you will offer us advice in the future.

Johnson Smith: You're too kind!

Wang Guo'an: Let's sit down and talk. (pouring tea) Please have some tea. Did you rest well last night?

Johnson Smith: I had a very nice rest. The hotel is comfortable, and the service is very attentive. Thank you for the arrangements.

Wang Guo'an: Don't mention it—it's [only] what we should do. If you have any problems while you're in Beijing, please contact me [or] Mr. Li anytime or let Miss Zhang Hong know.

Zhang Hong: Here's my business card with my telephone and cellular numbers.

Johnson Smith:
Lynn Petty: Thank you! Thank you!

Li Xinwen: President Wang, Miss Lynn Petty is our old friend. She stayed at the Great Wall Hotel when she came to Beijing last summer, too.

Wang Guo'an: That's great! Welcome to China once again, Miss Petty!

237

Lynn Petty: Thank you! Mr. Li was a great help to me last time, and it was a pleasure working together. I just love Beijing.

2. Explaining the Objectives of the Visit

Johnson Smith: Our purpose in making this trip to China is to confer with you about the new order for this fall and the conclusion of the agency contract. In addition, if it's possible we would like to visit a few factories to take a look at production conditions.

Wang Guo'an: Okay. We'd like to schedule the first talks for tomorrow morning. As for the matter of visiting the factories, Mr. Li is taking care of all the arrangements. We'll have him fill you in in a moment.

Lynn Petty: If there is time, we also hope to be able to visit special economic zones, such as Shenzhen, Zhuhai, Xiamen, and so on.

Li Xinwen: I don't think there will be a problem with any of these [requests]. We can discuss the itinerary arrangements this afternoon.

Johnson Smith: That's fine with us.

Zhang Hong: President Wang is planning to invite everyone to dinner tonight to welcome Mr. Smith and Miss Petty. Miss Petty, I'll pick you up at the hotel at 6:30, okay?

Lynn Petty: Okay! We'll be waiting for you in the lobby at 6:30.

Reading Passage

Etiquette of Meeting for Guests and Hosts

It is customary for Chinese people to shake hands to express welcome, gratitude or friendliness. When a guest and a host meet, the host should first shake the guest's hand as a gesture of greeting. Chinese are not accustomed to hugging. It's even uncomfortable for old friends to hug when they meet.

Many Chinese like to exchange business cards when they first meet someone. When somebody gives you a business card, you should accept it with both hands as an expression of courtesy. Business cards can help you remember his (or her) name, and they also make it easy to get in touch in the future. Incidentally, some people like to list a lot of official titles on their business cards. Don't worry—it's enough to remember the first title. Generally speaking, the title listed first is the most important one.

Lesson Four　Itinerary Arrangements

Johnson Smith and Lynn Petty plan to stay in China for about a week. Besides talking over business matters with their Chinese [associates], they are also going to visit [a few] factories and special economic zones. Their time is very limited, so they need a well-planned itinerary.

Dialogue

1. Discussing Itinerary Arrangements

Li Xinwen:　　Mr. Smith, Miss Petty, shall we talk over the itinerary arrangements now?

Johnson Smith:　Sure. We have a lot of matters to take care of during this trip to China, so we must plan [our schedule] carefully. We intend to stay in China for a total of eight days. Do you think that will be enough time?

Li Xinwen:　　If we schedule the activities a little closer together, there shouldn't be a problem.

Lynn Petty:　　Mr. Li is very experienced in planning itineraries. When I was in Beijing last year, he scheduled each day full [of activities]. We discussed business in the morning, toured in the afternoon, and watched performances at night. There wasn't even time to call my boyfriend! (laughing)

Li Xinwen:　　(laughing) I'm sorry, Miss Petty. This time we'll make sure to set aside a time just for you to make phone calls.

Lynn Petty:　　That won't be necessary! We've already broken up, anyway!

2. Revising Itinerary Arrangements

Li Xinwen:　　This is how I'm thinking of arranging the itinerary: [You'll spend] the first five days in Beijing and the last three days in Shanghai and Shenzhen—two days in Shanghai and one day in Shenzhen. What do you think?

Johnson Smith:　Isn't just one day too little time in Shenzhen? I've heard that several of Shenzhen's high-tech product companies are very interesting, and I'd really like the chance to take a look for myself!

Li Xinwen:　　In that case, we can change the schedule to four days in Beijing and two days each in Shanghai and Shenzhen. Will that work?

Lynn Petty:　　I think that will suit us better. Mr. Li, may I ask what activities you have planned for us in Beijing?

Li Xinwen:	In Beijing, besides discussing business, we will visit an apparel and a toy factory, [as well as] tour the Imperial Palace and the Great Wall.
Johnson Smith:	That's a good schedule. Mr. Li, we've put you into too much trouble!
Li Xinwen:	It's nothing more than what I should do. Also, tonight at 7:00 we have the welcome banquet, and tomorrow night Factory Director Qian of the apparel factory would like to take the two of you out to eat. The night after that I would like to treat you to Beijing roast duck...
Johnson Smith:	Mr. Li, you're too gracious!
Lynn Petty:	(to Johnson Smith) I guess now you know why I gained ten pounds last year? (laughing)

Reading Passage

Eat Well, Have Fun and Do Well in Business

China is a vast land with a large population and a very busy transportation system. Foreigners traveling in China not only have problems with the language; they also commonly run into unforeseen hassles. If you intend to go to China, you should definitely have your travel plans worked out [first]. You can either mail your itinerary to your Chinese [associates] prior to the trip, or let your host organization in China know what places you would like to visit and ask them to arrange the itinerary for you.

Whether you are going to China on business or on a personal visit, sight-seeing and banquets are both an indispensable part of Chinese itinerary arrangements. In particular, invitations to meals can be so frequent as to even become a burden. Chinese think that treating people to meals is conducive to establishing relationships and developing friendships. What person after eating a sumptuous dinner can still say "no" to the host?

Lesson Five   Attending a Banquet

President Wang Guo'an held a banquet to welcome Mr. Johnson Smith and Miss Lynn Petty on behalf of the Eastern Import & Export Corporation, and Director Ma of the Foreign Trade Bureau also attended. Johnson Smith and Lynn Petty both thought the banquet was very sumptuous.

Dialogue

1. Please Take the Seats of Honor

(at the restaurant)

Wang Guo'an: Mr. Smith, Miss Petty, you've arrived! Please come in!

Johnson Smith: Thank you!

Lynn Petty: This restaurant is beautifully decorated!

Zhang Hong: Yes, this is one of Beijing's most famous restaurants. Everyone likes to come here.

Wang Guo'an: Here, I'll introduce you. This is Director Ma of the Foreign Trade Bureau. This is Mr. Smith and Miss Petty of the American International Trading Company.

Director Ma: Welcome! Welcome to China! (shaking hands) This last couple of days must have been tiring!

Johnson Smith: Not too bad, really. We had a little jet lag, but we rested well yesterday. President Wang has taken care of everything for us.

Wang Guo'an: Everybody please take your seats! Mr. Smith, Miss Petty, you are our guests. Please be seated here at the seats of honor. Director Ma, please sit here also!

Director Ma: You are the host, [so] it's only right for you to sit with the guests!

Wang Guo'an: No, you are a [government] leader and should sit with our honored guests. I'll sit next to you. Come, everyone, please just take a seat anywhere you like!

2. Cheers!

Wang Guo'an: We've gathered here tonight to welcome Mr. Smith and Miss Petty. Why don't we all have a little something to drink first? Mr. Smith, would you like Maotai or red wine?

Johnson Smith: I've heard that Maotai liquor is legendary. I'll have the Maotai.

Wang Guo'an: And you, Miss Petty?

Lynn Petty: I'm really not much of a drinker. I'll have the wine, I guess.

Wang Guo'an: Now, let's drink a toast to welcome Mr. Smith and Miss Petty!
(everyone toasts)

Director Ma: Mr. Smith, please have something to eat. These are all hors d'oeuvres. In a little while [they'll bring out] the main dishes and the soup. Here, taste this! (Director Ma places some food on Mr. Smith's plate)

Johnson Smith: Thank you! I'll help myself.
(the waiters serve the food)

Zhang Hong: The dishes we're having today are all specialties of this restaurant. Miss Petty, try this. Do you like it? (Zhang Hong places some food on Miss Petty's plate)

Lynn Petty: Mmm...it's delicious!

Zhang Hong: Since it's good, eat some more! Now taste this. (again placing some food on Miss Petty's plate)

Lynn Petty: (laughing) Thank you. There are so many dishes on the table that I couldn't even begin to try them all!

Johnson Smith: Mr. Wang, I'd like to propose a toast to you in appreciation of the warm reception you all have given us!

Wang Guo'an: Okay. Let's drink together in anticipation of our satisfactory and successful cooperation!

Reading Passage

Chinese Banquets

Chinese food is famous throughout the world, and eating is naturally an extremely important matter in China. Chinese banquets are always very sumptuous. It's said that the celebrated "complete Manchu and Chinese banquet" had over 100 courses. Even ordinary banquets have over ten courses. During a banquet, distinguished guests and the host are placed at the seats of honor. Generally speaking, the seats facing the door or entrance are the seats of honor. Of course no banquet is complete without liquor. The meaning of "*ganbei*" is to finish drinking everything in your glass. If you don't want to become drunk immediately, however, you had better not finish your drink at one go. Chinese are accustomed to drinking and eating [various] dishes first and then eating rice and soup. So, the sequence of courses is: first, hors d'oeuvres; then, stir-fried dishes and the main dishes; and lastly, rice, soup and dessert. Another Chinese custom is that the host should serve the guest food. This expresses both sincerity and hospitality on the part of the host. If you are not used to this [custom], you can say to the host, "Thank you. I'll help myself."

Lesson Six Preliminary Negotiations

Today the representatives of the Chinese and American companies are going to conduct preliminary negotiations. The Eastern Corporation's [representatives] have made extensive preparations for these negotiations, and they've brought along a product catalogue and some samples. Johnson Smith and Lynn Petty are particularly interested in some of the new designs.

Dialogue

1. Looking at Samples

(in the conference room)

Wang Guo'an: Mr. Smith, Miss Petty, according to the itinerary, Mr. Li is supposed to acquaint the two of you with our products and prices today. Is that all right with you?

Johnson Smith: Sure. Discussing business is precisely why we've come. I'm really eager to know what all new things your company has this year.

Li Xinwen: Here is our product catalogue for this year. (to both Mr. Smith and Miss Petty) Please go ahead and look through it.

Johnson Smith: Mr. Li, are these all this year's new designs?

Li Xinwen: Eighty percent are new designs; only the ones in the back are traditional products that we continue to carry. I've also brought along some samples for you to take a look at. (picking up the samples)

Lynn Petty: Oh, how pretty! Mr. Li, I just love these designs, especially this sweater. The color and style are both very nice.

Li Xinwen: (smiling) This one? This was designed according to the suggestions you made last time. Have you forgotten, Miss Petty?

Lynn Petty: (laughing) Really? If that's the case, how do you plan to thank me?

2. Inquiring Prices

Johnson Smith: President Wang, the products your company is putting out this year have a lot of appeal, especially these new designs. May I ask if the prices listed in the catalogue are retail or wholesale prices?

Wang Guo'an: The prices in the catalogue are all retail prices. Wholesale prices are fifteen to twenty-five percent lower.

Lynn Petty:	Mr. Li, I noticed that there are some products with no price listed in the catalogue. Can you tell me their prices?
Li Xinwen:	The ones with no listed price are all trial items. (pointing to the catalogue) This pair of pants and this leather jacket, for instance, are both being produced by the manufacturer on a trial basis. If your company is interested, the prices can be negotiated individually using [the prices of] similar products as a reference.
Johnson Smith:	From what I understand, the price of your company's leather jackets appears to be a little higher than that of other companies. Why is that?
Li Xinwen:	I suppose our price being slightly higher has something to do with the product's quality and design. You can make further comparisons [if you like].
Johnson Smith:	Good. I would like to take this catalogue back with me and look through it carefully.
Wang Guo'an:	(looking at his watch) Oh, it's already after twelve o'clock. What do you say we eat lunch first and then continue our discussion?
Lynn Petty:	(jokingly) I agree—my stomach has already started negotiating with me!

Reading Passage

It Pays to Shop Around

Whether it's in shopping or in business, price is always one of the matters of most concern to both the buyer and the seller. China has an old saying that goes, "Compare the merchandise at three shops, and you won't come to grief." It [just] means that if you want to buy something, it's best to compare the prices at several different stores. This is the only way to avoid getting a bad deal; it's [also] the only way to buy quality things that are both inexpensive and satisfactory. Ever since the implementation of the policies of reform and opening to the outside world in 1979, China's market economy has expanded greatly. Customers now have more alternatives in the price, quality and variety of merchandise. On the one hand, market competition has brought more opportunities; but on the other hand, it has also brought more challenges. If you plan to do business in China, you definitely need to understand China's market conditions first. *The Art of War* says you can only be successful if you know yourself [as well as] know the enemy. This is also true in business.

Lesson Seven   Visiting a Factory

After the Chinese and American [representatives] concluded their first business discussion, Zhang Hong accompanied Johnson Smith and Lynn Petty on a tour of the toy factory [where] a batch of battery-operated toys from their company's last order was manufactured. They were deeply impressed by the toy factory's management and production efficiency.

Dialogue

1. In the Reception Room

Zhang Hong: Factory Director Chen, your guests have arrived!

Factory Director Chen: Welcome! Welcome to our factory! I'll introduce myself. My name is Chen Dafang, and I'm the factory director here. You must be Mr. Smith of the American International Trading Company!

Johnson Smith: That's right—I'm Johnson Smith. This is my assistant, Miss Lynn Petty.

Lynn Petty: How do you do, Factory Director Chen! Miss Zhang has said that a batch of battery-operated toys that we ordered last year was manufactured right here. Is that so?

Factory Director Chen: Yes, yes. I remember there was a rush to deliver that batch of toys before Christmas. Mr. Smith, Miss Petty, was your company satisfied with the products?

Johnson Smith: Very satisfied. We've come today [for two reasons]: first, to express our gratitude to your factory; and second, to take a look at production conditions with our own eyes.

Factory Director Chen: You're too gracious, Mr. Smith! How about I accompany you to see the workshop first? What do you say, Miss Zhang?

Zhang Hong: Sure! (to Johnson Smith and Lynn Petty) Why don't we listen to Factory Director Chen give an introduction [to the factory] as we walk?

Johnson Smith:
Lynn Petty: Okay!

2. At the Workshop

Factory Director Chen: This is our factory's assembly workshop. After products are assembled

	here, they're sent to the finished products workshop to undergo a quality inspection.
Lynn Petty:	Factory Director Chen, your workshop is not only well-run, the equipment is also state-of-the-art.
Factory Director Chen:	[modestly declines compliment] Last year we brought in these two assembly lines from abroad. Now not only have our costs gone down, but our output is also three times higher than it was two years ago. Our quality has also improved.
Johnson Smith:	Are these cartoon figures being assembled right now going to be exported?
Factory Director Chen:	Yes. These toys are all being manufactured for Disney. They're planning to put them on the market this fall, so time is pressing.
Lynn Petty:	They're too cute! I'm sure they'll be very popular!
Johnson Smith:	Factory Director Chen, I'm very impressed by your factory. I hope we can work together even more from now on.
Factory Director Chen:	That's great! Let's keep in close contact in the future!

Reading Passage

Chinese Enterprises

In general, there are two kinds of enterprises in China: state-owned enterprises and privately-owned enterprises. State-owned enterprises are funded and operated by the central government or local governments. Because they have government support, they enjoy a definite advantage [in access to] financial resources, raw materials, technology and marketing. However, many state-owned enterprises have been poorly managed and are suffering financial loss. Privately-owned enterprises in China have grown very rapidly over the last ten to twenty years, and they now provide state-owned enterprises with some stiff competition. Presently, the Chinese government is actively pushing the reform of state-owned enterprise, and encouraging privately-owned enterprises to take over those ineffective sate-owned enterprises by means of contract, lease, merger or acquisition. Privately-run enterprises are the new type of joint share enterprises that have emerged from this reform.

Enterprises are greatly impacted by the economic policies of the Chinese government. Whether state-owned or privately-owned, every business must accommodate its expansion plans to the government's economic policies. [At present,] spurred on by the Chinese government's policy of openness, many state-owned and privately-owned enterprises are actively seeking collaboration with foreign enterprises. This is an excellent opportunity to enter the Chinese market.

Lesson Eight   Price Negotiations

Today the Chinese and American companies are going to negotiate the order for this fall. The purchasing price and quantity will be the key points in the negotiations for both parties. Today's negotiations are one of the primary reasons Johnson Smith and Lynn Petty have made this trip to China.

Dialogue

1. Successful Negotiations

Johnson Smith: President Wang, over the last couple of days we have toured your factories and looked at quite a few products. Now I'd like to hear your prices.

Wang Guo'an: Sure! Do you have any particular products in mind?

Johnson Smith: I'd like to know the price of your sweaters and jeans.

Li Xinwen: The sweaters are 360 U.S. dollars per dozen; the jeans are 240 U.S. dollars per dozen.

Johnson Smith: Do the prices you've stated include freight charges?

Li Xinwen: Yes, they include cost and freight.

Lynn Petty: Mr. Li, the quote for the sweaters appears to be 10% higher than last year. Why is this?

Li Xinwen: This sweater is our new design. The style and quality are both greatly improved, and the cost is also higher than last year. We have no choice but to raise the price accordingly.

Lynn Petty: Even so, 360 U.S. dollars per dozen is still pretty expensive. We're longtime clients—can't you go a little lower, [say], give us a 5% discount?

Wang Guo'an: I'm afraid 5% is impossible. However, if your company orders over 1000 dozen, we can give a 2.5% discount.

Johnson Smith: H'm, we can consider this price. Also, I think your jeans are a little overpriced as well. There are a lot of manufacturers producing jeans at present, and competition is fierce. If we buy at this price, we won't make a profit!

Li Xinwen: But the quality of our products is internationally recognized, and they are competitive in the market.

Johnson Smith: Right! That's precisely why we hope to buy from your company. How about we order 2000 dozen each of the sweaters and jeans, and you give us a 3% discount on both?

Wang Guo'an: Okay! That's acceptable to us. It's settled then!

2. Failed Negotiations

Lynn Petty: Mr. Li, may I ask what your quote is for this type of leather jacket?

Li Xinwen: That leather jacket is [one of] our trial products for this year. In order to establish a place for it in the market, we're prepared to sell at the special price of 1800 U.S. dollars per dozen.

Lynn Petty: Mr. Li, you must not be very clear about the current situation on the international market. Your price is almost the same as the price of some world famous brands!

Li Xinwen: Miss Petty, I believe the design and quality of our product can compare favorably with certain world famous brands. Last month we signed a contract with a Japanese company at this very price. However, while our name recognition is still low, we are willing to lower our price accordingly. May I ask what your counteroffer is?

Lynn Petty: If [the price is lowered to] 1200 U.S. dollars per dozen, we can consider ordering 1000 dozen.

Li Xinwen: Our losses would be too great at 1200 U.S. dollars per dozen! The most we will go down is 200 dollars. How about 1600 U.S. dollars per dozen?

Lynn Petty: That's still too expensive! If sales aren't good, we will have to sell at a loss. Why don't we both concede 200 more [and settle on] 1400 U.S. dollars per dozen?

Li Xinwen: I'm sorry. 1600 is our bottom price—we can't go any lower.

Lynn Petty: That's too bad! It looks like we have no choice but to look for another supplier.

Reading Passage

Bargaining

Bargaining is an essential part of doing business. The saying, "quote a price so vast as to cover the heavens," is a bit of an exaggeration no doubt; but it really is a good illustration of the knack Chinese have for bargaining.

The success of business negotiations often rests on thoroughness and patience. Before begin-

249

ning to negotiate, [one should] diligently investigate market conditions, carefully compare the prices of various goods and thoroughly prepare for the coming negotiations. These are all basic determinants of success. However, foreigners doing business in China often run into some unexpected problems. This is not only due to differences in culture and customs; it's also a result of differences in social and economic systems. An adept negotiator must have patience. As long as you're willing to understand the other party and patiently communicate with him or her, you will always be able to find a solution to your problems. And your business dealings in China will certainly succeed.

Lesson Nine   Cultural Similarities and Differences

Johnson Smith and Lynn Petty have already been in China for several days now. Besides discussing business, they have also found time to stroll through shops, buy souvenirs and even visit the Great Wall. They've had some interesting experiences—some they found strange, but others were very moving.

Dialogue

1. How Strange!

(on the street)

Lynn Petty: Johnson, didn't you want to buy a gift for your wife? I know of a shopping center in this area with a good selection and reasonable prices. Why don't I take you there?

Johnson Smith: Okay. But I'd like to go to the bank and [get] some Renminbi first. Do you know where we can find a bank?

Lynn Petty: Yes—there's a bank not far from here. I changed money there once last year.

Johnson Smith: If it's on the way, let's go [there] first.

Lynn Petty: Okay. No problem!

(outside the bank)

Lynn Petty: That's strange! Why is the bank closed?

Johnson Smith: (looking at the business hours) Summer business hours...closed from twelve to two p.m.

Lynn Petty: (looking at her watch) It's just 12:10 now. What should we do?

Johnson Smith: Let's just forget it and go to the shops. I still have some pocket money.

(at the shopping center)

Johnson Smith: Wow. This place is really bustling with people and activity. (in a low voice to Lynn Petty) Lynn, have you noticed that a lot of people in China smoke? Some people are smoking in here now, even though there are "no smoking" signs.

Lynn Petty: I know. And I also noticed that Mr. Li always offers cigarettes when he's discussing business with clients. I guess this is a kind of civility?

Johnson Smith: Right. They have this custom in Taiwan, too. (suddenly) Oh! My stomach is hurting all of a sudden. I need to go to the restroom for a moment. I'm sorry—please wait for me. (walks off)

251

(a minute later, Mr. Smith walks back)

Lynn Petty:　　　　Are you feeling a little better now?

Johnson Smith:　　A lot better. But I sure didn't use [that] restroom.

Lynn Petty:　　　　Why?

Johnson Smith:　　(with a wry smile) Because the toilets in there aren't the kind you sit on—they're squat toilets. I just can't bring myself to use one!

2. Meeting Some Warm-hearted People

(at the base of the Great Wall)

Zhang Hong:　　　　Ah, we've made it to the Great Wall. Shall we take the cable car up or climb up?

Lynn Petty:　　　　Taking the cable car would require less effort, but climbing up ourselves might be more interesting.

(Tourist #1 and Tourist #2 pass by, [stopping to] greet Lynn Petty and Johnson Smith)

Tourist #1:　　　　(to Lynn Petty) Hello! Your Chinese is really good! Where are you from?

Lynn Petty:　　　　We're from America.

Tourist #1:　　　　The best way to see the Great Wall is to go up by cable car and then walk down. This way is fun, and it won't wear you out.

Lynn Petty:　　　　Great idea! We'll do that! Thank you!

Tourist #2:　　　　(to Johnson Smith) You'd better take a coat up with you. The wind is strong on the Great Wall, and it would be easy to catch a cold just wearing a T-shirt.

Johnson Smith:　　H'm, you're right. I really should take a coat up with me. Thank you! (looking at the jacket Tourist #2 is holding) That Great Wall jacket is truly beautiful. Where did you buy it?

Tourist #2:　　　　I bought it right at a gift shop east of here. Would you also like to buy one?

Johnson Smith:　　I should buy one for my wife. She really likes the Great Wall, too.

Tourist #2:　　　　(enthusiastically) If you'd like one, I can go with you to take a look.

Johnson Smith:　　That would be too much trouble. You don't need to do that.

Tourist #2:　　　　It's no trouble! It's right over there—not far at all!

Johnson Smith:　　It's not necessary, really. You're too kind! Thank you!

Tourist #1:　　　　(enthusiastically) There are also [vendors] selling mineral water there, it's cheap, and the brand is good, too. You should buy two bottles to take with you [so] you'll have something to drink if you get hot or thirsty. (pointing at the Great Wall) Things are super expensive on top!

Lynn Petty:　　　　You've been great. Thank you!

Johnson Smith:　　Thanks!

252

Zhang Hong: (smiling) Let me remind everyone that there aren't any restrooms on the Great Wall. If you'd like to use the bathroom, it would be best to go right now.

Reading Passage

When in Rome, Ask What the Romans Do

Because of differences in culture and habits, foreigners in China are sure to come across some things they find strange. [For example], a complete stranger on the street kindly leads you where you need to go, taking the initiative to help you out and give you some suggestions. But [then] somebody bumps into you on a crowded bus or subway and doesn't even say "sorry." A sales girl does everything she can to get you to buy her products, but when you've bought something you're not satisfied with, you find it very hard to return. [Or] a recent Chinese acquaintance makes you uncomfortable by bluntly asking how much money you make per year. Going Dutch is very rare when eating out with Chinese; everyone will vie to pay the bill, leaving you at a loss as to what to do. The Chinese have an idiom, "rujingwensu." It means that you should inquire about local customs when you first arrive at a new place. This is a good idea for foreigners visiting China for the first time.

Lesson Ten   Delivery and Payment

The Chinese and American [representatives] have already tentatively worked out the new order over the last couple days of negotiations. Now they're most concerned about the delivery schedule and method of payment, and this morning they are going to hold further talks to address these issues.

Dialogue

1. Delivery Schedule

Johnson Smith: I suppose today we should discuss the delivery schedule for this order.

Li Xinwen: Okay. Do you have any specific requirements concerning the time of delivery?

Johnson Smith: You understand the strong seasonal nature of the clothing [business]. The sweaters and jeans in this order will all go on the market this fall. Mr. Li, can you make the delivery sometime during the first ten days of August?

Li Xinwen: The first ten days of August? Mr. Smith, you aren't joking, are you? Last year we didn't deliver until September. Our current production schedule is already full.

Johnson Smith: (earnestly) I'm not joking. The peak sales period for sweaters is in September and October. Last year our merchandise went on the market two weeks later than that of other [companies], and it put us at a disadvantage. This year I definitely don't want to let the opportunity slip by again.

Li Xinwen: But it would indeed be difficult for us to adjust our production schedule and increase output immediately.

Lynn Petty: I realize this delivery schedule is rather tight, but we also have our difficulties. Mr. Li, we're old friends—please think of a way to help us out.

Li Xinwen: Miss Petty, I do want to help you and to help myself as well. But to make the delivery over a month ahead of time would truly not be easy.

Lynn Petty: I have an idea. Could we divide the garments into two separate shipments— half of the order to be delivered during the first ten days of August and the other half during the first ten days of September? Do you think this would work, Johnson?

Johnson Smith: H'm. That's a solution. What do you say, Mr. Li?

254

Li Xinwen:	Let me think it over... I need to call President Wang. Why don't we take a break first?
Johnson Smith:	
Lynn Petty:	Okay!

2. Method of Payment

Li Xinwen:	I'm sorry for keeping you waiting so long. I just talked with President Wang. We can accept the two shipments arrangement...
Johnson Smith:	That's great! Thank you!
Li Xinwen:	However, I must explain our requirements concerning the method of payment.
Johnson Smith:	Of course. I'm also concerned about this matter. May I ask what type of method you have in mind?
Li Xinwen:	We generally take payment by letter of credit, but your requesting an early delivery this time will have a definite impact on our flow of funds. Therefore we are asking that your company make 30% of the payment in advance and use a Irrevocable Letter of Credit for the remainder of the payment.
Johnson Smith:	We can have Citibank wire you the 30% advance payment. Can we pay the rest with a document against acceptance or another [type of] installment plan?
Li Xinwen:	I'm sorry, but we don't accept these payment methods at present. So as not to influence the time of delivery, please be sure to [have the bank] issue a letter of credit thirty days before loading and transport.
Lynn Petty:	Mr. Li, you're tough! When it comes to money, you show no mercy!
Li Xinwen:	(laughing) Haven't you heard the Chinese saying, "Even blood brothers keep careful accounts?"
Lynn Petty:	(laughing) No, this is more like, "no dough, no go!"

Reading Passage

Chinese Banks and Renminbi

China's central bank is the People's Bank of China. The major commercial banks include the Bank of China, the Industrial and Commercial Bank of China, the China Construction Bank, Agricultural Bank of China, Bank of Communications, etc. The Bank of China is China's largest bank specializing in foreign currency, and foreigners doing business in China will all have dealings with this bank. Perhaps you already noticed that Chinese banks are all national banks.

The government hopes to ensure the stability of the entire nation's finances and money markets through direct administration of the banks.

China's legal currency is the Renminbi. It has three units: yuan, jiao and fen. One yuan equals ten jiao; and one jiao equals ten fen. There are a total of thirteen denominations of Renminbi: 100 yuan, 50 yuan, 20 yuan, 10 yuan, 5 yuan, 2 yuan, 1 yuan, 5 jiao, 2 jiao, 1 jiao, 5 fen, 2 fen and 1 fen. At present, the circulation and use of Renminbi is limited to within China only. In foreign trade, China and its trade partners normally settle accounts using the more internationally prevalent hard currencies, such as the U.S. dollar, Japanese yen and euro, using internationally prevalent methods such as remittance, collection, and letter of credit to make the payment. In recent years, as the Chinese economy has expanded rapidly and China has joined the World Trade Organization, many foreign banks have set up branches or offices in China. In the future it will become more and more convenient for foreigners to do business in China.

Lesson Eleven   Sales Agents

The Chinese and American [representatives] just reached an agreement on the delivery schedule and method of payment, and Johnson Smith and Lynn Petty are both very satisfied. Now the two parties are going to continue their negotiations; the issue at hand is that the Eastern Corporation acts as the American International Trading Company's sales agent in China.

Dialogue

1. Sole Agency

Wang Guo'an: Mr. Smith, Miss Petty, Vice President Li told me that you reached an agreement on this fall's new order this morning. I'm very happy. May I ask if your company is satisfied?

Johnson Smith: We're very satisfied, especially since we were able to smoothly resolve the issue of the delivery schedule. That's very important. President Wang, thank you for looking after us.

Wang Guo'an: Not at all! Your company is a longtime client—we should do our best to satisfy your requests.

Lynn Petty: (smiling) President Wang, our company purchased over two million U. S. dollars (!) worth of your products this time. Are you planning to buy a little something from us?

Li Xinwen: (laughing) Miss Petty, I think that the really tough one here is *you*. For your information, President Wang has come this afternoon precisely to talk over this matter of distributing your company's products in China.

Wang Guo'an: It's like this. This was the Eastern Corporation's first year distributing your company's air conditioners, microwaves and other household appliances, and sales were very good. We would like to further expand our cooperation in this area.

Johnson Smith: Good. That's another reason we've made this trip to China. What particularly do you have in mind, Mr. Wang?

Wang Guo'an: We hope to become your company's sole agent in China.

Johnson Smith: As you know, we also have an agreement in place allowing a company in Guangdong to distribute our air conditioners. I'm afraid that giving you the right of sole agency might influence other business that we have with that company.

257

Li Xinwen: Mr. Smith, our company has excellent commercial networks all over the country. If we had the right of sole agency, we would surely do even better!

Johnson Smith: How's this—we can give you the right of sole agency for our microwaves. Besides that, we have a new type of household dishwasher that we plan to try out on the Chinese market, and if you're willing, we'd like you to be the sole agent. Mr. Wang, Mr. Li, what do you think?

Wang Guo'an:
Li Xinwen: Okay! It's settled!

2. Credit Check and Commission

Johnson Smith: Mr. Wang, seeing that your company is about to become our sole agent, we need to understand your credit situation a little better.

Wang Guo'an: You can inquire about our credit at the Beijing branch of the Bank of China.

Johnson Smith: I'm sure you also know that as sole agent, the Eastern Corporation must consent not to take on any similar products of other companies while our agreement is in effect.

Wang Guo'an: Yes, we're very clear on this point.

Johnson Smith: How much do you want to take as commission?

Wang Guo'an: When distributing foreign products, we normally draw a 10% commission.

Johnson Smith: 10% is too much! I think that 8% is more reasonable.

Wang Guo'an: If your company is willing to share half of the advertising expenses, we can reduce the commission to 8%.

Johnson Smith: How much can you guarantee for our yearly export value?

Wang Guo'an: Last year the gross sales for the microwaves [totaled] 1,400,000 [U.S. dollars]. As sole agent, we can import at least 2,800,000 U.S. dollars worth of your microwaves every year. However, this is the first time the dishwashers will be tried out in China, and it's not yet clear how they will sell. We need to do a market survey before we can decide.

Johnson Smith: How about this—we can sign a sole agency agreement for one year first and see how our products are received.

Lynn Petty: I'm sure Chinese women will like using a dishwasher.

Li Xinwen: (smiling) You're mistaken, Miss Petty! These days it's the men who do the dishes in China!

Reading Passage

Foreign Goods in China

In recent years, as China's trade with other countries has grown rapidly, more and more foreign products have come into China. From the basic necessities of life to high-tech products, Chinese interest in foreign goods is becoming stronger and stronger. Without a doubt, populous China is a huge market with immense potential, and foreign firms are now faced with an extraordinary business opportunity. However, for foreign companies unfamiliar with China, doing business there is by no means an easy matter. Foreign goods entering the Chinese market have different fates: some make a profit and some sell at a loss; still others sustain economic losses because of locally-made illegal imitations. In order to come out the victor in Chinese market competition, many foreign firms are commissioning Chinese companies with reliable credit as agents to sell their products. Generally speaking, there are three types of agency: general agency, sole agency and commission agency. General agents are fully authorized to represent foreign firms in all kinds of business dealings. Sole agents enjoy the exclusive right to sell a certain type of product. Commission agents have the authority to sell a certain type of product and to draw a commission, but they can't represent the firm, and they don't have exclusive selling rights. Sales agency not only can provide convenient commercial networks and ensure a steady sales volume for foreign firms; it also helps in establishing a good product reputation. It is a type of commercial trade beneficial to both parties.

Lesson Twelve   Advertising

During yesterday's negotiations, Johnson Smith agreed that his company would assume responsibility for half of the advertising expenses. Now he's anxious to know how much it costs to advertise in China. Johnson Smith and Lynn Petty will leave Beijing for Shanghai this afternoon, so early this morning Zhang Hong and Li Xinwen will accompany them for consultations at the advertising departments of a TV station and newspaper office, respectively.

Dialogue

1. At the Advertising Department of a TV Station

Zhang Hong: Let me introduce the two of you. This is Mr. Smith of the American International Trading Company; this is Manager Qian from this station's advertising department. Manager Qian is an old acquaintance of mine, Mr. Smith. If you have any questions, feel free to ask him!

Johnson Smith: Manager Qian, our company's new dishwasher is just about to go on the Chinese market, and we plan to hold a sales promotion to get sales rolling. Miss Zhang has said that your commercials are very entertaining, so we'd like for you to help.

Manager Qian: Miss Zhang has built us up too highly! However, I can guarantee one thing: no one who has seen our commercials has failed to buy [the product] yet! (laughing)

Johnson Smith: (laughing) Is that so? It must not be cheap to advertise here, then?

Manager Qian: Don't worry. You are a new client and one introduced by Miss Zhang at that. I will definitely give you the most preferential price.

Johnson Smith: That's great. Manager Qian, could you please tell me your specific charging criteria?

Manager Qian: Our fee is comprised of two parts: a production charge and a broadcasting charge. The production charge is determined on the basis of a client's particular demands; the broadcasting charge is calculated [at the rate of] 3000 yuan per fifteen seconds. There is some variation in fees for different time periods.

Johnson Smith: May I ask what you mean by "different time periods"?

260

Manager Qian:	The broadcasting charge is higher at night than during the daytime, for instance. It's [also] higher on weekends than on weekdays. And [the charge for] airing a commercial during a live telecast of exciting sports competitions or artistic performances is generally twice as high.
Johnson Smith:	Are these all the most preferential rates?
Manager Qian:	You can rest assured—our rates are always the most preferential ones!
Johnson Smith:	(thinking) H'm... I need to think it over first, and then I'll get back to you.

2. At the Advertising Department of a Newspaper Office

Li Xinwen:	Miss Zhou, I've brought you a visitor. This is an important client of ours from America, Miss Petty. Miss Petty, Miss Zhou is the head of the advertising department here.
Lynn Petty:	How do you do!
Miss Zhou:	How do you do! You've come to discuss placing an ad, right?
Lynn Petty:	Right. Our company has several types of household appliances that we're about to put on the Chinese market. I've brought along an ad that we'd like to run in your paper in order to build up name recognition. Please take a look first and see if it's suitable or not. I welcome any suggestions!
Miss Zhou:	Don't be so polite. H'm, microwaves and dishwashers. This ad is very attractive. May I ask if you plan to use any Chinese slogans in addition to the English description?
Lynn Petty:	We'll need your help for that. We'll pay the specified fee, of course.
Miss Zhou:	When do you plan to start running the ad?
Lynn Petty:	If it's possible, it would be best to start in the middle of December. [We'd like to] run it four times per week: as a half-page ad on Monday and Wednesday and as a whole-page ad on Friday and Saturday. [We'll try it] for one month first.
Miss Zhou:	Okay, no problem. These are our rates. Please take a look.
Lynn Petty:	May I ask if there are any price breaks for us as new clients?
Miss Zhou:	I'm truly sorry, but we only give appropriate discounts to long-time clients.
Li Xinwen:	Miss Zhou, we are sharing responsibility for these advertising expenses with the American [company], and the Eastern Corporation is certainly [one of] your long-time clients.
Miss Zhou:	In that case, I can give you the set 15% discount. How's that?
Li Xinwen:	What do you think, Miss Petty?
Lynn Petty:	It sure pays to work with you!

Reading Passage

Advertisements and the Chinese Mentality

Advertising is an essential part of doing business. Good advertisements not only can help firms break into the market; they also help in building up a product's name recognition. However, [when] doing business in China, one should understand the Chinese mentality toward product advertisements. Generally speaking, young people like name brands and new fashions, while those of middle and old age value good quality and reasonable prices. This seems to be the common pattern. It follows that the advertisements that can most easily attract Chinese consumers are both representative of modern life and suitable to the Chinese mentality. Firms that understand Chinese culture often rack their brains to find new and innovative ways to use Chinese idioms, common expressions and even poetry and song lyrics to [give] a Chinese "flavor" to their advertisements for foreign goods. For example, Nestle coffee ads use a tender scene and just a short slogan, "The flavor is wonderful," to create a warm and sweet atmosphere reminiscent of real life. [The Chinese names for] Coca-Cola and Pepsi are immediately pleasing to the ear of the Chinese, a people keen on seeking good fortune. And the Japanese firm, [Toyota], has its masterpiece: "When the carriage reaches the mountain, there will surely be a road; and where there's a road, there will surely be a Toyota." It's worth noting that the Chinese have traditionally felt that the best advertisement is the product itself. "If your wine really tastes good, you don't need to worry that your wineshop is located at the end of a narrow lane."—If you have an excellent product, you don't need to worry that nobody will buy it. In the eyes of Chinese consumers, overly exaggerated or overly beautiful advertisements are often untrustworthy. "When old lady Wang sold melons, she was always overstating her goods." What person doesn't like to say that his products are the best?

Lesson Thirteen   At a Trade Fair

Accompanied by Zhang Hong, the director of the Department of Public Relations for the Eastern Corporation, Johnson Smith and Lynn Petty flew from Beijing to Shanghai. They visited an international light industry trade fair the same day.

Dialogue

1. In the Exhibition Hall

Lynn Petty:	Oh, this is huge! Miss Zhang, I've heard that several hundred firms are taking part in this trade fair. Is that so?
Zhang Hong:	Yes, this is one of the largest trade fairs in the country this year. There are not only firms from all over the country—quite a few foreign companies are also taking part. Mr. Smith, Miss Petty, these two booklets introduce the firms taking part in the fair.
Johnson Smith:	(looking at the booklets) H'm... textiles, clothing, food items, medicine, household articles... Oh, there are also arts and crafts! There are so many goods on display! Very interesting! Miss Zhang, is your company taking part in the fair?
Zhang Hong:	Yes, our exhibit is right over there. In a little while we'll go take a look!
Lynn Petty:	Miss Zhang, seeing that this is a trade fair, can we place an order right now if we see something that we really like?
Zhang Hong:	Of course. The advantage of trade fairs is that you can look at samples, negotiate and strike a deal—all on the spot. It's very convenient for both the buyer and the seller.
Johnson Smith:	Miss Zhang, I have a question for you. Do you know what procedures our company would need to go through if we [decided] to take part in the next trade fair?
Zhang Hong:	It's very simple. All you have to do is apply in advance to the sponsoring organization, reserve a spot in the exhibition hall, and pay the required fees. If you're really interested, you can leave your company's address with them and ask them to mail the pertinent materials to you.
Johnson Smith:	It looks as if taking part in a trade fair is a good way to get into the Chinese market. We'll definitely come next time!

2. Doing Business at the Trade Fair

M. Rep[1]: Hello, Miss Zhang! It's been a long time. Are you also here to take part in the fair?

Zhang Hong: No, I'm escorting these two guests. This is the CEO of Asia for the American International Trading Company, Mr. Smith. This is Miss Petty. They are very interested in your products.

M. Rep: Mr. Smith, Miss Petty, it's a pleasure to meet you! We welcome your patronage!

Lynn Petty: We just looked at the silk products of several companies, but you have the largest and most beautiful selection here.

M. Rep: Thank you for the compliment! The truth is that our silks won the gold medal for top quality product in the country. If you're interested in Chinese silks, you've come to the right place! (taking out two booklets) This is our product catalogue. Please take a look!

Johnson Smith: (looking at the catalogue) You're right—these products really are appealing, and the prices are very competitive. May I ask if you have all of these products in stock?

M. Rep: That's guaranteed. Mr. Smith, if you intend to order right now, I can give you a special discount of 5%.

Johnson Smith: I'm afraid that I can't [decide] today. I need to think it over some more. Perhaps we'll come and confer with you again tomorrow.

M. Rep: That's okay. This is business—if not this time, then next time! You're welcome to get in touch with me anytime.

Zhang Hong: (jokingly) Hey, you're not trying to steal my clients, are you?

M. Rep: (laughing) How could that be? Everyone is here to do business!

Reading Passage

Chinese Trade Fairs

Commodity fairs, also called commodity exhibitions, are one of the major ways for Chinese firms to exhibit and sell products, exchange information and expand foreign trade. In order to promote economic growth, China holds a certain number of international commodity fairs at

---

[1] a representative of the manufacturer

regular intervals throughout the year. Some of these fairs are large, and some are small; and there is some variation in the type of fairs. The oldest and largest one is the Guangzhou Export Commodities Fair, called "*Guangjiaohui*" for short. It is held twice a year, once in the spring and once in the fall. Many Chinese firms consider it an honor to be able to exhibit their products at the Guangzhou Export Commodities Fair, and it could be said that this fair is one window through which we can understand Chinese economic growth. The China International Fair for Investment and Trade, held at Xiamen in September every year, is China's most important investment exhibition at the international level in recent years. Taking investment as its theme, the Xiamen Fair provides a complete list of all kinds of investment projects of the current year and is a bridge to investing in China.

As for foreign firms that would like to do business in China, taking part in a Chinese international commodity fair is undoubtedly an effective way to break into the market and to spread the word about their products. And if you want to import goods from China, a trade fair is an ideal place to get quality products at reasonable prices. As a large number of firms take part in the exhibitions, fierce competition is inevitable. Many firms [try to] attract buyers by lowering prices and offering all kinds of favorable terms. You don't want to miss such a great opportunity!

Lesson Fourteen   Special Economic Zones

Shenzhen is the last stop for Johnson Smith and Lynn Petty on this trip to China. After arriving in Shenzhen from Shanghai, Zhang Hong accompanied them as they toured the special economic zone and several Sino-foreign joint venture enterprises, including the Eastern Corporation's subsidiary in Shenzhen, the Eastern Technology Development Company. They were deeply impressed by the special economic zone's growth, construction and investment environment.

Dialogue

1. Discussing Special Economic Zones

Lynn Petty:	I can't believe how fast [Shenzhen] has grown!
Zhang Hong:	I know. Shenzhen has been utilizing foreign capital to develop its economy over the last several years, and it has already gone from being a small town to a large and modern city. More and more foreign firms are coming here to do business every year now, and many large companies from all over the world have investments in Shenzhen.
Johnson Smith:	Miss Zhang, what is it about the special economic zones that draws in foreign investment?
Zhang Hong:	I think it's primarily the desirable investment environment, particularly the excellent infrastructure and the favorable policies toward foreign investors.
Johnson Smith:	I know that the Eastern Technology Development Company is also a joint venture enterprise. May I ask how it has been doing?
Zhang Hong:	The Eastern Technology Development Company is a joint investment we have with a Japanese computer company. It primarily manufactures CD-ROMs and DVD players, and more than 75% of the products are exported. The results have been steadily good because of excellent management and state-of-the-art technology and equipment. Our exports weren't even affected by last year's Asian financial crisis.
Lynn Petty:	Is that so? [You know], a DVD player I bought in the U. S. was made in China. It could have been manufactured right here!

2. Discussing Joint Ventures

Johnson Smith: Miss Zhang, during today's tour I often heard the term, "*sanzi qiye*." This refers to three different kinds of enterprises which utilize foreign investment, right?

Zhang Hong: Right. "*Sanzi qiye*" refers to foreign single venture enterprises, Sino-foreign joint venture enterprises and Sino-foreign cooperative business operations. Many companies in Shenzhen are of one of these three types.

Johnson Smith: I'm very interested in joint ventures, but I'm still not very clear about the specific application procedures. Could you please tell me a little about them?

Zhang Hong: As far as I know, the application [process] for joint ventures can be divided into three steps: first, you apply for permission to set up the project; next, you obtain various forms; and lastly, you apply for a business permit. Oh, that's right. I have a booklet with me that gives a detailed explanation. If you want, you can keep it.

Johnson Smith: That's great. Thank you! I'll definitely read through it carefully after I get back to the States.

Lynn Petty: Miss Zhang, I've heard that the Chinese [company] often wants a 51% or higher controlling interest in joint venture enterprises. Is this true?

Zhang Hong: I don't think that's accurate. Taking our company as an example, the investment ratio is determined through consultations between the two parties. The Chinese party isn't adamant about having a controlling interest. If Miss Petty is willing to invest more money, we naturally welcome it! (laughing)

Reading Passage

China's Special Economic Zones

China began establishing its special economic zones after the implementation of the policies of reform and opening to the outside world. They are normally located in coastal areas where overseas contact is more convenient. In July of 1979, the Chinese government decided to start by opening up four special economic zones: Shenzhen, Zhuhai and Shantou in Guangdong province and Xiamen (Amoy) in Fujian province. These four SEZs are all on China's southeast coast near Hong Kong and Macao.

China's objectives in setting up the special economic zones were to attract foreign capital and to [help] the domestic economy develop at a faster rate. In order to meet these objectives, the Chinese government decided to implement special economic policies in the zones with the aim of creating a desirable investment environment. These special policies primarily include preferential treatment in such areas as taxes, importing and exporting, entering and leaving the country, and land usage. Joint ventures, for example, can receive large-scale corporate income tax breaks. And there are even more preferential measures when a large amount of money is invested, when the capital is invested over a long period of time or when the investment is in high-tech or new technology. Up to now, the special economic zones have already successfully attracted a large amount of foreign investment, becoming an important part of Chinese economic development.

Lesson Fifteen   Signing the Contract

Today is Johnson Smith and Lynn Petty's last day in China, and the Chinese and American [companies] are going to formally sign the contract. Vice President Li Xinwen of the Eastern Corporation flew from Beijing to Shenzhen early this morning, and he will represent the Eastern Corporation in today's signing ceremony.

Dialogue

1. Examining the Contract Drafts

Li Xinwen: Mr. Smith, Miss Petty, these are drafts of the two contracts we will sign today. One is the contract for this fall's order, and the other is a letter of intent for a long-term agreement. Please examine them, especially (pay attention to) items regarding quantity, amount of money, packing, delivery and payment, etc. If there are any oversights or objectionable points, please point them out immediately so that we can make corrections.

Johnson Smith: Okay! Lynn, let's each read through one draft, and when we're finished we can switch.

(Johnson Smith and Lynn Petty examine the drafts)

Lynn Petty: I have one problem, Mr. Li. The clause in the contract concerning the delivery schedule says that two deliveries will be made—one at the beginning of August and one at the beginning of September—but it doesn't give specific dates. That doesn't seem clear enough.

Li Xinwen: Right. I was just planning on confirming this with you. During our previous negotiations, both parties unanimously agreed that delivery would be made during the first ten days of August and the first ten days of September. If you have no objections, we can change this clause to, "One delivery shall be made before August tenth, and the other before September tenth." What do you think?

Lynn Petty: Johnson, do you think that will work?

Johnson Smith: I think so. That's consistent with the delivery times we agreed upon. However, I would like to add a clause like this in the contract: if a delay in delivery on the part of the seller leads to economic losses for the buyer, the buyer has the right to lodge an appeal and a claim for damages. To be honest with you, the delivery dates for this order are extremely important to us, and I

269

don't want there to be any mistakes. I hope you can understand, Mr. Li.

Li Xinwen: Our company [strongly believes in] taking our contracts seriously and honoring our word. We will definitely deliver on schedule. However, I completely understand your request, and we can write this clause in right away.

Johnson Smith: Thank you! In addition, I suggest that we add something like this in the long-term agreement: the two parties should henceforth hold talks once every six months in order to resolve as necessary any problems that might come up in the execution of the contract.

Li Xinwen: This clause is a necessity. I'll put it in at once. Thank you!

2. Formal Signing

Li Xinwen: Mr. Smith, here are the contract originals. We revised each problem area that you brought up this morning according to your suggestions. Please read through them once more. I hope that both parties will be satisfied this time.

Johnson Smith: (reading the contracts) H'm, I think that all of the clauses are detailed and clear, and I don't see anything else that needs to be changed or added. What do you think, Lynn?

Lynn Petty: I think everything [looks] great, too. Mr. Li, you've gone to a lot of trouble!

Li Xinwen: Not at all—it's my job. May I ask how many copies you need?

Johnson Smith: Please give me five copies of each contract.

Li Xinwen: Sure! If there aren't any other problems, I guess we can sign now. Mr. Smith, please sign here!

Johnson Smith: Okay. (signing) Mr. Li, this has been a very successful cooperation, and I'm delighted. I hope we'll have more opportunities to work with you and your company in the future.

Li Xinwen: Certainly! Certainly! Now that we have a long-term agreement, we will surely have more and more opportunities to work together! (pouring liquor) Come, let's drink a toast in celebration of our satisfactory and successful cooperation and to more [opportunities to] work together in the future!

(everyone toasts)

Lynn Petty: (jokingly) Mr. Li, it looks like I'll be coming to bother you in Beijing a lot from now on. It won't be a headache for you, will it?

270

Reading Passage

Laws and Regulations of the PRC Regarding
Foreign Economic Interests in China

In order to better utilize foreign capital and advanced technology to help develop the Chinese economy, the Chinese government began in 1979 to successively draft a series of laws and regulations regarding foreign economic interests. Up to now, China has already drafted and implemented such laws as the Law of Joint Ventures Using Chinese and Foreign Investment, the Foreign Economic Contract Law, the Law of Ventures Using Foreign Investment, the Law of Sino-Foreign Cooperative Ventures, and the Income Tax Law for Enterprises With Foreign Investment and Foreign Enterprises, etc. Affirming the policies of reform and opening to the outside world, these laws and regulations explicitly promise to protect the legal rights and interests of foreign investors and guarantee all kinds of conveniences and favorable considerations for foreign manufacturers, companies and individuals who invest in China. China's laws and regulations regarding foreign economic interests emphasize the fundamental principles of equality and mutual benefit, and at the same time stipulate four different channels of conflict resolution, namely, consultation, mediation, arbitration and litigation. In order to [ensure] that disputes are resolved in a fair and reasonable manner, China is also amenable to arbitration in a third country. Understanding the content of these laws and regulations is of great benefit to every foreigner who plans to invest or do business in China.

The implementation of China's laws and regulations regarding foreign economic interests has clearly improved China's investment environment, [thus] serving to encourage foreign investors. Present-day China is now attracting the interest of more and more foreign investors.

Lesson Sixteen   Farewell Dinner

Johnson Smith and Lynn Petty are about to return to America tomorrow. Li Xinwen is hosting an evening banquet for the Eastern Import & Export Corporation to celebrate the successful cooperation between the Chinese and American companies. It's also a farewell dinner for Mr. Smith and Miss Petty.

Dialogue

1. At the Farewell Banquet

Li Xinwen: Mr. Smith, Miss Petty, there are two reasons for tonight's banquet: one, to celebrate the successful cooperation between our two companies; and two, to bid farewell to the two of you. Please allow me to thank you on behalf of the Eastern Import & Export Corporation. Let me propose a toast to you! Thank you for all you did to ensure a satisfactory and successful conclusion to our negotiations. (everyone toasts)

Johnson Smith: Mr. Li, this has been a very fruitful trip, and we are very happy. I would also like to take this opportunity to thank you and the Eastern Import & Export Corporation on behalf of my company. We're thankful for the warm reception the Eastern Corporation has given us, and especially for all the arrangements you made for us during this trip.

Li Xinwen: Not at all. I was very happy to be able to work with you and Miss Petty. This trip has not only strengthened our business ties; it has also deepened our mutual understanding. I believe that with such a good foundation, we will definitely have even more commercial intercourse from this time forward.

Johnson Smith: I agree completely. During this trip I have seen China's development with my own eyes. China has already become a significant economic power. No wonder firms from so many countries want to do business here now. I dare say that many companies in America envy us for having such reliable "connections" as you and the Eastern Corporation. (smiling) Mr. Li, we hope you'll continue to look after us in the future!

2. Parting Words and the Presentation of Gifts

Lynn Petty: Time sure flies! It seems like I just arrived in China yesterday, but I'm already returning to the U.S. tomorrow morning!

Li Xinwen: Miss Petty, if you'd really like to stay in China a little longer, you would be more than welcome.

Lynn Petty: I would like to, but it depends on whether or not my boss is willing to give me a vacation.

Li Xinwen: I have a solution—perhaps we can include this issue in our next negotiations. What do you think, Mr. Smith?

Johnson Smith: (laughing) I'm sorry. There's absolutely no room for negotiation on this matter! Lynn Petty is my most capable assistant, and I couldn't get along without her!

Li Xinwen: (smiling) We'd be even more delighted if Mr. Smith planned a vacation in China, too!

Johnson Smith: I am actually thinking of bringing my wife along next time to do some traveling, it's just that I can't find time to do it. She is always saying that she'd like to come see the Great Wall and the terracotta soldiers.

Li Xinwen: Good. Please let me know when you decide, and I'll take care of the arrangements for you. Mr. Smith, Miss Petty, these are presents for you from our company. You can think of them as mementos from this trip!

Johnson Smith: Thank you!

Lynn Petty: Can I open it right now?

Li Xinwen: Of course. Go ahead!

Lynn Petty: Oh, a cloisonné vase. It's just beautiful! Thank you, Mr. Li.

Li Xinwen: Not at all. They're just a little something to keep as souvenirs.

Johnson Smith: Mr. Li, I also have a present for you.

Li Xinwen: You really shouldn't have! You're too kind!

Johnson Smith: Please accept it. I also have two gifts that I'd like to ask you to give to President Wang and Miss Zhang.

Li Xinwen: Okay. I'll take them, then. Thank you! Mr. Smith, Miss Petty, I have an important meeting tomorrow, so I won't be able to see you off. I'm very sorry. However, Miss Zhang will take you to the airport.

Johnson Smith: We're already very grateful that you accompanied us for so many days and [even] made this special trip here from Beijing!

Li Xinwen: It was nothing. You needn't be so polite. I wish you a pleasant trip! I hope we will meet again soon!

Johnson Smith:
Lynn Petty: Thanks! Good-bye!

Reading Passage

Establishing a Long-term Cooperative Relationship

When the word, "connections," is mentioned, many foreigners doing business in China immediately think of "going through the back door." It cannot be denied that "going through the back door" can often solve problems, but these kinds of "connections" are by no means safe. Sometimes "going through the back door" is not only not helpful; on the contrary, it [can] hold up your reputable business, and you might even [end up] being swindled. For foreigners planning to do business in China, making a solid effort to establish a working relationship based on equality and mutual benefit is more dependable than thinking of ways to "go through the back door."

Chinese value long-term cooperative relationships. If you are shrewd, you will make use of various occasions to let them know that your company also places great value on this kind of relationship. [When] doing business or interacting with Chinese people, there is no harm in speaking with frankness and sincerity [so that] the other party clearly understands your position. During intense negotiations, patience, understanding, respect and a friendly attitude are all essential. Don't let the Chinese think that you are a business person only concerned with present gains. In some cases, it doesn't hurt to make [reasonable] compromises in order to resolve a dispute. This way, the Chinese will not only feel like they have [kept] face; they will also be convinced that you are a reasonable friend with whom it is worthwhile to associate.

After the contract has been signed, the business transaction has been brought to a successful conclusion, and you have a great opportunity to solidify the relationship by striking while the iron is hot. Besides toasting, don't forget to express your company's hope to continue working together in the future [so that] your Chinese friends will be assured that your company is truly sincere about maintaining a long-term cooperative relationship. It's also a good idea to take advantage of this opportunity to give your Chinese friends a few meaningful little gifts. Chinese often say, "The gift is trifling, but the feeling is profound." Giving gifts both communicates your gratitude and shows that you value the friendship.

In short, gaining a better understanding of Chinese culture and the Chinese people will definitely help you as you do business in China.

I wish you success!

（二）词汇总表

拼音	汉字	课
A		
àn	按	L.7
ànshí	按时	L.15
ànzhào	按照	L.6
àomén	澳门	L.14
B		
Bái Lín	白琳	L.1
báitiān	白天	L.12
bǎifēn zhī…	百分之	L.6
Bǎishì Kělè	百事可乐	L.12
bǎiwàn	百万	L.11
bǎn	版	L.12
bàn bǎn	半版	L.12
bànshìchù	办事处	L.10
bàn shìqing	办事情	L.1
bàn shǒuxù	办手续	L.1
bāng	帮	L.2
bāng máng	帮忙	L.2
bàng	磅	L.4
bāokuò	包括	L.8
bāozhuāng	包装	L.15
bǎochí	保持	L.16
bǎohù	保护	L.15
bǎoliú	保留	L.6
bǎoxiǎn	保险	L.16
bǎozhèng	保证	L.10
bào jià	报价	L.8
bàopán	报盘	L.8
bàoqiàn	抱歉	L.10
bàoshè	报社	L.12
Běijīng Kǎoyā	北京烤鸭	L.4
běn chǎng	本厂	L.7

275

276

cǎo'àn	草案	L.15
cèsuǒ	厕所	L.9
chācuò	差错	L.15
chāyì	差异	L.9
cháxún	查询	L.11
chà bu duō	差不多	L.8
chǎnliàng	产量	L.7
chǎnpǐn	产品	L.4
cháng	尝	L.5
Chángchéng	长城	L.4
Chángchéng Fàndiàn	长城饭店	L.2
chángnián	常年	L.12
chángqī	长期	L.15
chǎnghé	场合	L.16
chǎngjiā	厂家	L.6
chǎngshāng	厂商	L.11
chǎngzhǎng	厂长	L.4
chē dào shān qián bì yǒu lù	车到山前必有路	L.12
chējiān	车间	L.7
chèn rè dǎ tiě	趁热打铁	L.16
chéngbāo	承包	L.7
chéngběn	成本	L.7
chéngduì jiāodān	承兑交单	L.10
chénggōng	成功	L.5
chéngjiāo	成交	L.13
chéngnuò	承诺	L.15
chéngpǐn	成品	L.7
chéngwéi	成为	L.4
chéngyì	诚意	L.16
chéngyǔ	成语	L.9
chīkuī	吃亏	L.6
chōu kòng	抽空	L.9
chōushuǐ mǎtǒng	抽水马桶	L.9
chū	初	L.15
chūbù	初步	L.6
chūcì	初次	L.3
chūkǒu	出口	L.1
chūkǒu'é	出口额	L.11
chūqián	出钱	L.14
chūrùjìng	出入境	L.14
chūshòu	出售	L.8
chūxí	出席	L.5

chūzhǔyi	出主意	L.9
chuántǒng	传统	L.6
chuánzhēn	传真	L.2
chuāngkǒu	窗口	L.13
chuàngbàn	创办	L.14
chuàngzào	创造	L.14
chuī	吹	L.4
chūnjì	春季	L.13
cìxù	次序	L.5
cùxiāo	促销	L.12
cuī	催	L.7
cuòguò	错过	L.10
cuòshī	措施	L.14

D

dáchéng	达成	L.11
dádào	达到	L.14
dǎ	打	L.8
dǎ jiāodào	打交道	L.10
dǎkāi	打开	L.1
dǎsuàn	打算	L.2
dǎ zhāohu	打招呼	L.9
dǎzhé	打折	L.13
dàcài	大菜	L.5
dàfúdù	大幅度	L.14
dàgōnggàochéng	大功告成	L.16
dàpī	大批	L.14
dàtīng	大厅	L.2
dāi	呆	L.4
dài	袋	L.2
dàilǐ	代理	L.3
dàilǐquán	代理权	L.11
dàilù	带路	L.9
dàiyù	待遇	L.14
dān	单	L.1
dānwèi	单位	L.10
dānwù	耽误	L.16
dānxīn	担心	L.1
dāngchǎng	当场	L.13
dāngdì	当地	L.7
dàngnián	当年	L.13
dàngtiān	当天	L.13

dǎo	倒	L.3
dào	道	L.5
dàodá	到达	L.1
dàodǐ	到底	L.11
dàoshì	倒是	L.16
dào … wéizhǐ	到……为止	L.14
délì	得力	L.16
dēng	登	L.12
dēngjì	登记	L.1
dēngjìkǎ	登记卡	L.1
děngděng	等等	L.3
děngyú	等于	L.10
díquè	的确	L.8
dísīní	迪斯尼	L.7
dǐjià	底价	L.8
dìqū	地区	L.3
dìsānguó	第三国	L.15
dìtiě	地铁	L.9
dìzhǐ	地址	L.13
diàndòng	电动	L.7
diànhuàcíkǎ	电话磁卡	L.2
diànhuì	电汇	L.10
diànnǎo	电脑	L.1
diànqì	电器	L.11
diànshìtái	电视台	L.12
diàochá	调查	L.8
dìngdān	订单	L.3
dìnggòu	订购	L.7
dìnghuò	订货	L.13
dìngqī	定期	L.13
dōngfāng	东方	L.1
Dōngfāng Jìnchūkǒu Gōngsī	东方进出口公司	L.1
Dōngfāng Kējì Fāzhǎn Gōngsī	东方科技发展公司	L.14
dōngnán	东南	L.14
dòuliú	逗留	L.4
dújiādàilǐ	独家代理	L.11
dújiādàilǐquán	独家代理权	L.11
dúzīqǐyè	独资企业	L.14
dùjià	度假	L.16
dùzi	肚子	L.2
duìfāng	对方	L.3
duì … gǎnxìngqù	对……感兴趣	L.6

Fújiàn Shěng	福建省	L.14
fúwùtái	服务台	L.2
fúzhuāng	服装	L.4
fù	副	L.1
fù	付	L.2
fùběn	副本	L.15
fùdān	负担	L.4
fù fèi	付费	L.12
fù kuǎn	付款	L.10
fùyàn	赴宴	L.4
fùzérén	负责人	L.12
fù zhàng	付账	L.9
fù zǒngjīnglǐ	副总经理	L.1

G

gǎigé	改革	L.6
Gǎigé Kāifàng Zhèngcè	改革开放政策	L.6
gǎijìn	改进	L.8
gǎishàn	改善	L.15
gān bēi	干杯	L.5
gǎn	赶	L.7
gǎndòng	感动	L.9
gāokējì	高科技	L.4
gāo xīn kējì	高新科技	L.14
gàobié	告别	L.16
gè dì	各地	L.11
gè fù gè de	各付各的	L.9
gèlèi	各类	L.13
gèrén	个人	L.15
gěiyǔ	给予	L.15
gēnjù	根据	L.15
gēn…yǒuguānxì	跟有……关系	L.6
gèngjiā	更加	L.16
gōngdao	公道	L.9
Gōnggòng Guānxì Bù	公共关系部	L.3
gōngrèn	公认	L.8
gōngsī	公司	L.1
gōngyì měishùpǐn	工艺美术品	L.13
gōngyìng	供应	L.13
gōngzhèng	公正	L.15
gǒnggù	巩固	L.16
gòngtóng	共同	L.12

gōutōng	沟通	L.8
gòumǎi	购买	L.7
gòuwù zhōngxīn	购物中心	L.9
gǔdiǎn	古典	L.12
gǔfènzhì	股份制	L.7
gǔlì	鼓励	L.7
gùgōng	故宫	L.4
gùkè	顾客	L.6
gùrán	固然	L.8
guānjiàn	关键	L.8
guānxì	关系	L.16
guānyú	关于	L.15
guānyuán	官员	L.1
guānzhào	关照	L.11
guānzhù	关注	L.15
guǎnlǐ	管理	L.7
guānggù	光顾	L.13
guānglín	光临	L.3
guāngpán	光盘	L.14
guǎngdōng	广东	L.11
guǎnggào	广告	L.11
guǎnggàobù	广告部	L.12
guǎnggàocí	广告词	L.12
Guǎngjiāohuì	广交会	L.13
Guǎngzhōu	广州	L.13
Guǎngzhōu Chūkǒu Shāngpǐn Jiāoyìhuì	广州出口商品交易会	L.13
guàng	逛	L.9
guīdìng	规定	L.2
guīlù	规律	L.12
guìbīn	贵宾	L.5
guójì	国际	L.1
guónèi	国内	L.10
guówài	国外	L.7
guóyíng	国营	L.7
guóyǒu	国有	L.7
guòfèn	过分	L.12
guòjiǎng	过奖	L.12
guòmù	过目	L.6

H

| hǎiguān | 海关 | L.1 |
| hǎiwài | 海外 | L.14 |

282

hángqíng	行情	L.6
háowúyíwèn	毫无疑问	L.11
hǎohāor	好好儿	L.4
hǎojiǔ	好久	L.1
hǎoshǒu	好手	L.8
hàokè	好客	L.5
hàomǎ	号码	L.3
héfǎ	合法	L.15
hélǐ	合理	L.11
hétong	合同	L.3
hézī	合资	L.14
hézī qǐyè	合资企业	L.14
hézuò	合作	L.3
hézuò jīngyíng	合作经营	L.14
hùzhào	护照	L.1
huāpíng	花瓶	L.16
Huāqí Yínháng	花旗银行	L.10
huàbié	话别	L.16
huàmiàn	画面	L.12
huánpán	还盘	L.8
huìfù	汇付	L.10
huìkèshì	会客室	L.7
huìtán	会谈	L.3
huò	货	L.6
huòbì	货币	L.10
huòdé	获得	L.13
huòkuǎn	货款	L.10
huòyuán	货源	L.8

J

jīchǔ shèshī	基础设施	L.14
jīhū	几乎	L.8
jīhuì	机会	L.6
jījí	积极	L.7
jīliè	激烈	L.8
jílì	吉利	L.12
jí	级	L.2
jí	即	L.11
jíjiāng	即将	L.12
jíshǐ	即使	L.3
jíyú	急于	L.12
jìdé	记得	L.7

jìjié	季节	L.10
jìjiéxìng	季节性	L.10
jìniàn	纪念	L.9
jìniànpǐn	纪念品	L.9
jìrán	既然	L.5
jìsuàn	计算	L.12
jì…yě	既……也	L.3
jì…yòu	既……又	L.3
jìxù	继续	L.6
jiā cài	夹菜	L.5
jiārù	加入	L.10
jiātíng yòngpǐn	家庭用品	L.13
jiāyòng diànqì	家用电器	L.11
jiāqiáng	加强	L.16
jiāshēn	加深	L.16
jiǎ	甲	L.9
jiàgé	价格	L.6
jiàqī	假期	L.16
jiàqián	价钱	L.6
jiānbìng	兼并	L.7
jiǎn	减	L.11
jiǎnchēng	简称	L.13
jiǎnmiǎn	减免	L.14
jiǎnyàn	检验	L.7
jiànkāng shēnmíngkǎ	健康申明卡	L.1
jiànlì	建立	L.4
jiànxíng	饯行	L.16
jiànyì	建议	L.6
jiāng	将	L.11
jiāngyào	将要	L.15
jiàngdī	降低	L.7
jiāohuàn	交换	L.3
jiāohuò	交货	L.7
jiāoliú	交流	L.8
jiāo péngyou	交朋友	L.1
jiāo shuì	交税	L.1
jiāotōng	交通	L.4
jiāowǎng	交往	L.14
jiāoyì	交易	L.13
jiāoyìhuì	交易会	L.13
jiàozǎo	叫早	L.2
jiēdài	接待	L.2

jiēdài dānwèi	接待单位	L.4
jiēfēng	接风	L.5
jiēshòu	接受	L.8
jiésuàn	结算	L.10
jiézuò	杰作	L.12
jiè	届	L.13
jiè	借	L.16
jièyòng	借用	L.12
jīn'é	金额	L.15
jīnhòu	今后	L.3
jīnjiǎng	金奖	L.13
Jīnlíng Fàndiàn	金陵饭店	L.2
jīnróng	金融	L.10
jīnróng wēijī	金融危机	L.14
jǐn	仅	L.10
jǐnguǎn	尽管	L.12
jìnchūkǒu	进出口	L.1
jìn huò	进货	L.8
jìnkǒu	进口	L.1
jìn lì	尽力	L.11
jìnniánlái	近年来	L.10
jìnrù	进入	L.7
jìnyíbù	进一步	L.10
jīngjì tèqū	经济特区	L.3
jīngjì xiàoyì	经济效益	L.14
jīngxiāo	经销	L.11
jīngyíng	经营	L.14
jǐngtàilán	景泰蓝	L.16
jìng	敬	L.5
jìngzhēng	竞争	L.6
jìngzhēngxìng	竞争性	L.8
jiǔdiàn	酒店	L.2
jiǔwǔzhé	九五折	L.13
jiǔ xiāng bú pà xiàngzi shēn	酒香不怕巷子深	L.12
júzhǎng	局长	L.5
jǔbàn	举办	L.13
jǔxíng	举行	L.5
jùdà	巨大	L.11
jùshuō	据说	L.5
jùtǐ	具体	L.10
jù wǒ suǒ zhī	据我所知	L.14

K

kǎ	卡	L.1
kǎtōng	卡通	L.7
kāi chéng bù gōng	开诚布公	L.16
kāichū	开出	L.10
kāifā	开发	L.14
kāifàng	开放	L.6
kāiwánxiào	开玩笑	L.10
kāizhǎn	开展	L.13
kāndēng	刊登	L.12
kànqilai	看起来	L.13
kàn yàng	看样	L.13
kànzhòng	看中	L.13
kǎochá	考察	L.4
kǎolǜ	考虑	L.8
kàojìn	靠近	L.14
kě'ài	可爱	L.7
kěkào	可靠	L.11
kěkǒukělè	可口可乐	L.12
kèhù	客户	L.8
kèrén	客人	L.2
kètào	客套	L.9
kěndìng	肯定	L.15
kōngtiáo	空调	L.11
kǒngpà	恐怕	L.8
kònggǔ quán	控股权	L.14
kǒutóuyǔ	口头语	L.12
kǔxiào	苦笑	L.9
kuājiǎng	夸奖	L.13
kuāzhāng	夸张	L.8
kuǎn	款	L.6
kuàngquánshuǐ	矿泉水	L.9
kuīsǔn	亏损	L.7
kuòdà	扩大	L.11

L

lǎnchē	缆车	L.9
lǎobǎn	老板	L.1
lǎohuà	老话	L.6
lǎonián	老年	L.12
lèyì	乐意	L.1
lèixíng	类型	L.13

286

lěngpán	冷盘	L.5
lí bu kāi	离不开	L.12
lǐjiě	理解	L.8
lǐmào	礼貌	L.3
lǐpǐndiàn	礼品店	L.9
lǐ qīng qíngyì zhòng	礼轻情义重	L.16
Lǐ Xìnwén	李信文	L.1
lǐyí	礼仪	L.3
lìchǎng	立场	L.16
lìhai	厉害	L.10
lìxiàng	立项	L.14
lìyì	利益	L.16
liè	列	L.3
lièrù	列入	L.16
liánghǎo	良好	L.11
língqián	零钱	L.9
língshòujià	零售价	L.6
lǐngqǔ	领取	L.14
lìngwài	另外	L.4
lìngyì	另议	L.6
liútōng	流通	L.10
lùxù	陆续	L.15
lǚguǎn	旅馆	L.2
lǚkè	旅客	L.2
lǚxíngshè	旅行社	L.2

M

mǎimài	买卖	L.8
mǎizhǔ	买主	L.6
màizhǔ	卖主	L.6
Mǎnhànquánxí	满汉全席	L.5
mǎnzú	满足	L.11
màn tiān tǎo jià	漫天讨价	L.8
Máotáijiǔ	茅台酒	L.5
màoyì	贸易	L.1
méi cuò	没错	L.12
méishénme	没什么	L.4
měifāng	美方	L.3
Měiguó Guójì Màoyì Gōngsī	美国国际贸易公司	L.1
měiyuán	美元	L.1
miǎn bu liǎo	免不了	L.9
miǎn shuì	免税	L.1

miàn	面	L.4
miànduì	面对	L.5
miànlín	面临	L.11
miànzhí	面值	L.10
miànzi	面子	L.16
miǎo	秒	L.12
mínyíng	民营	L.7
míngpái	名牌	L.8
míngpiàn	名片	L.3
míngquè	明确	L.15
míngyì	名义	L.16
mìngyùn	命运	L.11
mòshēngrén	陌生人	L.9
mǒu	某	L.8
mǒuxiē	某些	L.8
mǒu yì zhǒng	某一种	L.11
mùdì	目的	L.3
mùlù	目录	L.6
mùqián	目前	L.10

N

ń	嗯	L.5
nàixīn	耐心	L.8
nánchù	难处	L.10
nándé	难得	L.11
nánguài	难怪	L.16
nánmiǎn	难免	L.13
nánrén	男人	L.11
niúzǎikù	牛仔裤	L.6
nóng	浓	L.11
nǔshì	女士	L.11

O

ō	哦	L.13
ōuyuán	欧元	L.10

P

páizi	牌子	L.9
péi	陪	L.7
péiběn	赔本	L.8
péitóng	陪同	L.13
pī	批	L.7

pīfājià	批发价	L.6
píjiākè	皮茄克	L.6
pīnmìng	拼命	L.9
pínfán	频繁	L.4
pǐnzhǒng	品种	L.6
píngděng hùlì	平等互利	L.15
píng shí	平时	L.12
pútáojiǔ	葡萄酒	L.5
pǔtōng	普通	L.5
pǔtōng dàilǐ	普通代理	L.11

Q

qīdài	期待	L.16
qījiān	期间	L.3
qícì	其次	L.14
qíguài	奇怪	L.9
qítā	其他	L.6
qíyú	其余	L.10
qízhōng	其中	L.6
qǐdào…zuòyòng	起到……作用	L.15
qǐyè	企业	L.7
qìfēn	气氛	L.12
qiàtán	洽谈	L.3
qiāndìng	签订	L.3
qiānshǔ	签署	L.15
qiānzì	签字	L.15
qiánmiàn	前面	L.4
qiánlì	潜力	L.11
qiáng	强	L.10
qiángdiào	强调	L.15
qīn	亲	L.7
qiáoliáng	桥梁	L.13
qīnqiè	亲切	L.12
qīn xiōngdì, míng suànzhàng	亲兄弟,明算账	L.10
qīnyǎn	亲眼	L.7
qīnggōngyè	轻工业	L.13
qīngsōng	轻松	L.1
qíngmiàn	情面	L.10
qǐngjiào	请教	L.13
qǐngkè	请客	L.4
qǐng wù xī yān	请勿吸烟	L.9
qìngzhù	庆祝	L.15

qiūjì	秋季	L.3
qǔjué	取决	L.8
quánmiàn	全面	L.13
quánquán	全权	L.11
quányì	权益	L.15
quēshǎo	缺少	L.16
què	却	L.9
Quècháo Kāfēi	雀巢咖啡	L.12
quèrèn	确认	L.15

R

ràngjià	让价	L.8
rèchǎo	热炒	L.5
rènào	热闹	L.9
rèqíng	热情	L.9
rèxīn	热心	L.9
réndìshēngshū	人地生疏	L.11
rénkǒu	人口	L.11
rénkǒu zhòngduō	人口众多	L.11
rénmínbì	人民币	L.2
rìchéng	日程	L.3
rìyuán	日元	L.10
rúguǒ	如果	L.2
rùjìng	入境	L.1
rù jìng wèn sú	入境问俗	L.9
rùkǒu	入口	L.5
rù xí	入席	L.5
ruògān	若干	L.13

S

sānzī qǐyè	三资企业	L.14
shàntóu	汕头	L.14
shànyú	善于	L.8
shāngdìng	商定	L.10
shāngpǐn	商品	L.6
shāngwù	商务	L.2
shāngwù zhōngxīn	商务中心	L.2
shāngyè	商业	L.8
shàng cài	上菜	L.5
shàng dàng	上当	L.6
shàng wǎng	上网	L.2
shàngxún	上旬	L.10

292

Táiwān	台湾	L. 1
tàitai	太太	L. 16
tánpàn	谈判	L. 1
tǎo	讨	L. 12
tǎo jílì	讨吉利	L. 12
tǎo jià huán jià	讨价还价	L. 8
tàofáng	套房	L. 2
tèjià	特价	L. 8
tèsè	特色	L. 5
tèsè cài	特色菜	L. 5
tèshū	特殊	L. 14
tīxùshān	T恤衫	L. 9
tíchū	提出	L. 13
tígōng	提供	L. 11
tíqián	提前	L. 10
tíqǔ	提取	L. 11
tíxǐng	提醒	L. 9
tì	替	L. 9
tiān	天	L. 4
tián	填	L. 1
tiándiǎn	甜点	L. 5
tiáojiě	调解	L. 15
tiáokuǎn	条款	L. 15
tiáozhěng	调整	L. 7
tiǎozhàn	挑战	L. 6
tōngcháng	通常	L. 10
tōng qíng dá lǐ	通情达理	L. 16
tōngxíng	通行	L. 10
tónglèi	同类	L. 6
tóngshí	同时	L. 15
tóufàng	投放	L. 7
tóuqiàhuì	投洽会	L. 13
tóuténg	头疼	L. 15
tóuxián	头衔	L. 3
tóuzī	投资	L. 7
tóuzī huánjìng	投资环境	L. 14
tújìng	途径	L. 13
tǔdì	土地	L. 14
tuī chén chū xīn	推陈出新	L. 12
tuīchū	推出	L. 6
tuīdòng	推动	L. 7
tuīxiāo	推销	L. 9

wùbì	务必	L.10
wùměijiàlián	物美价廉	L.12

X

Xī'ěrdùn Fàndiàn	希尔顿饭店	L.2
xīyān	吸烟	L.9
xīyǐn	吸引	L.6
xīyǐnlì	吸引力	L.6
xǐwǎn	洗碗	L.11
xǐwǎnjī	洗碗机	L.11
xǐyīdài	洗衣袋	L.2
xǐyīfáng	洗衣房	L.2
xìxīn	细心	L.8
xiàjì	夏季	L.9
Xiàmén	厦门	L.3
xiānjìn	先进	L.7
xiàndàihuà	现代化	L.14
xiànhuò	现货	L.13
xiànjīn	现金	L.2
xiànmù	羡慕	L.16
xiànyú	限于	L.10
Xiānggǎng	香港	L.14
xiāngzi	箱子	L.1
xiángxì	详细	L.14
xiǎng bu dào	想不到	L.4
xiǎngfǎ	想法	L.10
xiǎngyǒu	享有	L.11
xiàngmù	项目	L.13
xiāofèi	消费	L.12
xiāofèizhě	消费者	L.12
xiāolù	销路	L.8
xiāoshòu	销售	L.7
xiāoshòu wǎngdiǎn	销售网点	L.11
xiāoshòu zǒng'é	销售总额	L.11
xiǎocèzi	小册子	L.13
xiàolǜ	效率	L.7
xiàoyì	效益	L.7
xiédìng	协定	L.15
xiéshāng	协商	L.14
xiéyì	协议	L.11
xīncháo	新潮	L.12
xīnlǐ	心理	L.12

总计：1040

(三) 句型总表

拼音	句型	课
A		
A bǐ B Adj. …	A 比 B Adj. ……	L.2
A bǐ B zǎo/wǎn V. …	A 比 B 早/晚 V.……	L.10
A bǐ B V. le …	A 比 B V.了……	L.7
A dàibiǎo B V. …	A 代表 B V.……	L.3
A de hǎochù jiùshì…	A 的好处就是……	L.13
A děngyú B	A 等于 B	L.10
A duì B yǒu yǐngxiǎng	A 对 B 有影响	L.7
A fēn wéi …	A 分为……	L.7
A gěi B … de yìnxiàng	A 给 B……的印象	L.7
A gěi B de yìnxiàng …	A 给 B 的印象……	L.7
A wèi B V. …	A 为 B V.……	L.2
A yě hǎo, B yě hǎo	A 也好,B 也好	L.7
A yǒulì yú B	A 有利于 B	L.11
A yǒuzhù yú B	A 有助于 B	L.4
ànzhào …	按照……	L.6
B		
bǎ Obj. fēnchéng…	把 Obj. 分成……	L.10
bǎ Obj. yìkǒuqì + V. + Comp.	把 Obj. 一口气 + V. + complement	L.5
bǎ A gǎichéng B	把 A 改成 B	L.15
biànyú	便于	L.3
bìngbù	并不	L.11
búdàn…érqiě…	不但……而且……	L.4
búdàn bù…fǎn'ér…	不但不……反而……	L.16
bùdébù	不得不	L.8
bùfáng + V.	不妨 + V.	L.16
búshì…ba	不是……吧?	L.10
búshì…érshì…	不是……而是……	L.9
búshì…ma	不是……吗	L.9
C		
chúle…yǐwài, yě/hái…	除了……以外,也/还……	L.4

S

sb. yǒuquán V. sth.	sb. 有权 V. sth.	L.15
shànyú…	善于……	L.8
shéi bù…(ne)	谁不…… 呢?	L.12
shǐ/ràng	使/让	L.1
shìděi/yīnggāi…	是得/应该……	L.4
shìlái/qù…de	是来/去……的	L.1
shǔyú…	属于……	L.14
shuōdào…	说到……	L.10
suànshì…	算是……	L.13
suīrán…dànshì/kěshì…	虽然……但是/可是……	L.5
suízhe…	随着……	L.10
suǒ V. de	所 V. 的	L.16

T

tì sb. V.	替 sb. V. ……	L.9
tōngguò	通过	L.10

W

wèile…	为了……	L.8
wèiyú…	位于……	L.14
wúlùn…háishì…	无论……还是……	L.4

X

xíguàn + V.	习惯 + V.	L.3
xiān…, zài…, zuìhòu…	先……, 再……, 最后……	L.5
xiàng A, B, C děngděng	像 A, B, C 等等	L.3
xièxie…	谢谢 + clause	L.1

Y

yī…jiù…	一……就……	L.12
(yī)kào…lái V. …	(依)靠……来 V. ……	L.14
yīshì…èrshì…	一是……二是……	L.7
yǐbiàn…	以便……	L.14
yǐ…de bànfǎ	以……的办法	L.13
yǐ…de míngyì	以……的名义	L.16
yǐ…jìsuàn	以……计算	L.12
…yǐshàng	……以上	L.1
yǐ…wéiróng	以……为荣	L.13
yǐ…wéi zhǔtí	以……为主题	L.13
yìbān shuō(lái)	一般说(来)	L.3
yìbiān V₁, yìbiān V₂	一边 V$_1$, 一边 V$_2$	L.7

305

总计 154 个

（四）重要网址

business. beijing. cn. net 中国商务电视信息网

  China Business Information Net

www. agri. gov. cn 中国农业信息网

  China Agricultural Information Network

www. bank-of-china. com 中国银行

  Bank of China

www. Businessonline. com. cn 中国商务在线

  China Business Online

www. cbg. org. cn 中国贸易指南

  China Business Guide

www. ce. net. cn 中国企业网

  China Enterprise Network

www. cecf. com. cn 中国出口商品交易会

  China Export Commodities Fair

www. cei. gov. cn 中国经济信息网

  China Economic Information Network

www. ceic. gov. cn 中国电子行业信息网

  China Electronics Industry Network

www. cheminfo. gov. cn 中国化工信息网

  China Chemical Information Network

www. china-appliance. com. cn 中国家电

  China Appliance

www. chinabidding. com. cn 中国采购与招标

www. ChinaBig. com 中华大黄页

  China Big Yellow Page

www. chinacars. com 中国汽车网

  China Cars

www. chinafair. com. cn 中国投资贸易洽谈会

www. chinafashion. com 中国服装信息网

  China Fashion Information Network

www. chinafdi. org. cn 中国国际投资促进网

www.chinainvest.com.cn　中国招商

www.chinamarket.com.cn　中国商品交易市场

China Market

www.china-medicine.com　中国医药网

China Medicine

www.china-realestate.com　中国房地产联合网

China Real Estate

www.chinasilk-info.com　中国丝绸纺织信息网

China Silk and Textile Network

www.chinatop100.com/yqlj.htm　中国 100 大商务网站

China Top 100 Business Web

www.cin.gov.cn　中国建设部

Ministry of Construction, P. R. China

www.clii.com　中国轻工业信息网

China National Light Industry

www.cnta.com　中国旅游

China Tourism

www.cpic.gov.cn　中国价格信息网

China Price Information Network

www.ctei.gov.cn　中国纺织经济信息网

China Textile Information Network

www.customs.gov.cn　中国海关

General Administration of Customs, P. R. China

www.fesco.com.cn　外企在线

China Association of Foreign Service Trades

www.healthcare.net.cn　中国保健养生网

China Healthcare Network

www.mei.net.cn　中国国家机械工业

State Machinery Industry, P. R. China

www.moftec.gov.cn　中国对外贸易经济合作部

Minister of Foreign Trade and Economic Cooperation, P. R. China

www.sinotex.net　纺织电子商务网

China Textile Electronic Commerce Center

www.snet.com.cn　中国航贸信息网

China Shipping and Trading Information Network

www.techfair.com.cn　中国技术出口交易会

Technology Export Fair of China

（五）中国地图

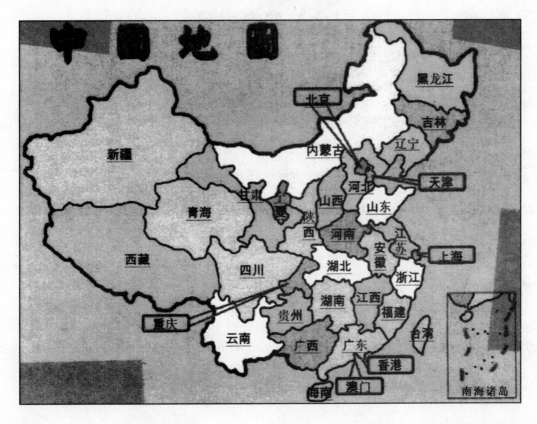

Anhui	安徽	Aomen（Macao）	澳门
Beijing	北京	Chongqing	重庆
Fujian	福建	Gansu	甘肃
Guangdong	广东	Guangxi	广西
Guizhou	贵州	Hainan	海南
Hebei	河北	Heilongjiang	黑龙江
Henan	河南	Hubei	湖北
Hunan	湖南	Jiangsu	江苏
Jiangxi	江西	Jilin	吉林
Liaoning	辽宁	Neimenggu（Inner Mongolia） 内蒙古	
Ningxia	宁夏	Qinghai	青海
Shaanxi	陕西	Shandong	山东
Shanghai	上海	Shanxi	山西
Sichuan	四川	Taiwan	台湾
Tianjin	天津	Xizang（Tibet）	西藏
Xianggang（Hong Kong） 香港		Xinjiang	新疆
Yunnan	云南	Zhejiang	浙江

（六）参考书目

国际贸易之基础
  吕金交 台北众文图书公司 1996 年修订版

国际商务汉语 International Business Chinese
  李忆民主编 北京语言文化大学出版社 1997 年第一版

汉语水平词汇与汉字等级大纲
  国家对外汉语教学领导小组办公室汉语水平考试部
  北京语言学院出版社 1992 年第一版

汉语外贸口语三十课 Thirty Lessons in Business Chinese Conversation
  张静贤主编 北京语言学院出版社 1991 年第一版

牛津英汉双解商务英语词典 Oxford Dictionary of Business English for Learners of English
  （英）Tuck, Allene 编，俞利军等译
  华夏出版社、牛津大学出版社 2000 年第一版

商业汉语 Business Chinese
  黎杨莲妮、李更新 华语教学出版社 1990 第一版

商业文选 Business Readings
  李振清主编 台湾师范大学国语中心编印 1992 年第二版

商业英文书信范例
  林季红 香港万源图书有限公司 1999 年版

商用汉语会话 Conversational Chinese for Business
  郭力编著 北京大学出版社 1993 年 10 月第一版

实用商业会话 Practical Business Conversations
  李振清主编 台湾师范大学国语中心编印 1992 年第二次修订版

外经贸常用应用文写作
  叶穗 上海科学技术文献出版社 1995 年第一版

外贸洽谈五百句 Business Chinese 500
  北京语言学院、北京对外贸易学院编 华语教学出版社 1997 年第四版

外贸写作　　Business Writing in Chinese
　　赵洪琴、吕文珍编　　北京语言学院出版社 1994 年第一版

中国法律简介　　Introduction to Chinese Law
　　翁松燃、张鑫　　香港明报出版社 1987 年第一版

中国经济百科全书　　Encyclopedia of the Chinese Economy
　　陈岱孙主编　　中国经济出版社 1991 年第一版

中国经济体制改革实用词典
　　陈家骥主编　　海潮出版社 1989 年第一版

中英文广告实用手册　　Chinese-English Advertisement Practical Handbook
　　丁树德等　　天津科技翻译出版公司 1995 年第一版

Dunung, Sanjyot P.: *Doing Business in Asia: The Complete Guide*, Lexington Books, New York, NY., USA, 1995.

Hong, Wei: *Practical Business Chinese*, 实用商业汉语 China Books & Periodicals, Inc., San Francisco, CA, USA, First Edition, 1997.

Kuo, Jane C.M.: *Open for Business*, 新世纪商用汉语高级读本 Cheng & Tsui Company, Boston, MA, USA, First Edition 2001.

Li, Jenny: *Passport China*, World Trade Press, San Rafael, CA, USA, 1996.

Schneiter, Fred: *Getting Along with the Chinese*, Heian International, Inc., Torrance, CA. USA, First American Edition, 1994.

Wu, Daming & Guo, Yannan: *Business Chinese: A Practical Guide*, Dept. of East Asian Studies, University of Durham, Elvet Hill, Durham DH1 3TH, UK 1996.